THE POLITICS OF THE *CHARTER*:
THE ILLUSIVE PROMISE OF CONSTITUTIONAL RIGHTS

Andrew Petter is a leading constitutional scholar who served from 1991 to 2001 as a British Columbia MLA and cabinet minister, including Attorney General. In *The Politics of the Charter*, Petter assembles a set of his original essays written over three decades to provide a coherent critique of the political nature, impact, and legitimacy of the *Canadian Charter of Rights and Freedoms*. Showing how *Charter* rights have been shaped by the institutional character of the courts and by the ideological demands of liberal legalism, the essays contend that the *Charter* has diverted progressive political energies and facilitated the rise of neo-conservatism in Canada.

Drawing upon his constitutional expertise and political experience, Petter evaluates the *Charter* in practical, legal, and philosophical terms. These essays, along with a new introduction and conclusion, map out Petter's political philosophy and review the entirety of the *Charter* record. *The Politics of the Charter* is vividly written, free of legal jargon, and accessible to a broad readership, and will provoke renewed discussion about how best to achieve a more compassionate and egalitarian Canadian society.

ANDREW PETTER is a professor in the Faculty of Law at the University of Victoria.

ANDREW PETTER

The Politics of the *Charter*

The Illusive Promise of Constitutional Rights

UNIVERSITY OF TORONTO PRESS
Toronto Buffalo London

ISBN 978-0-8020-9898-6 (cloth)
ISBN 978-0-8020-9599-2 (paper)

Library and Archives Canada Cataloguing in Publication

Petter, Andrew
  The politics of the Charter : the illusive promise of constitutional rights /
Andrew Petter.

Includes bibliographical references and index.
ISBN 978-0-8020-9898-6 (bound) – ISBN 978-0-8020-9599-2 (pbk.)

1. Canada. Canadian Charter of Rights and Freedoms.   2. Civil rights –
Canada.   3. Judicial power – Canada.   4. Legislative power – Canada.
5. Equality – Canada.   6. Canada. Supreme Court.   I. Title.

KE4381.5.P48 2010   342.7108'5   C2009-905516-3
KF4483.C519P48 2010

University of Toronto Press acknowledges the financial assistance
to its publishing program of the Canada Council for the Arts and the
Ontario Arts Council.

 Canada Council **Conseil des Arts**
for the Arts du Canada **ONTARIO ARTS COUNCIL**
CONSEIL DES ARTS DE L'ONTARIO

University of Toronto Press acknowledges the financial support for its
publishing activities of the Government of Canada through the Book
Publishing Industry Development Program (BPIDP).

*In memory of my parents
who encouraged me to question orthodoxy
and always to look for a better way.*

Contents

Acknowledgments

The essays in this collection represent my evolving critique of the political nature and legitimacy of the *Canadian Charter of Rights and Freedoms* from its enactment in 1982 to the present day. The introductory and concluding essays are new. The others were first published between 1986 and 2009 and are reprinted here with permission of the copyright holders. These essays are reproduced in their original form with only minor modifications designed to reduce duplicative and superfluous language, to clarify meaning, and to achieve consistency of style and form. A title and quotation have been attached to chapter 2, which is excerpted from a longer essay; and a few endnotes have been added or augmented to update citations and to provide information that has come to light since their initial publication.

My work on these essays has been greatly assisted by the generous support I have received from the Faculty of Law of the University of Victoria, where I have been a faculty member since 1986, and from Osgoode Hall Law School, where I was a faculty member from 1984 to 1986. My ability to complete the collection was further aided by a grant from the Law Foundation of British Columbia, and by a month-long residency in 2008 at the Rockefeller Foundation's Bellagio Center.

I wish also to extend my appreciation to the editors of the publications in which these essays first appeared, to the editors at the University of Toronto Press for their encouragement and assistance in bringing this collection to fruition, and to the anonymous reviewers of the manuscript for their helpful comments. Two of the essays are co-authored, and one derives from my contribution to a co-authored survey article. I am grateful to my co-authors both for their collaborations and for their permission to include these essays in this collection.

An enormous number of colleagues and friends have generously provided me with ideas and advice concerning these essays over the past three decades. They include Joe Arvay, Harry Arthurs, David Beatty, Edward Belobaba, Benjamin Berger, Allan Blakeney, John Borrows, Gwen Brodsky, Gillian Calder, Jamie Cameron, Jamie Cassels, Don Casswell, Sujit Choudhry, Cheryl Crane, Avigail Eisenberg, Robin Elliott, Gerry Ferguson, Colleen Flood, Hamar Foster, Judy Fudge, Donald Galloway, Harry Glasbeek, Donna Greschner, Reuben Hasson, Matthew Hennigar, Janet Hiebert, Peter Hogg, Grant Hushcroft, Martha Jackman, Tsvi Kahana, James Kelly, John Kilcoyne, Shauna Labman, Hester Lessard, Rod Macdonald, Patrick Macklem, Michael Mandel, Chris Manfredi, John McCamus, Ted McDorman, John McLaren, Michael M'Gonigle, Ally McKay, Mary Jane Mossman, William Moull, Danielle Pinard, Wes Pue, Kent Roach, Bruce Ryder, David Schneiderman, Lynn Smith, Lorne Sossin, Jeremy Webber, and John Whyte.

I am also fortunate to have benefited over these years from the work of some incredibly capable law students who have given me research assistance. Claudia Chender, Jessica Maude, and Richard Epstein provided outstanding research support in relation to one or more of these essays. Lorne Neudorf and Jennifer Bond did the same, while also devoting their precious time and talents to helping me prepare this collection for publication.

I owe special debts of gratitude to the following people: Jim MacPherson for the ongoing encouragement he has provided me in this and other endeavours since I was his constitutional law student at the University of Victoria; Patrick Monahan for the support he gave me as colleague and co-author early in my academic career; Margo Young for her friendship and for urging me to resume my *Charter* scholarship after I returned from politics to academe; and James Tully for his interest in my work and for persuading me to undertake this collection. Murray Rankin is a special friend who has provided me substantive and editorial advice throughout my academic career. Joel Bakan has been an extraordinary source of support and inspiration and has profoundly influenced my thinking. Allan Hutchinson has always been there for me personally and professionally and is a treasured comrade, colleague, and co-author. My son Dylan not only has suffered my obsessions with politics and the *Charter* over the years, but also has allowed me to engage him in discussion, from which I have benefited, on a multitude of thorny issues. And Maureen Maloney has been my toughest critic, my greatest supporter, and my dearest companion. In her multiple roles as colleague, friend, and life partner, she has borne the brunt of my commitment to this project; and it is she to whom I owe the greatest debt for making this and all my life's journeys worthwhile.

Andrew Petter

THE POLITICS OF THE *CHARTER*:
THE ILLUSIVE PROMISE OF CONSTITUTIONAL RIGHTS

Introduction

If I had to sum up my political philosophy in ten words, I would describe myself as a democrat who desires social equality and opposes political privilege. Democracy is a system of government by and for the people, though it has many variants. My vision of democracy is one that locates decision-making structures as closely as possible to citizens and that maximizes opportunities for public engagement. Equality, too, is a malleable concept, running the gamut from formal equality (which is preoccupied with the provision of equal treatment) to substantive equality (which is focused on the attainment of equal conditions). My commitment to equality leans strongly towards the substantive end of this spectrum, driven by a desire to reduce poverty and lessen disparities in wealth and power. Privilege, too, has a multitude of meanings. The form of privilege that most concerns me in the political context is the power of the few to hold sway, without popular direction or accountability, over the welfare of the many.

My critique of the *Canadian Charter of Rights and Freedoms*[1] is a product of this political philosophy. Even as a law student in the early 1980s, when the *Charter* was being promoted by Prime Minister Pierre Elliott Trudeau as necessary to ensure a just society, I worried that the promises made on its behalf were illusive and that its generalized rights would do little to improve conditions for the socially disadvantaged. At the same time, I feared that the authority judges would gain under the *Charter* would give rise to a new form of political privilege that would limit the scope for democratic decision making in Canada. Regrettably, the ensuing years have largely confirmed these suspicions.

The essays in this collection represent stages in a journey I have taken over the past three decades to pursue these concerns and, more generally, to explore the political nature and legitimacy of the *Charter*. That journey began when I was exposed to the earliest *Charter* decisions of the courts while working from 1982 to 1984 as an articling student and Crown solicitor at the Constitutional Law Branch of the Saskatchewan Ministry of Justice. The political philosophy that motivated me to embark upon that journey, however, was formed much earlier in my personal history.

∾

It is a well-worn political truism that where one stands on public policy issues depends upon where one sits. In my case the seats that influenced my political thinking were varied, ranging from seats I held in government to those I occupied while growing up around family tables at which discussion of social and moral issues was encouraged by my parents. Yet three seats stand out in my mind as having particularly shaped the political philosophy that later informed my *Charter* analysis.

The first of these seats is the one I took most summers as a boy in the late 1950s and early 1960s at the annual CCF and later NDP picnics at Sea Bluff Farm outside Victoria. Huddled on blankets on the ground after exhausting ourselves with three-legged races and hayrides, and having filled our stomachs with hot dogs and ice cream, I and other children were treated to some of the finest political oratory in the land. The speakers included such socialist luminaries as M.J. Coldwell, Robert Strachan, and Harold Winch, but the perennial favourite of adults and children alike was Tommy Douglas. With colourful tales about lands of mice controlled by cats, and cream separators used by the rich to skim the best for themselves, Tommy explained with his compelling parables and vivid metaphors why elites, for all their pretensions and reassurances, could not be trusted to protect the interests of those less fortunate than themselves, and why democratic mobilization by ordinary people offered the best hope of attaining social justice. They were lessons that spoke to my inchoate sense of justice and that enabled me to see the possibility of a society in which everyone could enjoy a decent standard of living and participate as equals. But they were also lessons that alerted me to the fact that these egalitarian values and goals are not shared by all and cannot be taken for granted; rather, they must be fought for in the democratic arena against the might and guile of those who are accustomed to using their power and influence to maintain their superior social positions.

A seat I held a decade later reinforced my belief in the progressive potential of democratic institutions. As executive assistant to the Minister of Housing in British Columbia's first NDP government, I became immersed in an activist social democratic administration seeking to advance social equality, economic security, and environmental sustainability. Passing 367 bills during its 1,200 days in office (about one every three days),[2] the government of Dave Barrett, among other things, transformed the province's welfare system, increased support for seniors, doubled parkland, created an agricultural land reserve, established a public automobile insurance corporation, and enhanced democratic accountability through legislative reforms.[3] Though the Barrett government was defeated in the 1975 election, I was impressed by how much it was able to achieve in this short time, and subsequently by how many of its accomplishments survived under successor administrations.[4] At the same time, the vilification of that government in the press, the vitriolic campaign waged against it by business and other established interests, and the coalescence of opposition politicians to defeat it, deepened my appreciation of the extent to which social elites are committed to maintaining their privileged position and of the lengths to which they will go to do so.

The following decade, I occupied a third seat that focused my attention on the potential dangers posed by an entrenched bill of rights to both progressive politics and democratic institutions. In the summer of 1981, during my transition from undergraduate to graduate law studies, I worked as a speechwriter for Saskatchewan Premier Allan Blakeney. That summer was a turbulent time in Canadian politics, with Prime Minister Trudeau waging his campaign to entrench a charter of rights in the Canadian Constitution over the objections of most provincial premiers. The position taken by Blakeney in this debate distinguished him from the federal NDP and from many other social democrats, whose tendency was to regard a charter of rights as an unqualified good. It also set him apart from his fellow premiers, whose opposition to the *Charter* was largely grounded in their concerns for preserving provincial jurisdiction. Blakeney's objection to the *Charter* was not that it would limit the powers of provinces but rather that it would limit the power of citizens to influence public policy through democratic engagement, which he, like Tommy Douglas, regarded as the best means of attaining social justice. Invoking memories of the *Lochner* era, a forty-year period in which the United States Supreme Court struck down almost two hundred laws regulating market activity,[5] he argued that an entrenched charter would enable the 'generally conservative' courts to 'oppose redistribution of power and wealth in society.'[6] More fundamentally, he regarded an entrenched charter as a setback in the hard-fought struggle of ordinary people to attain democracy and as a reassertion of power by social elites, whose interests were threatened by popular political institutions. He thus maintained that no social democrat 'should voluntarily hand power from the political forum, where the policies of the majority find expression, to the judicial forum.'[7]

Blakeney's assessment of courts' conservative nature reinforced the opinions I had formed in law school. His belief in the progressive potential of politics and his distrust of social elites resonated with the lessons I had learned from listening to Tommy Douglas[8] and working in the Barrett government. And his commitments to democracy and equality, which were the bases of his opposition to the *Charter*, coincided with my own developing political philosophy. Furthermore, his willingness to challenge conventional thinking among social democrats appealed to my iconoclastic tendencies as well as to my growing scepticism of leftist orthodoxies. While working with the Barrett government, for example, I was attracted by the views of Resources Minister Robert Williams, an admirer of American political economist Henry George.[9] Williams wanted to reform the government-managed forest tenure regime by introducing market mechanisms aimed at producing greater competition and fairer rents. When the large forest companies that had prospered under the state-run system tried to paint him as a dangerous socialist, Williams responded that he was a Georgist who was more committed to free enterprise than they were.

Like Williams and some others on the left in British Columbia,[10] I distrusted monolithic government structures and was attracted by arguments in favour of decentralization and diversity, such as those advanced by E.F. Schumacher in his influential 1973 book *Small Is Beautiful*.[11] This placed me at odds with long-standing NDP policies favouring centralized state planning and aligned me with French Canadian progressives including, ironically, Professor Pierre Elliot Trudeau, whose 1961 essay 'The Theory and Practice of Federalism' had captured my imagination when I first read it in the late 1970s.[12]

❧

It was with these attitudes and values that I encountered the first wave of *Charter* cases to come before the courts while working as an articling student and lawyer in the Constitutional Law Branch of the Saskatchewan Ministry of Justice. The more I immersed myself in these cases, the more aware I became not only of the normative nature of the issues they raised, but also of the political dimensions of the judicial process through which those issues were addressed and resolved. These dimensions included the costs of engaging in *Charter* litigation, the procedural and evidentiary requirements of the courts, the experiences and attitudes of the judges, and the ideological assumptions underlying *Charter* rights themselves.

This growing awareness was accompanied by surprise and consternation at the lack of attention given to these dimensions by constitutional scholars and legal experts who commented on early *Charter* cases. The approach taken by these authorities largely disregarded the politics of *Charter* decision making, focusing instead on whether courts had gotten particular decisions 'right' or 'wrong' according to the commentators' own constitutional predilections. In other words, they approached the *Charter* as a legal instrument to be evaluated from a juridical perspective rather than as a political instrument to be evaluated from an ideological perspective. More fundamentally, I was troubled by the supposition of many of these commentators that the *Charter* was an unquestionably positive innovation whose rights represented an unqualified social good. This supposition struck me as naive and untenable, particularly when viewed against the backdrop of *Charter* cases that I saw being brought before the courts each day. These cases were raising controversial issues of policy and practice, and the judicial decisions to which they gave rise often involved political assumptions and policy positions that I regarded as dubious and regressive. Furthermore, the outcome of a disturbing number of these cases appeared to advance the interests of those with, rather than those without, power in society.

My move to Osgoode Hall Law School in 1984 to take up a position as an assistant professor provided me with an opportunity to reflect upon these concerns in a vibrant academic milieu that valued theoretical approaches and critical thinking. The result, two years later, was publication of 'The Politics of the *Charter*' [*Politics*] in which I presented my thesis that, contrary to the claims of its supporters, the *Charter* is a regressive political instrument more likely to hinder than to advance the interests of disadvantaged Canadians. The reasons for this, I maintained, lay partly in the nature of *Charter* rights, whose primary function is to constrain government action, but more fundamentally in the nature of the judicial system charged with their interpretation and enforcement. Drawing upon the first nine *Charter* decisions of the Supreme Court of Canada, I sought to demonstrate that, beyond the confines of the criminal law, corporations and other powerful interests who oppose government intervention in the marketplace have the most to gain from *Charter* litigation, while the poor and other disadvantaged groups who rely on government action to protect their interests have the most to lose.

Politics marked my academic entry into the world of *Charter* politics, and it is the opening chapter in this collection. Influenced by the writings of Peter Russell,[13] Roderick MacDonald,[14] and J.A.G. Griffith,[15] and by the ideas of many of my Osgoode colleagues, this essay gained notice as one of the first political critiques of the Supreme Court of Canada's early *Charter* jurisprudence. Given its disregard for conventional *Charter* wisdom, and its departure in technique and tone from traditional legal writing, the essay stirred considerable controversy at the time, fuelling a debate among *Charter* critics and proponents that has since animated Canadian constitutional scholarship. The arguments advanced in *Politics*, while embryonic and unrefined, also provided the analytical framework and set the stage for my subsequent scholarship in this area.

The next two essays in this collection focus on particular Supreme Court of Canada decisions in order to delve more deeply into questions concerning the legitimacy of judicial review and the ideology of liberal legalism. Chapter 2, '*Charter* Legitimacy on Trial: The Resistible Rise of Substantive Due Process' [*Resistible Rise*], was written in 1986 as part of a survey of constitutional cases co-authored with Patrick Monahan. It examines the *British Columbia Motor Vehicle Reference*,[16] in which the Court held that section 7 of the *Charter* guarantees substantive as well as procedural due process. This ruling was significant because it disregarded the stated intentions of the *Charter*'s framers and opened the door to judicial review concerning the substance of public policy on issues such as abortion, social assistance, and public health insurance. *Resistible Rise* contests the Court's characterization of judicial review as being 'objective and manageable'; it also argues that judges who deny the political dynamics of *Charter* interpretation are unable to discharge their constitutional responsibilities in a manner that is responsive to those dynamics or that is sensitive to concerns regarding their lack of legitimacy and expertise. The result was a decision that stripped *Charter* adjudication of all political inhibitions and that sought to justify a judicial role in public policy making that went far beyond that envisioned by the *Charter*'s framers.

Chapter 3, 'Private Rights/Public Wrongs: The Liberal Lie of the *Charter'* [*Liberal Lie*] was written in 1987 following my return to British Columbia to assume a teaching position at the Faculty of Law of the University of Victoria. This essay, co-authored with Allan Hutchinson, explores the ideology of liberal legalism that underlies *Charter* adjudication. Focusing on the *Dolphin Delivery* case,[17] in which the Court excluded from *Charter* scrutiny a common law injunction against picketing private property, *Liberal Lie* shows how this ideology induces judges to treat private property entitlements and the laws that support them as a pre-political foundation on which *Charter* rights are bestowed and against which the constitutionality of state action is judged. As a result, the major source of inequality in society – the unequal distribution of such entitlements – is removed from *Charter* scrutiny, and the restraining force of the *Charter* is directed against those arms of the state best equipped to redress such inequality – the legislative and executive branches. The essay argues that judges are required to adhere to the ideology of legal liberalism in order to perpetuate the myth that their *Charter* role is legal rather than political, and to portray themselves as 'neutral arbiters' rather than governmental decision makers.

Chapter 4, 'Canada's *Charter* Flight: Soaring Backwards into the Future' [*Charter Flight*], was written in 1988 for a British audience, at a time when many in that country were urging the adoption of a constitutional bill of rights. Synthesizing arguments developed in *Politics* and my subsequent *Charter* essays, it reviews the first seven years of Supreme Court of Canada decisions to illustrate the political dangers associated with such a bill. This essay warns that the *Charter*'s impact on Canadian politics will, at best, be to divert progressive energies, inhibit market regulation, and legitimize prevailing inequalities in wealth and power; at worst, it could undermine social programs and block future reforms. *Charter Flight* reiterates the claim advanced in *Liberal Lie* that rights adjudication is unavoidably ideological. What *Charter* proponents describe as an alternative to politics is in reality the entrenchment of one particular political vision. Furthermore, that vision looks backwards rather than forwards, grounded as it is in nineteenth-century legal norms.

Chapter 5, 'Rights in Conflict: The Dilemma of *Charter* Legitimacy' [*Rights in Conflict*], written in 1989, returns to the question raised in *Resistible Rise* concerning the legitimacy of *Charter* adjudication. Here, however, the focus is on justificatory theories advanced by Canadian scholars. While these theories vary, they share a commitment to justifying *Charter* decision making by reference to values said to characterize

Canada as a community. At their root is the notion that *Charter* rights reflect a social consensus grounded in conventional norms, community relations, or an evolving tradition. *Rights in Conflict*, also co-authored with Allan Hutchinson, seeks to show that this approach fails to provide a satisfactory account of *Charter* legitimacy. *Charter* rights, far from representing social consensus, mask fundamental social and political conflicts. Using examples from court cases, this essay reviews three categories of conflict that arise in rights adjudication and discusses the inability of orthodox theorists to account for or respond to them. It concludes by suggesting that democratic politics provide a more promising and progressive venue than rights adjudication for building a genuine sense of social solidarity.

~

Having spent five years as a constitutional scholar arguing that the *Charter* is not a productive instrument for progressive politics, and that democratic engagement is a more rewarding means for seeking positive social change, it occurred to me that perhaps the time had come to act on my own advice. Thus in 1990 I put my political money where my academic mouth was and decided to seek election to the British Columbia Legislature. Having gained the NDP nomination in the newly formed constituency of Saanich South in Greater Victoria, I was elected by a narrow margin in the 1991 provincial election that brought the government of Mike Harcourt to power.

For the next ten years, I sat as an MLA, holding on to my seat by an even narrower margin in the 1996 provincial election. During this time, I served as a cabinet minister in the successive NDP administrations that held office in British Columbia from 1991 to 2001, carrying responsibility for numerous portfolios, including Aboriginal Affairs, Forests, Health, Intergovernmental Relations, Finance, Advanced Education, and Attorney General. This is not the place to review my record, or that of the governments in which I served, except to say that my time in government was as exciting and rewarding at some times as it was disheartening and frustrating at others. It is worth noting, however, that far from dampening my enthusiasm for democracy, these experiences persuaded me that the main deficiencies of our parliamentary system stem not from it being too democratic, but from it being not democratic enough. In particular, I found myself increasingly troubled by the extent to which the system lacked public accountability, concentrated power in the executive branch, and discouraged citizen engagement.

At the same time, my years in government reinforced my previous concerns regarding the undemocratic nature and political character of the *Charter*, whose influence upon public policy manifested itself not only through judicial decisions, but also through the daily legal advice provided to ministers and officials and through its regular invocation by politicians to advance, shield, and avoid policy positions.

~

When I returned as a professor to the Faculty of Law at the University of Victoria in 2001, having decided for personal reasons not to run in that year's provincial election, my intention was to shift my academic focus to issues of democratic governance and reform. After taking up the position of Dean of Law shortly after my return, however, I assigned myself a Civil Liberties seminar as a means of catching up on *Charter* developments over the ten years I had been absent from the classroom. That seminar turned out to be more of an eye-opener for me than for my students, as recounted in chapter 6, 'Rip Van Winkle in *Charterland*' [*Rip Van Winkle*]. This essay, written in 2003, takes a satirical yet serious look at the changes that occurred in *Charter* jurisprudence in the 1990s, with particular attention being given to the rise of dialogue theory as a justification for judicial review.

Dialogue theory intrigued me because of its abandonment of previous pretences concerning the objective nature of *Charter* decision making and also because of its ramifications for the scope and nature of judicial review. On the one hand, I was pleased that the theory supported a positive role for legislatures in *Charter* decision making and that it appeared to provide room for the courts to edge away from the regressive implications of liberal legalism. On the other hand, I was unconvinced by the theory's claim that judicial review can be understood as part of a 'democratic dialogue' with legislatures. *Rip Van Winkle* challenges this aspect of the theory, disputing its assumptions concerning the potency and finality of legislative power and pointing out that it offers no normative justification for judicial review. The essay also notes that there is a dark side to dialogue theory: because it treats *Charter* decision making as legitimate while acknowledging its political character, the theory is more willing to compromise democratic principles than previous theories seeking to legitimize judicial review.

While *Rip Van Winkle* examines the impact of dialogue theory upon the courts, chapter 7, 'Look Who's Talking Now: Dialogue Theory and the Return to Democracy' [*Look Who's Talking*], considers its implications for democratic institutions. This essay, written in 2004, begins by reviewing the rise of dialogue theory and its paradoxical reliance upon legislative supremacy to justify judicial review. The essay notes that this justification, while not compelling, signals a return to democracy as the dominant value underlying Canadian constitutional structures. By placing their faith in the finality of legislative power, dialogue theorists join *Charter* sceptics in claiming a significant stake in the democratic nature of the Canadian state. *Look Who's Talking* argues that this common investment in democracy should motivate both groups to give more urgent attention to the requirements of democracy and the need for democratic reform. Drawing from my experiences in government, the essay proposes a number of strategies to make Canadian political institutions more representative and responsive and to increase opportunities for citizen engagement and deliberation in political decision making.

Chapter 8, 'Wealthcare: The Politics of the *Charter* Revisited' [*Wealthcare*], reviews the political implications of the Supreme Court of Canada's landmark decision in *Chaoulli v. Quebec (A.G.)*,[18] in which a majority of judges held that prohibitions on private health insurance in Quebec violated rights to life and security of the person in the Quebec and/or Canadian charters of rights. The ruling called into question the constitutionality of Canada's single-payer Medicare system and reawakened concerns about the *Charter*'s regressive ideology and influence. *Wealthcare*, written in 2005, maintains that this decision disregards years of democratic struggle and serves as a powerful reminder of how *Charter* rights favour those with market power over those whose social well-being depends upon government action. The essay goes on to provide an updated political assessment of the *Charter* record. This assessment shows that, while judges have developed techniques over the years that allow them to moderate and ameliorate the *Charter*'s regressive tendencies, the underlying ideology and political nature of *Charter* rights remain much the same as those identified in my early *Charter* writings. The essay also considers the political role of dialogue theory, arguing that the theory has been used by some to embolden courts without regard to political consequences.

Chapter 9, 'Taking Dialogue Theory Much Too Seriously (or Perhaps *Charter* Dialogue Isn't Such a Good Thing After All)' [*Taking Dialogue Theory*], extends my previous critique of dialogue theory in response to a renewed defence of it by its original academic proponents.[19] This essay, written in 2006, challenges two central claims of these scholars: (1) that the frequency of legislative responses to *Charter* decisions invalidating laws in Canada shows that this country has a weaker form of judicial review than the United States, and (2) that dialogue theory can be reconciled with a justification for judicial review based on the need to protect individuals from appeals to the general welfare. *Taking Dialogue Theory* maintains that the first claim is not supported by the methodology and evidence presented by the authors, while the second lacks coherence and is self-defeating. At the same time, the essay concedes that dialogue theory is not soon likely to loosen its grip on Canada's constitutional imagination. By casting courts as part of a democratic decision-making process, the theory relieves them of responsibility for the consequences of their *Charter* actions without constraining their *Charter* powers. In the absence of a more compelling justification for judicial review, judges are unlikely to eschew a theory that offers them all of this and that comes with an imprimatur of academic approval.

Chapter 10, 'Legalize This: The *Chartering* of Canadian Politics' [*Legalize This*], explores the broader influences of the *Charter* upon Canadian governments and civil society. Written in 2007, it asserts that the *Charter* has produced two spheres of public discourse: a sphere of justice and rights that has become the domain of lawyers and courts, and a sphere of policy and interests that remains the preserve of politicians and legislatures. Moreover, there can be no question as to which sphere dominates where there are conflicts: for all the talk of 'dialogue' between courts and legislatures, those who speak in the language of justice and rights have a huge rhetorical and political advantage over those who speak in the language of policy and interests. *Legalize This* argues that this privileging of rights talk, while seen most obviously in the realm of *Charter* litigation, also pervades government and civil society. Drawing from my various experiences as a lawyer, politician, and scholar, this essay explains how the 'legalization' of politics has increased the authority of lawyers and legal discourse while diminishing the importance of politicians and democratic engagement within Canadian government and civil society.

The collection closes with a conclusion in which I review the *Charter* record of the Supreme Court of Canada and argue that the *Charter*'s most powerful political influences have been its tendencies to legalize political discourse and to legitimize neo-conservative policies. Noting that income inequality and poverty rates have risen in Canada during the *Charter* era, the conclusion reiterates that renewed commitments to political mobilization and democratic engagement offer the best hope for promoting a more egalitarian and inclusive society. At the same time, it urges adoption of new mechanisms and strategies to strengthen democratic institutions and to overcome the contemporary challenges of legalized politics and economic globalization.

~

I began this introduction by referring to these essays as stages in a journey that I have taken over the past three decades to explore the political nature and legitimacy of the *Charter*. As with any journey of this duration, my perceptions have varied over time as I have encountered changing landscapes and gained new perspectives. For example, the *Dolphin Delivery* case, which is the focus of *Liberal Lie*, drew my attention to the extent to which *Charter* rights are driven by an ideology of liberal legalism; the rise of dialogue theory discussed in *Rip Van Winkle* gave me new insights into the capacities of judges to moderate the impacts of that ideology when it suits their purposes; and the decision in *Chaoulli*, which is the subject of *Wealthcare*, reminded me of the *Charter*'s destructive potential when that ideology is given its full force. Similarly, my experiences in government heightened my awareness of the *Charter*'s extensive influence upon political institutions and civil society described in *Legalize This*, and increased my appreciation of the urgent need for reform of democratic institutions discussed in *Look Who's Talking*.

Notwithstanding these variations, the political philosophy that has guided me has remained remarkably constant throughout this adventure, as have my underlying concerns for the *Charter*'s undemocratic character and regressive tendencies. Whether readers find this philosophy agreeable and these concerns convincing is something they will determine for themselves. At minimum, I hope that in joining me on this journey they will gain greater insight not only into my own evolving critique of the *Charter* over the past three decades, but also into the varying views and shifting approaches taken by judges and other scholars over the same period.

NOTES

1 Part I of the *Constitution Act, 1982*, being Schedule B of the *Canada Act, 1982* (U.K.), 1982, c. 11.
2 K. Carty, *Politics, Policy, and Government in British Columbia* (Vancouver: UBC Press, 1996) at 321.

3 See generally J.T. Morley, N.J. Ruff, N.A. Swainson, R.J. Wilson, & W.D. Young, *The Reins of Power: Governing British Columbia* (Vancouver: Douglas and McIntyre, 1983).

4 The Agricultural Land Reserve and the Insurance Corporation of British Columbia, for example, have survived to the present day.

5 S. Choudhry, 'The Lochner Era and Comparative Constitutionalism' (2004) 2 Int'l J. Const. L. 1 at 45–6.

6 R. Romanow, J. White, & H. Leeson, *Canada ... Notwithstanding: The Making of the Constitution 1976–1982* (Toronto: Carswell/Methuen, 1984) at 110.

7 *Ibid.*

8 Some may see an irony in my invocation of Tommy Douglas, in that his government enacted the *Saskatchewan Bill of Rights Act*, 1947, S.S. 1947, c. 35, which was the first general law prohibiting discrimination in Canada. It should be noted, however, that Douglas's *Bill of Rights* was different from the *Charter* in three critical respects: first, it was not entrenched and therefore was subject to legislative amendment; second, it did not purport to be paramount over other legislation; and third, it applied to private as well as public institutions and actors: R. Rempel, 'Fundamental Freedoms, Private Actors and the Saskatchewan Bill of Rights' (1991) 55 Sask. L. Rev. 263.

9 For an excellent summary of Henry George's economic philosophy, see L. Wasserman, 'The Essential Henry George,' in R.V. Andelson, ed., *Critics of Henry George: A Centenary Appraisal of Their Strictures on Progress and Poverty* (London: Associated University Presses, 1979), 23.

10 See *e.g.* W. Magnusson, C. Coyle, R.B.J. Walker, & J. Demarco, eds., *After Bennett: A New Politics for British Columbia* (Vancouver: New Star Books, 1986).

11 E.F. Schumacher, *Small Is Beautiful: Economics as if People Mattered* (New York: Perennial Library, 1973).

12 P.E. Trudeau, 'The Theory and Practice of Federalism,' in *Federalism and the French Canadians* (Toronto: Macmillan, 1968), 138. The essay originally appeared in Michel Oliver, ed., *Social Purpose for Canadians* (Toronto: University of Toronto Press, 1961).

13 P. Russell, 'The Political Purposes of the Canadian Charter of Rights and Freedoms' (1983) 61 Can. Bar Rev. 30.

14 R.A. MacDonald, 'Postscript and Prelude – The Jurisprudence of the Charter: Eight Theses' (1982) 4 Sup. Ct. L. Rev. 321 at 346.

15 J.A.G. Griffith, *The Politics of the Judiciary*, 3rd ed. (London: Fontana Press, 1985).

16 *Reference Re s. 94(2) of Motor Vehicle Act (British Columbia)*, [1985] 2 S.C.R. 486. (This was a case in which I appeared as counsel for the intervener the Attorney General of Saskatchewan.)

17   *Dolphin Delivery Ltd. v. Retail, Wholesale and Department Store Union, Local 580,* [1986] 2 S.C.R. 573.
18   *Chaoulli v. Quebec (A.G.),* [2005] 1 S.C.R. 791.
19   P.W. Hogg, A.A. Bushell Thornton, & W. Wright, '*Charter* Dialogue Revisited – or "Much Ado about Metaphors"' (2007) 45 Osgoode Hall L.J. 1. Hogg and Bushell (as she then was) presented their original thesis in P.W. Hogg & A.A. Bushell, 'The *Charter* Dialogue between Courts and Legislatures (or Perhaps the *Charter of Rights* Isn't Such a Bad Thing After All)' (1997) 35 Osgoode Hall L.J. 75.

1 The Politics of the *Charter**

Introduction

When the *Canadian Charter of Rights and Freedoms* was proclaimed into law on 17 April 1982, it was an occasion of much rejoicing. Across the country, politicians, judges, civil servants, academics, lawyers, and earnest civil libertarians gathered together to celebrate the advent of the new *Charter*. At long last, Canadians were told, their rights and freedoms were constitutionally protected from government encroachment, never again to be subject to the vagaries of the political process.

Far away from the ceremonies, beyond the sound of the champagne bottles being popped and the clinking of glasses, the news of their new rights and freedoms may have struck a strange note to some Canadians. To the single mother depending upon government-subsidized day care and the laid-off steelworker collecting unemployment insurance, to the pensioner cashing her guaranteed income supplement and the hospital patient receiving public health care, the suggestion that government was the major adversary of rights and freedoms must surely have sounded peculiar. Some may also have been surprised to learn that the institution responsible for protecting their rights and freedoms from government encroachment was the judiciary, an institution that has traditionally shown little enthusiasm for the 'eccentric principles of socialist philanthropy' upon which such benefits are founded.[1]

Still, while some may have been surprised, relatively few seemed perturbed. No matter what one thought about the roles of govern-

* Originally published in (1986) 8 Sup. Ct. L. Rev. 473–505. Copyright © 1986 by Andrew Petter.

ments and courts in our society, surely there was nothing to lose in having more rights and more freedoms. And, if there were smouldering doubts, they were quenched by the support that the *Charter* received from the federal New Democratic Party, from anti-poverty groups, and from numerous other agencies that purported to speak on behalf of the socially and economically disadvantaged. Surely these agencies could not have been mistaken as to the *Charter*'s political impact?

The purpose of this essay, put bluntly, is to argue not just that these agencies could have been mistaken as to the *Charter*'s political impact, but that they *were* mistaken. Far from advancing the interests of disadvantaged Canadians, the *Charter* is much more likely to work to the detriment of those interests. The reasons for this lie partly in the nature of the rights themselves, but more fundamentally in the nature of the judicial system charged with their interpretation and enforcement.

Many of the groups that supported the *Charter* seem to have viewed it as a distributive instrument that would give to everyone without taking from anyone. Thus, while they contemplated how the *Charter* might promote interests that they favoured, they gave relatively little consideration to the ways in which the *Charter* could harm those same interests. Furthermore, to the extent that they did consider such harm, they assumed that it could be minimized by expanding some rights, such as equality rights, with which they identified, and by omitting others, such as property rights, to which they were ideologically opposed.

These groups fundamentally misconceived the nature of a charter of rights and of its impact upon society. First, it simply is not accurate to view a charter as being distributive in nature. This is because rights are not commodities that can be given away; rather, they are entitlements governing the relationships among people within a community. The extent to which one person's rights and entitlements are expanded is the extent to which the rights and entitlements of others are contracted. In other words, the conferral of rights under a charter is a zero-sum rather than a positive-sum game.[2]

The 1976 decision of the Supreme Court of Canada in *Harrison v. Carswell*[3] provides a good illustration of this point. In that case, the owner of a shopping centre brought charges under the *Petty Trespasses Act*[4] against a person who sought to picket her employer, a tenant of the centre. The question for the Court was whether the property rights of the owner with respect to the common area of the centre were sufficient to enable him to sustain an action in trespass. The majority decided that they were. By protecting the owner's property rights, however, the

Court simultaneously limited the ability of employees and others to exercise their rights to free speech and assembly.

The view of a charter of rights as a distributive document is wrong not only because it fails to take account of the interrelationship amongst rights and entitlements, but also because it fails to take account of the true function of a charter in a liberal democracy. A charter distributes nothing because it has nothing to distribute. When we say that a person has rights and freedoms under a charter what we really mean is that government must not interfere with that person in particular ways.[5] Thus a charter gives to citizens only insofar as it takes from government. Governments, however, do not act in vain. Through redistribution of economic resources and regulation of private conduct, governments seek to pursue political purposes that benefit particular social interests. Viewed in this light, one can see that the function of a charter of rights is not to distribute or even to redistribute – it is to regulate the way in which governments go about distributing and redistributing.

The irony, of course, is that the very groups that supported the *Charter* in the name of disadvantaged Canadians are ones that advocate greater intervention by government as a means of achieving social justice. By bringing about the enactment of the *Charter*, they have inhibited the ability of government to engage in the very activities that they espouse.

But what of the rights themselves? Does not the broad guarantee of equality rights and the absence of property rights ensure that the *Charter* cannot be used in socially or economically regressive ways? Those who believe so misunderstand the nature of a rights document and the role of the judicial system in relation to that document. First, we must bear in mind what has just been said about the function of a charter of rights: it gives to citizens only insofar as it takes from government. For example, the guarantee of equality rights in the *Charter* does not give people a guarantee of social equality; it does not even commit government to guaranteeing social equality. Its role is much more limited. What it does is inhibit government from implementing measures that would bring about or perpetuate inequality.

Still, what can be wrong with preventing government from treating people unequally? In the abstract, of course, there is nothing wrong. We can all agree that people ought to be treated equally. The problem comes when we try to define what is meant by equality. As Justice Frankfurter once observed, '[c]lassification is inherent in legislation.'[6] We tax the rich to fund programs for the poor. We impose special obligations upon employers. We give special benefits to senior citizens. Most governmental measures treat one person or group differently from another. Thus, a commitment to some abstract notion of equality is not particularly useful. The idea of equality becomes meaningful only when it is animated by a particular social or political idea. A person who regards markets as fair allocators of wealth, for example, will likely view a system of taxation that imposes higher rates of taxation on higher income earners as a denial of equality. A person who believes that markets do not allocate wealth fairly, on the other hand, will view such a system of taxation as an instrument for promoting equality.[7]

Other rights in the *Charter* are no different. Rights to freedom of expression, freedom of conscience, freedom of association, liberty, and fundamental justice are just as amorphous unless and until they are infused with political content. Furthermore, the *Charter* leaves open for interpretation not only the scope of rights and freedoms, but also how they interact with one another and with other societal values.[8] As was stated by Jacques J. in a recent decision of the Quebec Court of Appeal:

> The power to determine the constitutionality of the legislation [under the *Charter*] imposes on the judge the obligation to 'fill in the gaps in the law, to resolve potential contradictions, to choose one or the other interpretation of the legal text' ... and finally to rank the various rules which come into play.[9]

What happens, for example, when one person's right to freedom of expression or property collides with another person's right to equality? The political nature of the process of interpreting and reconciling values such as these has never been acknowledged more clearly than by the Supreme Court itself. In the words of Dickson J., speaking for a majority of the Court in *Harrison v. Carswell:*

> The submission that this Court should weigh and determine the respective values to society of the right to property and the right to picket raises important and difficult political and socio-economic issues, the resolution of which must, by their very nature, be arbitrary and embody personal economic and social beliefs.[10]

The 1979 decision of the Supreme Court in *Gay Alliance Toward Equality v. The Vancouver Sun*[11] drives home the point. At issue in that case was whether the British Columbia *Human Rights Code* guaranteed a gay rights group equal access to the classified advertising section of a newspaper. In order to resolve this issue, the Court had to decide whether the classifieds were a 'service ... customarily available to the public' within the meaning of section 3 of the Code. Martland J., speaking for a majority of the Court, decided that they were not. He based this decision upon the view that to apply the Code to the advertising section would undermine freedom of the press, which he characterized as the freedom of the *Sun*'s owners to control the content of their newspaper. And he did so even though he acknowledged that there was at the time 'no legislation in British Columbia in relation to freedom of the press similar to the First Amendment [of the United States Constitution] or the Canadian Bill of Rights.'[12]

The only way to make sense of this judgment is to understand it in terms of the political ideas that underlie it. One such idea is that freedom of the press protects commercial as well as editorial expression in a newspaper. A second is that freedom of the press is essentially a property right shared only by newspaper owners. A third is that this property right, though unprotected by legislation, is more worthy of protection than a legislative guarantee of equality. No doubt there are more, but the point is made. The key to understanding the impact of a charter lies less in understanding its text than it does in understanding the political nature of the judicial system that is charged with its interpretation. As *Gay Alliance* shows, even the absence of an articulated right, such as a right to property, is unlikely to influence the political importance attached to that right by the courts or to inhibit the courts from giving priority to that right over competing rights and freedoms.

Thus far, I have sought to establish that the conferral of rights and entitlements under a charter is a zero-sum game, that a charter only gives to citizens insofar as it takes from government, and that a charter's ultimate impact is dependent less upon its text than upon the political nature of the judicial system that is charged with its interpretation. These propositions provide a framework for understanding the politics of the *Charter*. At the same time, they leave to be answered the most important question of all: What is the political nature of the Canadian judicial system?

This essay will seek to answer this question through an examination of two interrelated dimensions of the adjudicative process. One concerns access to that process, and the other concerns the nature of the process itself. Each of these dimensions will be examined against the backdrop of the early *Charter* cases decided by the Supreme Court of Canada.[13] In the first part, I shall examine the extent to which barriers to access affect the utility of the *Charter* to different groups in society. For this purpose, I will refer to the early *Charter* cases decided by the Supreme Court mainly to illustrate the points I am making. In the second part, I shall look to the political character of the Canadian judicial system and consider how that political character has manifested itself in the early Supreme Court decisions. Because my concern is the impact of the *Charter* upon the allocation of wealth and power in society, the focus here will be less on the doctrinal aspects of the Court's reasoning than upon the political assumptions and themes underlying its decisions.

Access to the Judicial Process

Though the *Charter* expressly states that it 'guarantees the rights and freedoms set out in it,'[14] it does nothing of the kind. Carrying a copy of the *Charter* in one's pocket does not 'guarantee' that the rights it sets out will be respected by others. The *Charter* enumerates certain rights and freedoms, albeit in vague and general terms, but they are 'guaranteed,' if at all, by the state and, in particular, by the courts.

This does not mean that the *Charter* will have no impact outside the judicial arena; clearly it will. Some legislation, government policies, and police practices have already been modified in anticipation of judicial interpretation of the *Charter*, and further changes will occur on an ongoing basis as the meaning of the *Charter* is 'revealed.' The fact remains, however, that it is the judiciary that will ultimately determine the nature of *Charter* rights and, consequently, their impact upon society. As Professor Peter Russell has put it:

> [T]he judicial branch will be the most important forum for the systematic application of *Charter* standards. Judicial opinions will be authoritative on the specific meanings to be given to the *Charter*'s general principles. In most instances judicial decisions will be final and definitive on the proper limits of rights and freedoms.[15]

Thus the main avenue available to Canadians who wish to mobilize their *Charter* rights is to raise a claim in court. But courts are places that are not easily accessible to most Canadians. The procedures are complex, and the language of adjudication is difficult to fathom; the formality and adversarial nature of court proceedings are intimidating.[16] Furthermore, the hierarchical structure of the Canadian judicial system means that, in order to obtain an authoritative ruling, one must be prepared to carry, or to defend, one's claim through numerous appeals all the way to the Supreme Court.

These factors make it unthinkable for most Canadians to consider raising a *Charter* claim without first retaining legal counsel. This, combined with other costs associated with litigation,[17] makes the process of vindicating *Charter* rights in court an extremely expensive one. Just how expensive a process this can be is illustrated by some of the early *Charter* cases decided by the Supreme Court. For example, the successful action mounted by Southam Newspapers to have a search of its offices by anti-combines officers struck down under the *Charter* took over two-and-one-half years and cost Southam about $200,000.[18] The unsuccessful action brought by Operation Dismantle to have cruise missile testing declared unconstitutional cost that organization about $50,000 even though its lawyers worked for reduced fees and the litigation never progressed beyond preliminary issues.[19]

In some cases, of course, public funding is available to raise a *Charter* claim. A poor individual who is charged with a serious criminal offence will usually be able to obtain funding from a provincial legal aid plan.[20] The federal government has also established a fund for equality and language rights claims 'of substantial importance,'[21] and in a few provinces, legal aid plans and community clinics have allocated some resources to assist with non-criminal *Charter* claims.[22]

As substantial as this funding may seem, it cannot begin to break down the barrier that stands between most Canadians and their rights under the *Charter*.[23] Virtually the only context in which disadvantaged Canadians are guaranteed an opportunity to raise a *Charter* claim is in the course of defending themselves from criminal charges brought against them. This is an important area to be sure, both because most *Charter* cases are criminal[24] and because a large number of people charged with criminal offences are poor;[25] but it is also the area in which the issues raised are of the most limited social and economic significance. The rights asserted by persons in the context of criminal proceedings are predominantly procedural, the benefit of the *Charter* largely defensive, and the claims made usually have little relevance beyond the criminal context. Furthermore, the victims of crime, particularly crimes against the person, tend also to be drawn from lower income categories.[26] Thus, to the extent that the *Charter* provides additional protection to persons charged with criminal offences, it may also serve to weaken the ability of the state to protect those in society who are most vulnerable to criminal activity.[27]

If the *Charter* were concerned solely with legal rights in a criminal context, its overall political impact would be marginal. But the *Charter* purports to protect many other rights (such as freedom of expression, freedom of association, and equality) whose relevance extends well beyond the context of criminal proceedings. Furthermore, some of the so-called legal rights in the *Charter* (such as liberty, security of the person, and freedom from unreasonable search or seizure) may be invoked to protect interests unrelated to those arising in a criminal context. The political implications of these non-legal rights, and of legal rights in their application to non-criminal situations, are more far-reaching. They enable the courts to impose limitations on all manner of government regulatory and redistributive activity. Yet it is in the non-criminal area that public funding to raise *Charter* claims is most limited.

My purpose is not to advocate that the government expand public funding in this area. Even if there was the political will to do so, I think it would be bizarre for governments in this country to pour more money into encouraging Canadians to look to the courts for political solutions to their problems. My purpose here is limited to demonstrating that, beyond the confines of criminal law, the impact of having chosen the courts as the adjudicative mechanism for resolving *Charter* claims is to favour those who have the economic resources to fight an action in court. It is significant to note, for example, that of the six non-criminal *Charter* cases decided by the Supreme Court to date,[28] two involved *Charter* claims made by corporations,[29] one by a publicly funded institution,[30] and another by a broadly based political group.[31] In just two of the six cases was the *Charter* invoked by individuals,[32] and in only one of these could the individuals be identified as economically disadvantaged.[33]

To their credit, some members of the Supreme Court have spoken out about the problems of accessibility to courts in *Charter* cases.[34] Moreover, the Court has been sensitive to these problems in some of its decisions. In *Singh*,[35] for example, the Court appointed counsel for six appellants who were unrepresented at the time they made application for leave and who lacked the means to hire counsel themselves. In *Skapinker*,[36] the Court awarded costs to an individual respondent and an individual intervener, even though it ultimately dismissed their *Charter* claim and allowed the Law Society's appeal.

While these cases reflect judicial concern about accessibility and costs, they also illustrate the limited means available to the judiciary to overcome monetary obstacles. It is beyond the judicial mandate, even under the *Charter*, to establish a comprehensive legal aid scheme for persons wishing to assert their constitutional rights in court. Judges can, in exceptional cases like *Singh*, appoint counsel when a case reaches court. Under section 10(b) of the *Charter*,[37] they may also be able to order that counsel be provided at public expense to persons subject to arrest and detention. And they can award costs so as to favour those who are least able to afford counsel. But these measures by themselves cannot possibly overcome the monetary barriers raised by *Charter* litigation.

Besides, the signals sent out by the Supreme Court have been conflicting. The reassuring signal given to individual litigants in *Skapinker* was offset by the Court's decision to award costs to the government in *Operation Dismantle*.[38] If the government had chosen to collect them, these costs would have added about $15,000 to the peace group's legal bills.[39] The federal Justice Minister has suggested that the reason for the Court's decision on costs was that it regarded the appellant's arguments to be 'thin and frivolous.'[40] However, this explanation is difficult to accept given that the initial issue decided by the Supreme Court was raised on a preliminary motion by the government and was decided in favour of Operation Dismantle by the trial judge. At the very least, the Court could have articulated its reasons for awarding costs to the government, especially in light of its disposition of costs in *Skapinker*. The Court did not do so and, as the decision stands, it can only have a chilling impact on those with limited financial resources who are contemplating bringing *Charter* actions against public authorities.

Finally, some may see in the process that gave rise to the decision of the Court in *Operation Dismantle* a positive sign about the ability of ordinary Canadians to band together to bring before the courts issues of collective concern. This, in my view, would be a mistake for several reasons. First, notwithstanding that Operation Dismantle claimed to represent more than one-and-a-half million Canadians opposed to cruise missile testing, the case put severe financial strains on the organization and diverted energy and resources from other forms of political action in which it could have engaged.[41] Second, the process cannot be disassociated from the decision to which it gave rise. Even if ordinary Canadians could regularly band together to bring their collective concerns before the courts under the *Charter*, the case illustrates the inappropriateness of their doing so. Issues that are of sufficient concern to attract broad political support, yet that do not find favour with the government of the day, invariably occupy a prominent place in the mainstream of political debate. This fact heightens their political appearance and thereby weakens the courts' authority and their desire to intervene.

It is undoubtedly true, as Wilson J. points out in her concurring opinion in *Operation Dismantle*, that questions such as those concerning the dangers posed by cruise missile testing are no more problematic than many other issues addressed by the courts.[42] But this is something that most judges would prefer not to acknowledge. Perhaps this is why the rest of the Court shuns Wilson J.'s reasons, preferring to seek refuge in Dickson J.'s holding that the allegations of the peace group were incapable of being proven.[43] The reason why the Court regards them as incapable of being proven, it seems, is that the Court is reluctant (and understandably so) to confront an issue so transparently close to the mainstream of political debate.[44] Judicial discretion compels the Court to view the allegations as lying 'in the realm of conjecture'[45] rather than, as Wilson J. would have it, as provable 'statements of intangible fact.'[46]

Thus, even if persons of lower and average economic status could regularly band together to bring issues of collective concern before the courts, the nature of such issues militates against court action succeeding, except where the wording of the *Charter* confers upon the courts a specific political mandate to support such action (as was the situation in *Quebec Association of Protestant School Boards*,[47] in which the Court struck down provisions of Quebec's language laws under the unequivocal wording of section 23 of the *Charter*).

The Politics of the Judicial Process

The institutional barrier created by money not only denies the disadvantaged access to the courts; in doing so, it also serves to shape *Charter* rights. As I have already suggested, most of the rights and freedoms set out in the *Charter* are indeterminate in nature. Furthermore, rights and freedoms must be limited in ways that take account of competing rights and freedoms and other societal goals. For these reasons it is impossible to ascertain from the language of the *Charter* the meaning of most of its guarantees. The way in which they will derive meaning will be through a process of judicial interpretation. This process takes place on a case-by-case basis in response to the particular facts and interests brought before the courts.

If the issues raised in non-criminal *Charter* cases tend to represent the interests of those with economic resources in society, the interpretation of rights will necessarily respond to and, over time, reflect those interests. The suggestion here is not that judges will consciously seek to privilege such interests or that such interests will prevail in every case. The point I wish to make is more subtle. It is that, over time, the disproportionate attention that these Interests command will shape the courts' perception of the purpose of rights and, hence, will influence the courts' interpretation of their meaning and scope.

Perhaps there would be less reason for concern on this score if the courts had an equal understanding of, and empathy for, the problems of all segments of Canadian society. Unfortunately, there is no reason to suppose that this is the case. There are few public institutions in this country whose composition more poorly reflects, and whose members have less direct exposure to, the interests of the economically and socially disadvantaged. Canadian judges are 'exclusively recruited from the small class of successful, middle-aged lawyers,'[48] and if not of wealthy origin, most became wealthy or at least achieved a degree of affluence before accepting their judicial appointments. The majority made their name in private practice, where they held themselves out as business people and shared business concerns. Furthermore, unless they practised criminal or family law, much of their professional time was spent catering to the needs of the business community. In short, there is nothing about the Canadian judiciary to suggest that they possess the experience, the training, or the disposition to comprehend the social impact of claims made to them under the *Charter*, let alone to resolve those claims in ways that promote or even protect the interests of lower-income Canadians.[49]

At a more fundamental level, the attitudes of lawyers and judges tend to reflect the values of the legal system in which they were schooled and to which they owe their livelihood. As Professor John Griffith has said with respect to British judges:

> These judges have by their education and training and the pursuit of their professions as barristers, acquired a strikingly homogeneous collection of attitudes, beliefs, and principles, which to them represent the public interest. They do not always express it as such, but it is the lodestar by which they navigate.[50]

Given the relative lack of social mobility in British society, the British judiciary's view of the 'public interest' is probably easier to identify than that of Canadian judges. However, with respect to at least one aspect of the 'public interest' – the protection of private property – the attitudes of judges in both countries are remarkably similar:

Here the tradition stems from the common law so much of which arose specifically for the purpose of settling disputes relating to land and settlements. ...

Not only the attitude but the very *function* of the judiciary in modern society are exemplified and emphasised by the difference in the protection of property rights and of personal human rights. Indeed 'rights' itself has two separate meanings in this context. Property rights are vested in individuals by the operation of law. Contracts, leases, trusts, wills, and settlements are all ways of creating and transferring these rights in law. And the protection of these rights is the primary purpose of a legal system.[51]

I would add this to Griffith's analysis: property rights have pre-eminent status not only because they are vested by law, but also because the assumption underlying the law is that such rights flow from a natural system of private ordering. Belief in the existence and legitimacy of such a system is what fuels the common law. Thus the law of contracts is seen not as a positive body of rules imposed upon the social order, but rather as a natural body of rules flowing from the social order. From this perspective, one can see that property rights – the body of 'natural' rules governing the ownership and exchange of property – is the core political value underlying the common law.

The centrality of property rights in the collective consciousness of the Canadian judiciary is apparent from such cases as *Harrison v. Carswell*, in which the Supreme Court gave primacy to property over free speech, and *Gay Alliance*, in which the Court upheld an owner's right to free speech so as to defeat a legislative guarantee of equality rights. Again, I am not trying to suggest that a desire to protect private property is the sole force driving the Canadian judiciary, nor am I suggesting that the interests of those who hold property will prevail in each and every case. What I am suggesting, however, is that deep in the judicial ethos there exists a special concern and reverence for property rights – a concern and reverence that over the course of time will guide and constrain judicial decision making in *Charter* cases.

This does not imply that judges have any conscious desire to see the *Charter* used in ways that will help the privileged and harm the disadvantaged. If anything, their conscious desire is probably the opposite. Thus where the interests of the disadvantaged do come before the courts, and where those interests coincide (or at least do not collide) with values such as the protection of private property, one can expect a result favourable to the disadvantaged. A good example of this is the

Singh case, in which the Supreme Court struck down a law denying illegal immigrants the opportunity of a hearing to determine their eligibility for refugee status. But such cases will be the exception rather than the rule. In the majority of non-criminal cases before the courts, the interests of the disadvantaged will not be heard or, if they are heard, will (as in *Harrison v. Carswell* and *Gay Alliance*) conflict with judicial notions of the 'public interest.' In sum, regardless of what judges aspire to do, the social context and political nature of judicial decision making ensures that *Charter* rights will be shaped predominantly by the needs of the economically privileged in Canadian society.

(1) Corporate Rights

One area in which institutional barriers and judicial attitudes have already combined to influence the nature of rights under the *Charter* relates to corporations. Of the first nine *Charter* cases decided by the Supreme Court, two concerned the rights of corporations. In *Big M Drug Mart*,[52] a corporation invoked the *Charter* guarantee of freedom of religion to successfully defend itself against charges under section 4 of the federal *Lord's Day Act* for conducting business on a Sunday. In *Southam*,[53] a corporation brought a successful action to strike down search and seizure provisions of the *Combines Investigation Act* on the basis that those provisions violated its right to be free from 'unreasonable search and seizure.'

More disturbing than the results of these cases are the assumptions made by the Court in reaching these results. In both cases, the Court speaks in the abstract about rights and freedoms under the *Charter* being *human* rights. In *Southam*, Dickson J. refers throughout his judgment to the purpose of the *Charter* being to protect 'the public's interest'[54] and 'the right of the individual.'[55] In *Big M Drug Mart*, he refers to freedom being 'founded in respect for the inherent dignity and the inviolable rights of the human person.'[56] In light of these sentiments, one might expect the Supreme Court to look with scepticism upon *Charter* claims brought before it by non-human entities such as corporations. Yet, as *Southam* in particular demonstrates, this has not been the case.

Nowhere in his reasons in *Southam* does Dickson J. even consider whether the rights enjoyed by corporations under section 8 of the *Charter* might be different from those enjoyed by human beings. This is especially disquieting given that he goes out of his way to identify the right to be free from unreasonable search or seizure as a privacy right rather than a property right. A corporation, after all, is an artificial entity whose function is economic in nature. While the privacy interests of human beings relate to their needs for psychological and bodily security, in addition to economic security, the privacy interests of corporations do not. Thus, while Dickson J. insists that section 8 is a privacy right and not a property right, his application of it to a corporation renders illusory the distinction he purports to make. To grant a corporation a privacy right is to grant it a property right pure and simple. It was for this reason that the United States Supreme Court held in *Bellis v. United States* that 'a substantial claim of privacy or confidentiality cannot often be maintained with respect to the financial records of an organized collective entity.'[57]

Furthermore, the powers and capacities of corporations flow from legislation. These powers and capacities permit corporations to accumulate capital in ways not available to individuals, and to protect their shareholders, officers, and directors from personal liability. To accept uncritically that these entities should be entitled to the same degree of privacy from the state as human beings is to disregard the fact that the extraordinary powers they wield are themselves a product of state action, and require commensurate constitutional authority in government to guard against their abuse.

Indeed, surely it is bizarre that corporations should be granted *any* protection under the *Charter*. Why should an artificial entity whose powers flow from the state and whose function is economic be entitled to share in rights founded in respect for 'the human person'? I do not mean to suggest by this that the shareholders, directors, officers – or, for that matter, the clients or employees – of a corporation should be denied a right of privacy under the *Charter*. But it is one thing to suggest that a search of corporate records might affect the privacy interests of an individual who is associated with a corporation; it is quite another to suggest that such a search affects the privacy interests of the corporation itself. The effect of giving corporations a right of privacy is to place in the hands of those who own and manage corporations the right to invoke special constitutional protection with respect to corporate property independent of any privacy interests that they as individuals might enjoy in that property. Perhaps such a right could be defended if the relationship of all shareholders and directors to all corporations were the same; but clearly this is not the case. The privacy interest of a shareholder or director of a closely held company with respect to corporate records is likely to be vastly different from the privacy interest of a shareholder or director of a widely held conglomerate.[58] To evaluate the privacy interest in each case on the basis that they are both corporations and thus both entitled to equivalent degrees of privacy is to disregard the underlying human values at stake. Furthermore, to treat corporations as having privacy interests of their own is to give corporations preferred status over unincorporated businesses whose owners must presumably found their rights to privacy under the *Charter* solely on the basis of the nature of their personal interests in the business.

To Canadian judges, many of whom served corporations in private practice and who are used to treating them like any other litigant, the suggestion that corporations should not be accorded 'personhood' under the *Charter* must sound peculiar. Just how peculiar is evident not only from *Southam*, but also from the words of Dickson J. in *Big M Drug Mart*. Before making the statement that freedom is founded on respect for the 'human person,' he says: 'Section 24(1) sets out a remedy for individuals (whether real or artificial ones such as corporations) whose rights under the *Charter* have been infringed.'[59] What is revealing about this sentence is the choice of the word 'individuals' to include corporations. The noun 'individual' is traditionally employed in law and common parlance to denote a natural person. I am not suggesting that this means that the Court will necessarily extend to corporations the benefit of equality rights, which the *Charter* limits to 'individuals'[60] (though Dickson J.'s phrasing is certainly encouraging to those who wish this result).[61] I *am* suggesting, however, that the use of the term 'individuals' in this context is a further indication that judges are unable to distinguish between the social interests of purely economic entities and those of human beings, particularly socially disadvantaged human beings.

The judicial tendency to equate the interests of corporations under the *Charter* with those of human beings is an ominous portent. It suggests that rights which were placed in the *Charter* to serve peculiarly human needs will be employed uncritically by the courts to protect purely economic interests. It further suggests that corporations which owe their powers to the state may be able to use the *Charter* to deny the state the ability to restrain those powers in the public interest.

(2) Conceptions of Liberty

One of the concerns often expressed by those who oppose entrenched charters of rights is that such charters can be used to undermine the ability of the state to control the use and abuse of private economic power.

Underlying this concern is a belief that a charter of rights embodies a theory that favours a minimal state, and that the courts will reinforce this theory by interpreting freedom under the *Charter* solely in terms of freedom from state intervention.

In Canada, this concern has been dismissed as ideological hysteria by some. Others, however, have given it more serious attention. Professor Roderick MacDonald, acknowledging the legitimacy of the concern, has argued that the courts should resist the temptation to interpret the *Charter* 'as the entrenchment of the anarchical fallacy that freedom arises only when constraint is absent.'[62] Freedom, he urges, must be understood as having both positive and negative aspects. Hence, government regulation can be seen as facilitating freedom where its purpose and effect are to enhance opportunities for fuller participation in the economic and political system:

> On the above analysis, the interpretation of any particular term of the [*Charter*] must not be reduced to a literal proscription on state activity. Evaluation of substantive enactments must balance the positive freedom such legislation facilitates against the restraint it imposes ... [A]ll rights elaborated in the *Charter* and all state activity measured against it must be evaluated by the following standard: does the restriction enhance the ability of all citizens to participate meaningfully in the process of the state?[63]

Essentially, MacDonald posits two distinct conceptions of freedom and, thus, of the relationship between individuals and the state. Under one conception, state action and individual freedom are inimical to each other; under the other, state action can be seen as a precondition to the attainment of individual freedom. The validity of the first conception is wholly dependent upon an ideological commitment to free markets and on faith in the ability of the unregulated marketplace to allocate resources fairly. The validity of the second conception is grounded in the notion that the marketplace is an insufficient protector of individual freedom and that private power poses as great a threat to individual liberty as does public power.

Each of these competing conceptions has political and cultural roots in Western democracy, though some democratic states have traditionally been more sympathetic to one conception than to the other. Indeed, MacDonald's advocacy of the latter conception can be seen as an appeal to Canadian political traditions over American ones. The American state was founded upon a commitment to limited government; the

Canadian state was not. And while the rhetoric of American politics takes for granted the value of free market economics, Canadian politics is more accepting of the need for state action to direct market forces and to compensate for deficiencies in the marketplace.[64]

Thus MacDonald's views reflect a concern not only that the courts refrain from using the *Charter* as an instrument to strip individuals of the benefits and protections they are afforded by state action but also, at a more basic level, that the *Charter* not be used to undermine the fundamental political character of the Canadian state. His prescription is to urge the courts to embrace a notion of freedom that is sensitive to the underlying political values of the country, and particularly to the view that government can act as a facilitator, as well as an inhibitor, of individual rights.

The early *Charter* decisions provide strong evidence that the Supreme Court embraces a wholly negative conception of freedom: a conception that views government solely as an inhibitor of freedom and that discounts the interests of individuals who depend upon the state to guarantee their freedom. In his majority decision in *Big M Drug Mart*, Dickson J. states that '[f]reedom can primarily be characterized by the absence of coercion or constraint.'[65] In her concurring opinion in *Operation Dismantle*, Wilson J. defines the 'right to liberty' in section 7 of the *Charter* as 'the right to pursue one's goals free from government restraint.'[66] It is again *Southam*, however, that illustrates most graphically the Court's vision of freedom and its relationship to the state.

The *Southam* case arose from a search conducted by combines officials of the business records of the *Edmonton Journal*, a Southam newspaper. The search was authorized by the Director of Investigation and Research of the Combines Investigation Branch in accordance with subsections 10(1) and (3) of the *Combines Investigation Act*. These provisions empowered the Director, on receiving a certificate from a member of the Restrictive Trade Practices Commission, to authorize a search of 'any premises on which [he] believes there may be evidence relevant' to an inquiry under the Act.

In his decision, Dickson J., writing for a unanimous Court, concludes that these provisions violate the 'right to be secure from unreasonable search and seizure' guaranteed by section 8 of the *Charter*. What is interesting, however, is the process of reasoning by which he reaches this result. While acknowledging that the meaning of the word 'unreasonable' in section 8 is indeterminate, Dickson J. seeks to establish a meaning by considering 'the purpose underlying s. 8.' He identifies that purpose as the protection of 'individuals from unjustified state intrusions upon their privacy.'[67] Thus the word 'unreasonable,' he says, indicates

> that an assessment must be made as to whether in a particular situation the public's interest in being left alone by government must give way to the government's interest in intruding on the individual's privacy in order to advance its goals, notably those of law enforcement.[68]

Based on this 'purposive interpretation,' Dickson J. concludes that, in order to meet the requirements of section 8, a search must be authorized by prior warrant issued by a person 'capable of acting judicially,' and that such warrant should only be issued where there are 'reasonable and probable grounds, established upon oath, to believe that an offence has been committed and that there is evidence to be found at the place of the search.'[69] The provisions of the Act fail to meet this standard, he says, first because members of the Restrictive Trade Practices Commission are not sufficiently neutral or detached to be capable of acting 'in a judicial capacity,' and second because the Director is empowered to authorize searches without first having to establish that an offence has been committed.

The first thing worth noting about this analysis is that it discounts entirely a role for the state in promoting rights and freedoms. In balancing the rights of the individual against the interests of the state, Dickson J. characterizes the state's interest under the *Combines Investigation Act* as being 'simply law enforcement.'[70] There is no reference in his judgment to the underlying purpose of that enforcement or to the interests it serves. There is no consideration of the possibility that the actions of the state might be understood and justified in terms of the freedom that such actions bestow upon other individuals. These omissions are particularly noteworthy given the nature of the *Combines Investigation Act*. The Act is not aimed at protecting interests that are peculiar to the state; nor is it, like most criminal statutes, aimed at activities that can be considered morally reprehensible.[71] Its purpose is to promote freedom in the marketplace. In particular, it is to protect the interests of small entrepreneurs and consumers who might otherwise be subject to coercion at the hands of private economic interests powerful enough to undermine competitive market forces.

It is ironic that, in the context of a judgment that claims, above all, to be 'purposive,' Dickson J.'s consideration of the state's interest in enacting the *Combines Investigation Act*, and of the freedom that Act bestows upon others, should be so dismally purposeless.[72] Nowhere does he consider the public interest served by the *Combines Investigation Act*, nor does he consider how that public interest might be undermined by requiring a judicialized warrant procedure or, more significantly, by making proof that an offence has been committed a precondition to a 'reasonable' search and seizure by the state.[73] The only explanation that adequately accounts for this purposeless approach to assessing the interests of the state is that the Court subscribes to the 'anarchical fallacy' to which MacDonald refers. The judgment reflects a hostility to state action of any character and an unwillingness to give weight to the correlative rights of those who rely upon state action for protection of their freedom.

Further evidence of the hostility with which the Court views state action can be found in Dickson J.'s treatment of the appropriate onus of proof. It should be remembered that the word 'unreasonable' is incorporated into section 8 as a part of the right: 'the right to be secure against unreasonable search or seizure.' Since the onus for proving that a right has been breached under the *Charter* falls on the person alleging the breach, one would expect that a 'purposive' interpretation of section 8 would place the onus for proving the 'unreasonableness' of the search or seizure upon Southam. Otherwise, the framers of the *Charter* would have omitted the word 'unreasonable' from section 8 and left it to government to justify its actions under section 1. Dickson J., however, seems to ignore the logic of the section by effectively placing on government the onus of proving that its search and seizure powers are reasonable. He does this first by holding that warrantless searches are *prima facie* unreasonable,[74] and second by deciding that searches conducted in the absence of a reasonable belief that an offence has been committed are necessarily unreasonable (at least where the state's interest is 'simply law enforcement').

In these ways, the judgment in *Southam* takes some dangerous steps down the road of negative freedom. By ignoring the possibility that government action might facilitate individual freedom and by placing the onus upon government to justify the reasonableness of its searches, the Court jeopardizes the interests of the less powerful in society, who depend upon government action to provide and protect their rights and freedoms.

The ultimate irony of the *Southam* case, however, only becomes apparent when the judgment is looked upon as a whole. The consequence of the Court's failure to distinguish between the privacy interests of corporations and those of human beings is to protect the right of artificial entities to wield economic powers granted to them by the state. At the same time, the effect of its adherence to a wholly negative notion of freedom is to curb the ability of the state to control those powers in the name of individual entrepreneurs and consumers. The result is a decision that sides against the interests of individuals and of competitive markets, the two touchstones of classical liberal thought.[75]

(3) Procedural and Substantive Rights

The rhetoric of the Supreme Court of Canada in its early *Charter* decisions reflects two conflicting desires. On the one hand, the Court wishes to be viewed as a progressive force in society. Accordingly, it has gone out of its way to free itself from the shackles of its *Canadian Bill of Rights* jurisprudence and, in almost every case, has pledged to interpret the *Charter* in a broad and liberal manner. On the other hand, the Court clearly wants to retain its identity as a judicial rather than a legislative body and has sought to refrain from taking too active a role. The Court has sought to accommodate these conflicting desires by giving its most expansive interpretations in relation to procedural rights[76] and by avoiding, where possible, any overt balancing of substantive policy.[77] Indeed, the Court has been circumspect with respect to its treatment of all substantive claims under the *Charter*.

Of the five cases involving claims to substantive rights,[78] the Court favours the persons invoking those rights in three of them. In two of these three cases, the Court takes an extremely cautious approach, striking down the legislation on the narrowest grounds possible and, by avoiding section 1 of the *Charter*,[79] sparing itself the necessity of having to appear to balance one substantive policy against another. In *Big M Drug Mart*, for example, the majority founds its decision on the religious purpose of the legislation and rejects the broader reasoning of Wilson J., who would have struck down the Sunday closing law on the basis of its effects. The majority's approach leaves unanswered questions concerning the constitutionality of secular Sunday closing laws and enables the Court to avoid having to consider under section 1 secular justifications for the law.[80]

In *Quebec Association of Protestant School Boards*, after deciding that parts of Quebec's *Charter of French Language* violate minority-language education rights, the Court refuses to consider two other questions relating to funding and pupil access. The Court also refuses to consider justifications for the law under section 1 of the *Charter* because, it says, the denial of section 23 is so blatant that it cannot constitute a 'reasonable limit' within the meaning of section 1. Professor Hogg has stated that the decision of the Court not to consider section 1 is based upon 'an amorphous distinction' that 'introduces an unnecessary and inappropriate complexity into the application of s. 1.'[81] But that, of course, is its purpose. The distinction between denials of rights that are and are not susceptible to being upheld under section 1 serves the same function as the distinction in *Operation Dismantle* between allegations that are and are not capable of being proved.[82] Both distinctions enable the Court to avoid the appearance of engaging in substantive balancing of competing political interests. They are expedients that permit the Court to protect its neutral and apolitical image as a judicial body.

The approach taken by the Court to the resolution of the substantive issues in the *Southam* case is less conservative. The Court interprets section 8 of the *Charter* as preventing government from using search powers for law enforcement except where there is evidence that 'an offence has been committed and that there is [further] evidence to be found at the place of the search.'[83] The rhetoric employed by the Court to support its decision is interesting. While claiming, on the one hand, to take a broad and purposive approach, the Court goes out of its way to demonstrate that the standards it adopts are grounded in 'Anglo-Canadian legal and political traditions.'[84] Thus, while the constitutionalization of this standard represents a significant judicial usurpation of legislative power, the Court is able to convey the appearance that its decision is merely an extension of abiding societal values.

The generally cautious approach of the Court in relation to substantive rights stands in stark contrast to the overt activism of its procedural decisions under the *Charter*. Of the five cases involving claims to procedural rights,[85] the Court favours the persons invoking the rights all five times. In *Southam* the Court devises a comprehensive procedural code governing the issuance of search warrants. In *Singh* the Court finds procedural defects in the system used by the federal government to determine whether illegal immigrants should be accorded refugee status. It is true that three of the six members involved in the judgment founded their decision upon the *Canadian Bill of Rights* rather than upon section 7 of the *Charter*, but this likely reflects a particular concern for that provision – one that has the potential to wear both substantive and procedural masks. In *Therens, Rahn*, and *Trask*[86] the Court holds that persons asked to submit to breathalyzer tests under section 235(1) of the *Criminal Code* are detained within the meaning of section 10 of the *Charter* and thus are entitled to be informed of their right to retain and instruct counsel without delay. The more startling aspect of these three cases, however, is the majority's holding that the introduction of direct evidence obtained in contravention of the *Charter* would necessarily 'bring the administration of justice into disrepute.'[87] Though the Court does not say so, the result seems to be the creation of an absolute exclusionary rule requiring the exclusion of any evidence obtained as a direct consequence of a *Charter* violation. This last holding may be explained in part as another example of the Court's unwillingness to be seen as engaging in balancing interests, even in relation to the exclusion of evidence. But it also reflects the relative enthusiasm with which the Court views procedural rights.

What accounts for the greater activism of the Court in relation to procedural as opposed to substantive rights, and what are its consequences? The causes can easily be explained. Because procedural rights do not directly address questions of substantive policy, they appear less disruptive of the political process. The substantive goals of legislation that is struck down for procedural defects can usually (though not always) be accommodated within a reformed procedural framework. Furthermore, the judiciary has traditionally assumed a creative role in resolving procedural issues, particularly in the context of administrative and criminal law. Procedure is an area with which the judiciary is thought to have superior expertise. Thus the Court can afford to assume an activist stance with respect to procedural rights, thereby strengthening its reputation as a progressive force, without doing serious damage to its image as a judicial body.

The very reasons that permit the judiciary to be more activist with respect to procedural rights make the protection afforded by such rights less socially significant. For example, the *Singh* decision permits the government to continue to apply the same criteria to deny immigrants refugee status provided the procedure for applying those criteria are modified to provide for an oral hearing at some stage in the process. The decisions in *Therens, Rahn*, and *Trask* do not limit the powers of the police to require drivers to submit to breathalyzer tests provided the police go through the motions of advising drivers of their right to counsel.

What this suggests is that, in the short term, the most dramatic impact of *Charter* adjudication upon public policy will be to strengthen the procedural framework in which policy is implemented rather than to alter the policy itself. The fight for substantive reform under the

Charter will be more difficult and protracted. For this reason, it is a fight that favours those who have the economic resources to sustain the battle. Furthermore, the circumspection that the Court has displayed with respect to substantive rights suggests that it is a fight that is more likely to be won by those who assert rights whose content and context reflect traditional judicial values, or values with which the judiciary can easily identify. It is significant that two of the three cases in which the Court has found substantive *Charter* rights to have been violated concerned the rights of property owners: one a corporation's right to privacy in its property,[88] and the other a corporation's right to be free from government regulation in the conduct of its business.[89] Conversely, both of the cases in which the Court has found substantive rights not to have been violated involved rights unrelated to property: one the right of non-Canadians to earn a livelihood,[90] and the other the right of the public to be free from the alleged dangers created by cruise missile testing.[91]

Conclusion

The *Charter* saga has just begun, and it would be foolhardy to predict at this stage what its precise social and economic impacts will be. The political themes and directions that underlie the early Supreme Court of Canada decisions, however, are discouraging for those who look upon the *Charter* as an instrument for advancing the interests of socially and economically disadvantaged Canadians. Furthermore, the institutional variables that shape *Charter* adjudication strongly suggest that these themes and directions are likely to be continued and embellished in the future.

Some, no doubt, are still pinning their hopes on section 15 of the *Charter*, the equality rights section, which has just recently come into force. Though section 15 does not afford explicit protection from discrimination on the basis of social or economic status, some of the grounds of discrimination it does enumerate (such as race, ethnic origin, and sex) coincide with social and economic cleavages in Canadian society. Thus many see in section 15 a major vehicle for redressing social and economic disparities.

While I think it is improbable that the Supreme Court will give section 15 the short shrift that it gave to equality rights under the *Canadian Bill of Rights*, the performance of the Court in the *Bill of Rights* cases stands as a stark reminder of the inherent conservatism and lack of competence of the judiciary in relation to claims founded upon principles of equality.[92] Coupled with the caution that the Court has already displayed with respect to other substantive claims, this will likely result in the Court using section 15 to redress only the most obvious instances of inequality under the law.

The consequence could be decisions that are actually socially and economically regressive. The major manifestations of social and economic inequality in our society stem not from explicit legislative edict, but from underlying systemic practices. At the same time, provisions that are clearly directed against groups that are socially disadvantaged have been expurgated from most statute books over the past few decades in response to changing political attitudes. The apparently discriminatory provisions that remain are, in many instances, those which favour the socially disadvantaged. A white paper released by the Saskatchewan Department of Justice, for example, shows that the majority of provisions on that province's statute books that distinguish between people on the basis of their gender are those that bestow social and economic benefits exclusively upon women.[93] It is true that such provisions, insofar as they reflect the paternalistic view that women are less able to care for themselves, can be characterized as reflecting a discriminatory attitude against women. The economic impact of eliminating such benefits, however, would be to further disadvantage women in the name of equality.[94]

In sum, the politics of the *Charter* suggest that even a seemingly 'liberalized' attitude towards equality rights is unlikely to address the underlying causes of social inequality in Canada. At best, courts may lash out at the few remnants of overt governmental discrimination, such as the treatment of women in the military, thereby diverting attention from more deeply rooted manifestations of social injustice. At worst, court decisions could serve to legitimize measures directed against the disadvantaged and produce results that exacerbate social inequalities.

NOTES

1 The quoted words come from the judgment of Lord Atkinson in *Roberts v. Hopwood*, [1925] A.C. 578 at 594 (H.L.).
2 See W.N. Hohfeld, 'Some Fundamental Legal Conceptions as Applied in Judicial Reasoning' (1913) 23 Yale L.J. 16. For a discussion of Hohfeld's analysis, see D. Kennedy & F. Michelman, 'Are Property and Contract Efficient?' (1980) 8 Hofstra L. Rev. 711 at 748–58.

3 *Harrison v. Carswell*, [1976] 2 S.C.R. 200 [*Harrison v. Carswell*].

4 *Petty Trespasses Act*, R.S.M. 1970, c. P-50.

5 Section 32(1) of the *Charter* provides that the *Charter* applies 'to the Parliament and government of Canada' and 'to the legislature and government of each province.' Some writers have argued that this section merely establishes a floor of applicability, not a ceiling, and that the *Charter* ought also to be applied directly to private action: see D. Gibson, 'The Charter of Rights and the Private Sector' (1982) 12 Man. L.J. 213; M. Manning, *Rights, Freedoms and the Courts* (Toronto: Emond/Montgomery, 1983) at 115–26. This view, however, is contrary to the intent of the drafters and is not subscribed to by most commentators: see P.W. Hogg, *Constitutional Law of Canada*, 2nd ed. (Toronto: Carswell, 1985) at 674–78; J.D. Whyte, 'Is the Private Sector Affected by the Charter?' in L. Smith, ed., *Righting the Balance: Canada's New Equality Rights* (Saskatoon: Canadian Human Rights Reporter, 1986); K. Swinton, 'Application of the Canadian Charter of Rights and Freedoms' in W.S. Tarnopolsky & G.A. Beaudoin, eds., *The Canadian Charter of Rights and Freedoms: Commentary* (Toronto: Carswell, 1982). Of course, if the application of the *Charter* is limited to governmental action, one is forced to confront the question of whether a coherent line can be drawn between governmental and private action: see B. Slattery, 'Charter of Rights and Freedoms: Does It Bind Private Persons' (1985) 63 Can. Bar Rev. 148; Whyte, *ibid.*; D. Gibson, 'Distinguishing the Governors from the Governed' (1983) 13 Man. L.J. 505; Y. de Montigny, 'Section 32 and Equality Rights' in A. Bayefsky & M. Eberts, eds., *Equality Rights and the Canadian Charter of Rights and Freedoms* (Toronto: Carswell, 1985).

6 *Morey v. Doud*, 354 U.S. 457 at 472 (1957).

7 Anyone who doubts the contingent nature of the notion of equality should consider the following tax schemes: one that taxes everyone at 10 per cent of their total income; one that taxes everyone at 100 per cent of that portion of their income under $10,000; one that taxes everyone at 100 per cent of that portion of their income over $10,000. All three schemes subject taxpayers to a uniform tax formula and, in that sense, treat people equally. Yet the relative economic impact of each scheme on different income earners varies tremendously.

8 Section 1 of the *Charter* gives the courts the mandate to uphold legally prescribed limits on *Charter* rights that they deem to be 'reasonable' and 'demonstrably justified in a free and democratic society.'

9 *Alliance des Professeurs de Montreal v. Attorney-General of Quebec*, [1985] C.A. 376 (Qc.), trans., quoting C. Perelman, *Le raisonnable et le déraisonnable en droit* (Paris: Librairie générale de droit et de jurisprudence, 1984).

10 *Harrison v. Carswell, supra* note 3 at 218.
11 *Gay Alliance Toward Equality v. The Vancouver Sun*, [1979] 2 S.C.R. 435 [*Gay Alliance*].
12 *Ibid.* at 454.
13 At the time of writing, the Supreme Court had engaged in *Charter* interpretation in nine cases. They are, in the order in which they were decided: *Skapinker v. Law Society of Upper Canada*, [1984] 1 S.C.R. 357 [*Skapinker*]; *Quebec Assn. of Protestant School Boards v. Quebec (A.G.)*, [1984] 2 S.C.R. 66 [*Quebec Assn. of Protestant School Boards*]; *Hunter v. Southam Inc.*, [1984] 2 S.C.R. 145 [*Southam*]; *Singh v. Canada (Minister of Employment & Immigration)*, [1985] 1 S.C.R. 177 [*Singh*]; *R. v. Big M Drug Mart Ltd.*, [1985] 1 S.C.R. 295 [*Big M Drug Mart*]; *Operation Dismantle Inc. v. R.*, [1985] 1 S.C.R. 441 [*Operation Dismantle*]; *R. v. Therens*, [1985] 1 S.C.R. 613 [*Therens*]; *R. v. Trask*, [1985] 1 S.C.R. 655 [*Trask*]; *R. v. Rahn*, [1985] 1 S.C.R. 659 [*Rahn*]. (I was counsel for the appellant the Attorney General of Saskatchewan in the *Therens* case.) This number does not include cases in which *Charter* issues were raised but subsequently abandoned, or cases in which the Court was able to decide the issues without reference to a *Charter* claim.
14 Section 1 states: 'The *Canadian Charter of Rights and Freedoms* guarantees the rights and freedoms set out in it subject only to such reasonable limits prescribed by law as can be demonstrably justified in a free and democratic society.'
15 P. Russell, 'The Political Purposes of the Canadian Charter of Rights and Freedoms' (1983) 61 Can. Bar Rev. 30 at 47.
16 Recognition of these factors might cause one to wonder: Why did those who brought about the enactment of the *Charter* choose the courts as the forum for resolving rights claims? There were alternatives. The structure of human rights commissions, for example, allows complainants to pursue their claims without the assistance of lawyers and with little or no economic resources. Why did the drafters of the *Charter* not establish an independent agency modelled after human rights commissions to adjudicate *Charter* disputes? It is not as though the resolution of rights questions is a peculiarly legal function requiring peculiarly legal skills. Indeed, I suggest later in this essay that the judiciary is peculiarly ill-equipped to deal with the kinds of issues that arise under the *Charter*. So why not an independent adjudicative agency made up of workers, feminists, philosophers, and social activists?
17 Even if persons with limited means could find lawyers willing to fight *Charter* cases on a 'pro bono* basis, most Canadians would have difficulty raising the money to cover the cost of disbursements, let alone the costs

of the other side should they lose. For example, criminal lawyer Edward Greenspan has estimated the costs of disbursements resulting from taking a criminal appeal to the Supreme Court of Canada at $9,500; in the *Southam* case, copying costs alone for the two-and-one-half-year court battle amounted to $8,000: *The Toronto Star* (23 April 1985) at A11.

18 *Ibid.* This figure presumably represents the total of all legal bills paid by Southam before collecting costs that were awarded to it by the Supreme Court.

19 Telephone interview of Jim Stark, President, Operation Dismantle Inc. (7 August 1985). This figure does not include the costs that Operation Dismantle was ordered to pay the government.

20 The Ontario and British Columbia legal aid schemes, for example, provide funding where the conviction of an accused would likely result in imprisonment. Also, a government that wishes to appeal a criminal acquittal to test some legal proposition will sometimes offer to pay the accused's legal fees. This occurred in *Therens*, *supra* note 13, where the Saskatchewan government agreed to pay the respondent's legal fees in relation to its appeal to the Supreme Court of Canada.

21 On 25 September 1985 the federal government announced that it would provide $9 million over five years to fund 'important test cases' under equality rights provisions of the *Charter* and to continue federal funding of cases relating to constitutional language rights. See Government of Canada, News Release (25 September 1985). [Federal funding for *Charter* test cases was extended in the 1990s but terminated in 2006.]

22 In Ontario the legal aid plan has provided funding for some *Charter* claims, but this is not the case in most other provinces. In some provinces, legal aid schemes do fund certain family law matters and, presumably, *Charter* claims that arise in the context of such matters. The Ontario government has also made a $1 million grant to the Women's Legal Education Action Fund to assist with *Charter* claims on behalf of women.

23 See D.V. Smiley, 'The Case against the Canadian Charter of Human Rights' (1969) 2 C.J.P.S. 277 at 283.

24 See F.L. Morton, 'Charting the Charter – Year One: A Statistical Analysis' in W. Pentney & D. Proulx, eds., *Canadian Human Rights Yearbook, 1984–85* (Toronto: Carswell, 1985).

25 See B. Bell-Rowbotham & C. Boydell, 'Crime in Canada: A Distributional Analysis' in C. Boydell, C.F. Grindstaff, & P.C. Whitehead, eds., *Deviant Behavior and Societal Reaction* (Toronto: Holt, Rinehart & Winston, 1972).

26 See Law Reform Commission of Canada, 'East York Community Law Reform Project' in *Studies on Diversion* (Ottawa: Information Canada, 1975).

27 See Russell, *supra* note 15 at 49. A good illustration of this point is provided
    by recent *Charter* decisions striking down provisions of the *Criminal Code*
    protecting complaints in sexual assault trials from being cross-examined
    on their sexual histories. These provisions were inserted in the *Criminal
    Code* to encourage victims of sexual assault to come forward and to protect
    them from being subjected to further psychological trauma in court. Nev-
    ertheless, a number of superior courts have held that these provisions vio-
    late an accused's rights to a fair trial and fundamental justice: *R. v. Oquataq*,
    [1985] N.W.T.R. 240 (S.C.); *R. v. LeGallant* (1985), 47 C.R. (3d) 170 (B.C.S.C.)
    [subsequently rev'd in (1986), 6 B.C.L.R. (2d) 105 (C.A.)]; *R. v. Seaboyer, R.
    v. Gayme* (22 November 1985), (Ont. H.C.) [subsequently aff'd in (1987), 61
    O.R. (2d) 290 (C.A.) and by S.C.C. in [1991] 2 S.C.R. 577].

28 The criminal cases are *Therens, Trask*, and *Rahn, supra* note 13. I am not
    using the term 'criminal' here in the same sense that it is used in the
    context of federalism cases. Thus, though the *Combines Investigation Act*
    (R.S.C. 1970, c. C-23) and the *Lord's Day Act* (R.S.C. 1970, c. L-13) have been
    characterized as criminal law for the purpose of upholding their constitu-
    tionality under section 91 of the *Constitution Act, 1867*, I have not identified
    Southam, supra note 13 (search under the *Combines Investigation Act*) or *Big
    M Drug Mart, supra* note 13 (charges under the *Lord's Day Act*) as criminal
    cases. Both statutes are concerned with the regulation of business conduct,
    and both are aimed at behaviour that today is considered less morally
    reprehensible than it is socially or economically deleterious: see *C.N.
    Transportation Ltd. v. Canada (Attorney General)*, [1983] 2 S.C.R. 206 at 274
    [*C.N. Transportation*], Dickson J., and *Big M Drug Mart, supra* note 13 at
    351.

29 *Southam* and *Big M Drug Mart, supra* note 13. Though Operation Dismantle
    is an incorporated entity, it is more appropriately identified as a political
    group as opposed to a corporation in the traditional sense.

30 *Quebec Assn. of Protestant Schools Boards, supra* note 13. The school boards in
    this case received financial assistance from the fund created by the federal
    government to support *Charter* litigation based upon constitutional lan-
    guage rights.

31 *Operation Dismantle, supra* note 13.

32 *Skapinker* and *Singh, supra* note 13.

33 *Singh, ibid.*, was initiated by a number of illegal immigrants of apparently
    little means seeking refugee status in Canada. *Skapinker, ibid.*, on the other
    hand, concerned the right of two lawyers, one of whom was already a
    member of the Massachusetts Bar, to practise law in Ontario.

34 See *e.g.* B. Dickson, 'Address to the Mid-Winter Meeting of the Canadian
    Bar Association' (2 February 1985) N.A.C. 139:10.

35 *Singh, supra* note 13.

36 *Skapinker, supra* note 13.

37 Section 10(b) provides: 'Everyone has the right on arrest or detention ... (b) to retain and instruct counsel without delay.'

38 *Operation Dismantle, supra* note 13.

39 This is the estimate given by the federal Justice Minister: *House of Commons Debates,* (4 May 1985) at 4721 (Hon. John Crosbie). After intense lobbying by peace groups and opposition politicians, the government decided not to collect these costs.

40 *Ibid.* at 4722.

41 Jim Stark, *supra* note 19. See also M. Mandel, 'The Rule of Law and the Legalization of Politics in Canada' (1985) 13 Int'l J. Soc. L. 273 at 279–85.

42 *Operation Dismantle, supra* note 13 at 475–9.

43 *Ibid.* at 450–5.

44 The Supreme Court has confronted some highly charged political issues in the context of division-of-powers cases such as the *Reference re Anti-Inflation Act,* [1976] 2 S.C.R. 373 and the *Patriation Reference,* [1981] 1 S.C.R. 753. In these cases, however, the substantive political debate was masked by a jurisdictional dispute between two orders of duly elected government. Hence the Court could purport to arbitrate based upon impersonal, institutional criteria and thus appear to resolve the issues without engaging in a substantive evaluation of the policies at stake. In *Charter* cases the Court does not act as an arbitrator between governments and cannot claim to be applying purely institutional criteria. *Charter* cases require the Court to substitute its opinion concerning the effect and merits of a policy for that of all governments, especially in considering whether a policy that violates a *Charter* right can nevertheless be upheld under section 1. In short, while in division-of-powers cases the Court can satisfy itself, and others, that the nature of the judicial decision-making process is qualitatively different from the nature of the political decision-making process, in *Charter* cases it cannot credibly do so. See P.J. Monahan, 'Judicial Review and Democracy: A Theory of Judicial Review' (1985) [unpublished] [subsequently published in (1987) 21 U.B.C.L. Rev. 87].

45 *Operation Dismantle, supra* note 13 at 454.

46 *Ibid.* at 479.

47 *Quebec Assn. of Protestant School Boards, supra* note 13.

48 Hogg, *supra* note 5 at 98.

49 Professor Schmeiser has put it this way:

> The assumption underlying judicial review of legislation is that courts will act better than government, that they will act more in the interest of

the people. The difficulty with this assumption is that legal practice and old age can produce conservative persons who are suspicious of social change. In the Great Depression, the United States Supreme Court used its judicial review power to block urgently needed social reform. The Canadian judicial attitude to administrative tribunals and to statutory interpretation also reveals a lack of awareness on occasion of social needs.

D.A. Schmeiser, 'Disadvantages of an Entrenched Canadian Bill of Rights' (1968) 33 Sask. L. Rev. 249 at 250–1.

50 J.A.G. Griffith, *The Politics of the Judiciary*, 3rd ed. (London: Fontana Press, 1985) at 198 [emphasis omitted].

51 *Ibid.* at 202–3.

52 *Big M Drug Mart, supra* note 13.

53 *Southam, supra* note 13.

54 *Ibid.* at 159.

55 *Ibid.* at 160.

56 *Big M Drug Mart, supra* note 13 at 336.

57 *Bellis v. United States*, 417 U.S. 85 at 92 (1974). This case dealt with self-incrimination and not search or seizure, but the principle is the same. Furthermore, while the United States Supreme Court has held that the Fourth Amendment, which protects the right to be secure in one's person and one's papers against unreasonable searches and seizures, applies to corporations, this can be explained on the basis of the specific wording of that amendment, which contemplates protection of property independent of privacy interests. What is disturbing about Dickson C.J.'s judgment is that he seems to want it both ways. He wants to say that section 8 is principally a privacy right, and thus more worthy of judicial protection than a mere property right, but he then goes on to apply it in a way that engages no interest beyond property.

58 In the first instance, for example, the shareholder might live on the premises and keep her personal records in the same place as her business records, while in the second, the shareholder might never have even visited the corporation's offices.

59 *Big M Drug Mart, supra* note 13 at 313.

60 Section 15(1) of the *Charter* states: 'Every individual is equal before and under the law and has the right to the equal protection and equal benefit of the law without discrimination and, in particular, without discrimination based on race, national or ethnic origin, colour, religion, sex, age, or mental or physical disability.'

61 See E. Gertner, 'Are Corporations Entitled to Equality?' (1986) 19 C.R.R. 287.

62 R.A. MacDonald, 'Postscript and Prelude – The Jurisprudence of the Charter: Eight Theses' (1982) 4 Sup. Ct. L. Rev. 321 at 346.

63 *Ibid.* at 345–6. Professor Russell expresses a similar concern when he states: 'It would be a pity if adoption of a constitutional charter of rights blunted our capacity to recognize that the state is not the only centre of power in our society capable of restricting freedom or equality or of abusing rights': *supra* note 15 at 50.

64 See Monahan, *supra* note 44.

65 *Big M Drug Mart, supra* note 13 at 336.

66 *Operation Dismantle, supra* note 13 at 488.

67 *Southam, supra* note 13 at 160.

68 *Ibid.* at 159–60.

69 *Ibid.* at 168.

70 *Ibid.*

71 See *C.N. Transportation, supra* note 28 at 365, Dickson J.

72 Indeed, the characterization of the state's purpose as 'simply law enforcement' is doubly ironic given that it was Dickson J. who one year earlier went out of his way in *C.N. Transportation, ibid.* to characterize the offence provisions of the *Combines Investigation Act* as being in relation to trade and commerce (as well as criminal law) because they were part of a scheme that sought to regulate 'economically deleterious' conduct: *ibid.* at 274.

73 The impact of the latter requirement, it should be noted, is to limit severely the substantive powers of the state to use search and seizure as a means of detecting and regulating anti-competitive behaviour. Nothing in the Act suggested that the search power could be used only to garner evidence of an offence, let alone that the Director had to have reasonable and probable grounds to believe that an offence had been committed. On the contrary, the Act permitted the Director to invoke his search powers for the purpose of garnering evidence 'relevant to' an inquiry, regardless of whether an offence had been established or not.

74 *Southam, supra* note 13 at 160–2. I am not arguing that a warrant procedure should never be required by section 8. What I am suggesting is that a 'purposive' interpretation of that section, and one that recognizes a role for government as a facilitator as well as an inhibitor of freedom, would place the onus on the party alleging the breach to demonstrate that the interests of government in conducting warrantless searches, and the correlative freedoms of others (who are unrepresented in court), are outweighed by the individual's right to privacy. Presumably this onus would be easy to

discharge where the government's objectives could be met through a warrant procedure. My concern, however, is for the myriad of administrative and regulatory searches to which warrants can have no application. The consequence of the *Southam* decision is to place upon government the onus for showing that its substantive objectives, and the interests of the public, in carrying out health and safety inspections, for example, outweigh the privacy interests of the 'individuals' being searched.

75 Furthermore, if the Court is not prepared to recognize the public interest represented by a liberal piece of legislation like the *Combines Investigation Act*, we can only wait with trepidation to see how the Court will regard attempts by the state to facilitate freedom through redistribution of wealth and other interventionist measures.

76 By procedural rights, I mean rights that relate to the *way* in which a policy must be achieved as opposed to rights that determine *whether* that policy can be achieved at all. Thus, in *Southam* I would identify that part of the judgment relating to when and by whom a warrant must be issued as 'procedural' and that part of the judgment specifying a standard of proof that must be met before a search can be conducted as 'substantive.' I recognize, of course, that the line between substantive and procedural rights is somewhat murky and that procedures can have a profound influence upon substance (indeed, that is the thesis of much of the first part of this essay).

77 See Monahan, *supra* note 44.

78 The five cases in which substantive claims were made are *Skapinker* (right to work); *Quebec Assn. of Protestant School Boards* (right to education in English); *Southam* (right not to be searched in absence of certain substantive criteria); *Big M Drug Mart* (right to operate one's business on a Sunday); and *Operation Dismantle* (right to be free of the alleged dangers of cruise missile testing), see *supra* note 13.

79 *Supra* note 14.

80 In the words of Dickson C.J.: 'The appellant can no more assert under s. 1 a secular objective to validate legislation which in pith and substance involves a religious matter than it could assert a secular objective as the basis for the argument that the legislation does not offend s. 2(a).': *Big M Drug Mart, supra* note 13 at 353.

81 Hogg, *supra* note 5 at 683.

82 See notes 42 to 46 and accompanying text at 26.

83 *Southam, supra* note 13 at 168. See also note 73.

84 *Ibid.* at 167.

85 The five cases in which procedural claims were made are *Southam* (right not to be searched in the absence of certain procedural criteria); *Singh*

(right to a hearing); and *Therens, Rahn,* and *Trask* (right to be informed of one's right to counsel prior to giving breathalyzer evidence), see *supra* note 13.

86 *Therens, Rahn, Trask, supra* note 13.

87 *Therens, ibid.,* at 621–2, Estey J.

88 *Southam, supra* note 13.

89 *Big M Drug Mart, supra* note 13. The third case in which a substantive right was held to have been violated concerned the right of certain parents in Quebec under section 23 of the *Charter* to have their children educated in English: *Quebec Assn. of Protestant School Boards, supra* note 13. However, given the narrow and specific language of section 23, this case is not typical of *Charter* adjudication.

90 *Skapinker, supra* note 13.

91 *Operation Dismantle, supra* note 13.

92 See generally W.S. Tarnopolsky, *The Canadian Bill of Rights,* 2nd rev. ed. (Toronto: McClelland and Stewart, 1975); Hogg, *supra* note 5 at 787–94. It is worth remembering that a number of members of the Court, including Chief Justice Dickson, concurred in perhaps the most egregious of the *Canadian Bill of Rights* decisions, *Bliss v. Canada (A.G.),* [1979] 1 S.C.R. 183, in which the Court decided that a provision denying regular unemployment benefits to a person whose employment was terminated due to pregnancy was not discrimination on the basis of sex. See J.C. MacPherson, 'Developments in Constitutional Law: The 1978–79 Term' (1980) 1 Sup. Ct. L. Rev. 77 at 111–29; M. Gold, 'Equality before the Law in the Supreme Court of Canada' (1980) 18 Osgoode Hall L.J. 336.

93 G. Lane, *Compliance of Saskatchewan Laws with the Canadian Charter of Rights and Freedoms* (Regina: Saskatchewan Department of Justice, 1984).

94 A similar process could occur in relation to criminal legislation that provides special benefits and exemptions to women and children. The Court could decide to strike down such legislation unless these benefits and exemptions are extended to men and to adults.

2 *Charter* Legitimacy on Trial: The Resistible Rise of Substantive Due Process[*]

Because things are the way they are,
things will not stay the way they are.

Bertolt Brecht

Introduction

It is not surprising that in Canada, as in the United States, questions regarding the legitimacy of judicial review under the Constitution would arise in relation to the interpretation of the 'due process clause.'[1] Section 7 is the most broadly framed and potentially expansive guarantee in the *Canadian Charter of Rights and Freedoms*. Positioned under the heading 'Legal Rights,' it provides:

> Everyone has the right to life, liberty and security of the person and the right not to be deprived thereof except in accordance with the principles of fundamental justice.

The scope of the guarantee in section 7 hinges upon the answers to a number of interpretative questions, including what is meant by the words 'life, liberty and security of the person,' whether the section guarantees one right or two, and what is the content of 'the principles of fundamental justice.' The Supreme Court of Canada's decision in the

[*] Originally published in (1987) 9 Sup. Ct. L. Rev. 78–102 as part of P.J. Monahan & A. Petter, 'Developments in Constitutional Law: The 1985–86 Term' (1987) 9 Sup. Ct. L. Rev. 69. Copyright © 1987 by LexisNexis Canada Inc. Reprinted by permission of P.J. Monahan and LexisNexis Canada Inc.

British Columbia Motor Vehicle Reference[2] touches upon all of these issues. The significance of the decision, however, stems from the Court's holding that 'the principles of fundamental justice' are substantive as well as procedural in nature. Because this holding is so clearly contrary to what was intended by the framers of section 7, and because of its implications, the case raises serious questions about the character of the adjudicative process and the scope of judicial power under the *Charter*.

Section 94(2)

In *Motor Vehicle Reference*, the Court was asked to assess the constitutional validity of section 94(2) of the British Columbia *Motor Vehicle Act*.[3] Section 94(1) of the Act made it an offence to drive while prohibited or while one's licence was suspended and imposed a mandatory prison term for all offenders. Section 94(2) provided that this offence was one of 'absolute liability ... in which guilt is established by proof of driving, whether or not the defendant knew of the prohibition or suspension.' The question for the Court was whether section 94(2), by making an offence that called for mandatory imprisonment one of absolute liability, violated an accused's right under section 7 of the *Charter* not to be deprived of liberty 'except in accordance with the principles of fundamental justice.' This, in turn, required the Court to consider whether these principles were substantive as well as procedural in nature. The case made against section 94(2) was not that it denied an accused a fair procedure; rather it was that, by omitting *mens rea* from the offence, it denied an accused a substantive defence.

History of Section 7

In order to appreciate the significance of this issue, one must look both to the history of section 7 and to American constitutional law. Section 7 derives from the 'due process' clause contained in the Fifth and Fourteenth Amendments of the United States Constitution. Yet the framers of the section were wary about certain aspects of the American experience with due process, particularly in relation to substantive due process.

From 1897 to 1937, during the so-called '*Lochner* era,'[4] American courts relied upon the due process clause to give substantive protection to laissez-faire economic liberties such as freedom of contract. These decisions were eventually abandoned when, in an effort to save New Deal legislation, President Franklin Roosevelt threatened to pack the

Supreme Court with his own appointees. But substantive due process did not die in the United States. While the American courts have shied away from giving substantive protection to economic rights since 1937, they have recently invoked substantive due process to protect rights of privacy and personal integrity, especially with respect to issues of contraception and abortion.[5]

The American experience with substantive due process, both before and after 1937, has been an ongoing source of controversy in the United States. The testimony given before the Special Joint Committee on the Constitution discloses that the framers of section 7 were aware of this controversy and sought to avoid it in Canada by adopting language that they believed would eliminate the possibility of section 7 being interpreted as a substantive guarantee.[6] Accordingly, they dropped the words 'due process' and replaced them with 'principles of fundamental justice.'

The choice of the phrase 'principles of fundamental justice' was perhaps unfortunate. As the federal Assistant Deputy Minister of Justice, B.L. Strayer, conceded during questioning before the Special Joint Committee, '[t]he term … has not been used very much in legislation.'[7] The one place in which it had been used was in section 2(e) of the *Canadian Bill of Rights*, which guarantees a person 'the right to a fair hearing in accordance with the principles of fundamental justice for the determination of his rights and obligations.' In *R. v. Duke*,[8] Fauteaux C.J. offered the following definition of 'the principles of fundamental justice' in section 2(e):

> Without attempting to formulate any final definition of those words, I would take them to mean, generally, that the tribunal which adjudicates upon his rights must act fairly, in good faith, without bias and in a judicial temper, and must give to him the opportunity adequately to state his case.[9]

This definition has been equated with the procedural guarantees afforded by the rules of natural justice.[10] The framers seem to have assumed that the *Duke* definition would automatically be applied by the courts in interpreting section 7. In doing so, however, they discounted an important contextual difference between section 7 of the *Charter* and section 2(e) of the *Bill of Rights*. While the former uses the phrase 'principles of fundamental justice' free from contextual limitations, the latter uses the phrase in the context of a provision that specifically addresses 'the right to a fair hearing.'

Still, while the intention of the framers might have been better served by the words 'natural justice,' 'procedural fairness,' or 'procedural due process,' there can be no doubt as to what their intention was. In the words of B.L. Strayer, speaking to the Special Joint Committee:

> Mr. Chairman, it was our belief that the words 'fundamental justice' would cover the same thing as what is called procedural due process, that is the meaning of due process in relation to requiring a fair procedure. However, it in our view does not cover the concept of what is called substantive due process, which would impose substantive requirements as to the policy of the law in question.
>
> This has been most clearly demonstrated in the United States in the area of property, but also in other areas such as the right to life. The term due process has been given the broader concept of meaning both the procedure and the substance. Natural justice or fundamental justice in our view does not go beyond the procedural requirements of fairness.[11]

The decision to limit review in section 7 solely to procedural values reflects the reluctance of the framers of the *Charter* to abandon entirely Anglo-Canadian traditions of parliamentary sovereignty. While they were prepared to permit the judiciary to evaluate the procedural adequacy of legislation, they were not prepared to relinquish to the courts the right to question its substantive adequacy on the basis of a standard as broadly and amorphously expressed as 'due process' or 'fundamental justice.'

Moreover, the framers had good reason to believe that, whatever words they used in section 7, the courts would be sympathetic to their concern to exclude substantive review. Time and again under the *Canadian Bill of Rights,* members of the Supreme Court had shied away from substituting their values for those of legislators, even in relation to apparently explicit substantive guarantees such as equality. In *R. v. Curr,*[12] Laskin J. declined to interpret the due process clause of the *Canadian Bill of Rights* as permitting substantive review of legislation, saying that, in the absence of a constitutional mandate to do so, compelling reasons relating to 'objective and manageable standards' would have to be advanced, and that he was 'not prepared in this case to surmise what they might be.'[13] He then went on to review the 'checkered history' of substantive due process in the United States, referring to the 'bog of legislative policy-making' that a court enters when it attempts 'to enshrine any particular theory ... which has not been plainly expressed in the Constitution.'[14] Thus the whole thrust of *Canadian Bill of Rights* jurisprudence, and the *Curr* judgment in particular, stood against the courts engaging in substantive review under a broadly framed due process guarantee, especially in the absence of a clear mandate from Parliament and the legislatures to do so.

The Decision of the Court

Despite the intentions of the framers, the American experience, and the circumspection of Laskin J. and others in *Canadian Bill of Rights* cases, the seven-member Court in *Motor Vehicle Reference* unanimously decided that the words 'principles of fundamental justice' in section 7 conferred upon the courts the power to review the substantive as well as the procedural adequacy of legislation. Lamer J., writing for himself and four others,[15] held that section 94(2) violated this substantive guarantee by permitting the punishment of those who were 'morally innocent.' McIntyre J. wrote a concurring opinion that endorsed Lamer J.'s reasoning, and Wilson J. reached the same result for somewhat different reasons.[16]

How did the Court justify this result, and what are its implications? The reasoning of the majority judgment of Lamer J. can be divided into three parts: the first is a defence of the legitimacy of judicial review under the *Charter*; the second seeks to support a substantive interpretation of section 7; and the third addresses the meaning of the 'principles of fundamental justice' in their substantive sense.

(1) Legitimacy of Judicial Review

Justice Lamer starts off by defending the legitimacy of judicial review under the *Charter*, particularly in relation to substantive due process. Essentially, his argument is that substantive review of legislation by the courts is nothing new in Canada. Such review took place under sections 91 and 92 of the *Constitution Act, 1867*, 'albeit within the more limited sphere of values related to the distribution of powers.'[17] From this he concludes that, under the *Charter*, 'it is the scope of constitutional adjudication which has been altered rather than its nature, at least, as regards the right to consider the content of legislation.'[18]

Lamer J. then goes on to respond to suggestions that a substantive reading of section 7 would require the courts to 'question the wisdom of enactments.'[19] This he denies, saying that, whether procedural or substantive, the task of the courts under section 7 is not to question the wisdom of legislation, but rather to measure the content of legislation against the 'objective and manageable standards' that are disclosed by a purposive analysis of its terms.[20]

Replying to allegations that a substantive interpretation of the section would transform the courts into a 'super legislature,' Lamer J. states:

> This is an argument which was heard countless times prior to the entrench-ment of the *Charter* but which has in truth, for better or for worse, been settled by the very coming into force of the *Constitution Act, 1982.* It ought not to be forgotten that the historic decision to entrench the *Charter* in our Constitution was taken not by the courts but by the elected representa-tives of the people of Canada. It was those representatives who extended the scope of constitutional adjudication and entrusted the courts with this new and onerous responsibility. Adjudication under the *Charter* must be approached free of any lingering doubts as to its legitimacy.[21]

A number of things need to be said about this analysis. The first is that it seeks to obscure the obvious and fundamental differences between federalism review and review under a charter of rights. Review on fed-eralism grounds is based upon a theory of exhaustion of powers, which in turn is firmly grounded in the doctrine of parliamentary sovereign-ty. Federalism review, in other words, is a means of allocating powers within a system dedicated to majoritarian democracy. The sole ques-tion for the courts in relation to federalism disputes is which majority, national or provincial, has the right to make a particular decision.

By contrast, *Charter* review is predicated upon a counter-majoritari-an principle. It asks the courts to determine whether *any* majority has the right to make a particular decision. For this reason, *Charter* review calls upon the courts to evaluate legislation in an entirely different way than federalism review. While federalism review requires the courts to examine the content of legislation merely to decide where the power to enact the legislation lies, *Charter* review calls upon the courts to evalu-ate that content against particular *Charter* norms and general notions of reasonableness. Thus, it simply is not true to suggest, as Lamer J. does, that under the *Charter* 'it is the scope of constitutional adjudica-tion which has been altered rather than its nature.'[22]

Second, the suggestion that the courts can resolve *Charter* cases with-out questioning the wisdom of policy is untenable. Rights issues, by their nature, concern the allocation of political entitlements in a society.

A rights claim is a claim in favour of expanding the entitlements of some at the expense of others. Consider the case of *Hunter v. Southam*,[23] in which the Supreme Court held that search provisions of the *Combines Investigation Act* violated the guarantee against unreasonable search and seizure in section 8 of the *Charter*. The immediate beneficiaries of this ruling are corporations being investigated for violations of the Act. But the costs associated with the decision extend far beyond officials in the Combines Investigation Branch. Ultimately, those costs will be borne by consumers and other entrepreneurs who have the most to gain from a rigorously enforced competition policy. What this illustrates is that *Charter* adjudication is, at root, a process of interest balancing that calls upon the courts to decide which interests are more important than others. Of course, the *Charter* may provide some guidance as to how certain interests ought to be balanced, but more often than not it will not do so or, at least, the guidance that it offers will not be determinative. As *Motor Vehicle Reference* demonstrates, the language of the *Charter* is so broad and amorphous that it leaves for judicial determination not only the precise nature and scope of certain *Charter* rights, but whether those rights exist at all.[24]

Furthermore, even if *Charter* rights were spelled out with crystal clarity, this would not obviate the need for interest balancing by the courts. This is because rights guaranteed by the *Charter* can never be absolute. There will always be competing interests and values that must be taken into account. It is for this reason that section 1 of the *Charter* subjects *Charter* rights to 'such reasonable limits prescribed by law as can be demonstrably justified in a free and democratic society.' Thus whether through interpretation of the rights themselves or through the subsequent application of section 1 (or both), interest balancing is inherent to *Charter* adjudication.

Once this is conceded, then the argument that the courts need not question the wisdom of policy under the *Charter* is revealed to be the chimera that it is. Interest balancing is essentially a political function. It calls upon the decision maker to offer subjective judgments concerning the relative importance to individuals and to society of competing values. When a court strikes down legislation under the *Charter*, what it is doing is offering an alternative assessment of how interests should be balanced from that of the legislature. To put it differently, it is 'questioning the wisdom' of the balance struck by the legislature. Consider *Motor Vehicle Reference* itself. The ostensible purpose of section 94 was to promote road safety by providing tough, mandatory penalties for those who drove while their licences were under suspension.[25] Section 94(2), by making the offence one of absolute liability, effectively placed upon persons with bad driving records the affirmative responsibility of ensuring that their licences still entitled them to drive.[26] Thus the legislature struck a balance between the public interest in road safety and the individual interest of persons with bad driving records in a way that strongly favoured the former over the latter. The determination by the Court that section 94(2) violated the right to liberty under the *Charter* was just another way of saying that the balance struck by the legislature was wrong: that it gave too much weight to the public's interest and failed to take sufficient account of the individual's interest.

This is evident from Lamer J.'s own characterization of how the Court should evaluate the British Columbia government's contention that section 94(2) should be upheld under section 1 of the *Charter*:

> I do not take issue with the fact that it is highly desirable that 'bad drivers' be kept off the road. I do not take issue either with the desirability of punishing severely bad drivers who are in contempt of prohibitions against driving. *The bottom line of the question to be addressed here is: whether the Government of British Columbia has demonstrated as justifiable that the risk of imprisonment of a few innocents is, given the desirability of ridding the roads of British Columbia of bad drivers, a reasonable limit in a free and democratic society.*[27]

Lamer J.'s subsequent determination that the law was not 'justifiable' was simply a rejection of the legislature's view as to what is a 'reasonable limit in a free and democratic society.'

A third thing that should be noted about Lamer J.'s analysis is that it ignores the admonitions of Laskin J. in *Curr* concerning the danger of the courts engaging in judicial review based upon a substantive standard as broad and amorphous as 'fundamental justice.' Indeed, it is ironic that Lamer J. should adopt Laskin J.'s phrase 'objective and manageable standards' to justify substantive review under section 7. Laskin J. employed the phrase in the context of a decision that doubted whether such standards existed in relation to substantive due process and cautioned that 'the appellant's right to the security of his person without due process of law must be grounded on more than a substitution of a personal judgment for that of Parliament.'[28]

Finally, Lamer J.'s suggestion that the legitimacy of *Charter* adjudication is no longer in doubt shows a disturbing disregard for the limits of the judicial function in a constitutional democracy. While it is beyond dispute that the *Charter* gives the courts a mandate to engage in *some* forms of judicial review, it does not follow that it entitles them to engage in *any and all* forms of such review. The rule of law, so often touted by the courts, is premised upon the belief that there is no such thing as unlimited discretion, even judicial discretion. Just as one may question the legitimacy of a decision of an administrative agency on the basis that it exceeds the bounds of its legislative mandate, so too can one question the legitimacy of a court's decision on the ground that it exceeds the bounds of its judicial mandate. This is no less true of a *Charter* decision than it is of any other judicial function. Thus, while the general exercise of judicial review powers under the *Charter* may be beyond doubt, one may still question the legitimacy of the Court interpreting section 7 as a substantive guarantee.

(2) A Substantive Interpretation of Section 7

Justice Lamer offers three justifications for adopting a substantive interpretation of section 7: one based upon the nature and derivation of the distinction between substantive and procedural due process; one based upon the text of section 7; and one based upon the relationship between section 7 and sections 8 to 14.

Lamer J.'s first justification for a substantive interpretation of section 7 essentially boils down to the assertion that the distinction between substantive and procedural due process is too categorical and too American:

> The substantive/procedural dichotomy narrows the issue almost to an all-or-nothing proposition. Moreover, it is largely bound up in the American experience with substantive and procedural due process. It imports into the Canadian context American concepts, terminology and jurisprudence, all of which are inextricably linked to problems concerning the nature and legitimacy of adjudication under the U.S. Constitution.[29]

Related to this justification are two additional arguments. The first is that the outer boundaries of substantive and procedural due process 'are not always clear and often tend to overlap,'[30] making it difficult to distinguish between the two concepts. 'Such difficulties', Lamer J. says, 'can and should, when possible, be avoided.'[31] The second is that there are certain 'truly fundamental structural differences'[32] between the *Charter* and the United States Bill of Rights that militate in favour of a substantive interpretation of section 7. In particular, Lamer J. notes that the United States Constitution 'has no s. 52 nor has it the internal checks and balances of sections 1 and 33.'[33] It is worth examining each of these points in turn.

It is, of course, true that the distinction between substantive and procedural due process is categorical, but for the *Charter*'s framers, its categorical nature was its virtue. By limiting courts to procedural issues under section 7, they could ensure that the judicial function would not trample too deeply into substantive policy matters. With respect to the argument that the dichotomy is too American, there is a certain irony here. Clearly the terminology of 'substantive' and 'procedural due process' is drawn from American jurisprudence, but what Lamer J. seems to forget is that section 7 itself derives from the American experience. Furthermore, regardless of its derivation, it is clear that the dichotomy was one that held the attention of the Canadian drafters of the section and, as the *Curr* case demonstrates, previously commanded the attention of the Supreme Court. It is a bit late in the day, therefore, to be asserting its lack of relevance to Canadian constitutional law. Finally, though the terminology may be American, the argument advanced in favour of restricting section 7 to procedural values is contrary to the American experience. Thus while Lamer J. decries the rhetoric of substantive and procedural due process as being American, he does so in aid of a result that, by disregarding the boundary between substantive and procedural due process, mimics the position of the American courts.

As for his concern regarding the boundaries of substance and procedure, the line dividing substantive from procedural due process is undoubtedly muddy. But what line in law is not? Moreover, muddy as it may be, it appears as a small puddle next to the 'bog of legislative policymaking' (to borrow Laskin J.'s phrase from *Curr*) that the Court enters when it takes upon itself the task of articulating the substantive values embodied by 'the principles of fundamental justice.'

The assertion that sections 1, 33, and 52 represent 'truly fundamental structural differences' between the Canadian and American constitutions is also unconvincing. The differences to which Lamer J. alludes are either illusory or do not cut clearly in favour of substantive over procedural due process. For example, while there is no clause in the United States Constitution that, like section 52 of the *Constitution Act, 1982*, explicitly provides that laws inconsistent with the constitution are 'of no force or effect,'[34] the power of the American courts to strike down laws that conflict with the Bill of Rights has been established in the United States since *Marbury v. Madison*[35] in 1803, some sixty-five years before the due process clause in the Fourteenth Amendment was ratified by the States and one hundred years before the doctrine of substantive due process started to assert itself in American jurisprudence. Similarly, though it is true that there is in the United States Bill of Rights no explicit limitation clause like section 1 of the *Charter*, this has not prevented the American courts from reading in limits where they have felt it desirable.

With respect to section 33, the override clause, this is the one provision to which Lamer J. refers that has no analogue in American constitutional experience. But two points must be made here. The first is that the political pressures against overriding the *Charter* make it extraordinarily difficult for governments to make use of section 33. Thus, governments will be loath to invoke section 33 to protect all but the most vital aspects of their legislative program. Second, the presence of section 33 cuts as strongly against broad *Charter* review by the courts as it does in favour of it. While the section, at least theoretically, permits governments a final say over most questions of public policy, it also reflects a latent distrust of civil liberties review in the American model. It is therefore somewhat bizarre to interpret section 33 as inviting the courts to expand judicial review in disregard of the American experience.

Lamer J.'s second justification for a substantive interpretation of section 7 is a textual argument based upon the wording of the section itself. According to Lamer J., the right protected by section 7 is the right to 'life, liberty and security of the person and the right not to be deprived thereof.' The words 'except in accordance with the principles of fundamental justice' he identifies as 'a qualifier of the right not to be deprived of life, liberty and security of the person.' From this he concludes that to interpret these qualifying words as restricting the right to procedural matters would be to 'strip the protected interests of much, if not most, of their content' and would be contrary to a 'purposive interpretation' of the rights protected by section 7.[36]

The problem with this analysis is that it ignores context and history. It separates the section into two components; then, by labelling one 'the right' and the other a 'qualifier to the right,' it presupposes that the first takes priority over the second. In other words, it asserts what it purports to ascertain: that the purpose of the section is to create a substantive right.

Furthermore, if Lamer J. views his task as one of giving a 'purposive interpretation' to the section, one has to wonder whose purpose it is that concerns him. Clearly it is not the purpose of those who drafted the section nor of the politicians who relied upon their advice. As Lamer J. concedes, the evidence of the Special Joint Committee of the Senate and the House of Commons on the Constitution of Canada discloses that senior federal civil servants and politicians who appeared before the Committee were united in their view that section 7 was confined to questions of procedural justice.[37] Yet, while Lamer J. acknowledges that such evidence is admissible for the purpose of interpreting the *Charter*, he refuses to attach to it 'any significant weight.' To do so, he says, would be to assume that 'the comments of a few federal civil servants' represented the views of the 'multiplicity of individuals who played major roles in the negotiating, drafting and adoption of the *Charter*.'[38]

Such a position might be more convincing if there were some evidence in the record of events leading to the adoption of section 7 that a substantial number of the political actors did not take seriously the advice given before the Joint Committee, or that they desired broader scope for section 7. In the absence of any such suggestion, and given the importance attached to that advice by governments and others, Lamer J.'s dismissal of the testimony before the Joint Committee can only be described as cavalier.

Moreover, Lamer J.'s decision to disregard the stated intentions of the *Charter*'s framers reveals the hollow nature of the so-called 'purposive' approach to *Charter* interpretation espoused by the Supreme Court. If the Court is unwilling to give serious weight to those stated intentions, how can it possibly identify even the broad purposes of those who enacted a guarantee as amorphously expressed as 'the principles of fundamental justice'? The answer is that it cannot. What the Court's 'purposive' approach really amounts to is a means of ascribing to the framers of the *Charter* values that seem appropriate to the judiciary. The word 'purposive' is a rhetorical device designed to cloak in objective garb the infusion into the *Charter* of a subjective judicial preference.

This assessment is confirmed by Lamer J.'s final rationale for refusing to interpret section 7 in light of the intentions of its framers. To do so, he says, would mean that 'the rights, freedoms and values embodied in the *Charter* [would] in effect become frozen in time to the moment of adoption with little or no possibility of growth, development, and adjustment to changing societal needs.'[39] What this argument suggests is that, in fact, the Court is not much concerned with adhering to the true purposes of those who enacted the *Charter*, since to rely upon those purposes would inhibit the judiciary from interpreting the 'rights, freedoms and values' to reflect 'changing societal needs.'

Of course, Lamer J. is right on one level. It would be unrealistic to expect the courts to heed blindly the opinions of the framers as to how the *Charter* should be applied in each and every circumstance. But it is one thing to say that the framers' intentions concerning specific applications of the *Charter* may not be determinative; it is quite another to hold that the courts can ignore the intentions of the framers with respect to fundamental issues concerning the nature and scope of judicial review under the *Charter*. As Professor John Whyte has stated with respect to *Motor Vehicle Reference:*

> [T]he issue raised in this case is not one of specific application. Whether s. 7 is limited to procedural protections is a large, general and constitutive question. The legislative record examined in the case goes to the question of the *Charter*'s fundamental purposes.[40]

By implying that the Court is entitled to reinvent the *Charter* wheel in accordance with its vision of 'changing societal needs,' Lamer J. succeeds in undermining not only the Court's claim to 'purposive' interpretation, but also his earlier insistence that the *Charter* embodies 'objective and manageable standards.' In doing so, he adds further fuel to concerns regarding the limits and legitimacy of the judicial function. Lamer J.'s third justification for a substantive interpretation of section 7 is based upon the relationship between section 7 and sections 8 to 14 of the *Charter*. According to Lamer J., the rights protected by sections 8 to 14 of the *Charter* are specific examples of the general right guaranteed by section 7:

> To put matters in a different way, sections 7 to 14 could have been fused into one section, with inserted between the words of s. 7 and the rest of those sections the oft utilised provision in our statutes, 'and, without limiting the generality of the foregoing (s. 7) the following shall be deemed to be in violation of a person's rights under this section.'[41]

Since some of the rights in sections 8 to 14 represent substantive guarantees, Lamer J. concludes that section 7, 'the general concept from which they originate,'[42] must also embody a substantive guarantee.

This final argument has an 'Alice in Wonderland' quality to it. While Lamer J. may be correct in saying that sections 7 to 14 'could have been fused into one section,'[43] the obvious response is: they were not. Because they were not, there is absolutely nothing to back up his assertion that all of the rights embodied within sections 8 to 14 can be accommodated within section 7.[44] Furthermore, it is difficult to see how some of the rights in sections 8 to 14 are capable of being so accommodated. For example, does Lamer J. seriously mean to suggest that the denial of an interpreter to a witness in any proceeding[45] amounts to a denial of that witness's right to 'life, liberty and security of the person'?

The presence of specific substantive rights in sections 8 to 14 and elsewhere in the *Charter* could have signalled to Lamer J., as it did to Laskin J. in *Curr*, that 'extreme caution' should be exercised by the Court with respect to the interpretation of a general due process guarantee. Instead, he relies upon the unsupported claim of a necessary link between sections 8 to 14 to expand the scope of the general right contained within section 7. Perhaps Lamer J. believes that the relationship he asserts between section 7 and sections 8 to 14 assists in limiting the scope of the former guarantee. In fact, it has the opposite effect. The implication of his argument is that every interest that is protected by sections 8 to 14 must also be protected by section 7. In *Southam*, for example, the Supreme Court unanimously held that the right 'to be secure against unreasonable search and seizure' in section 8 of the *Charter* conferred upon a corporation a substantive right to privacy. The effect of this ruling was to create a property right in favour of corporations.[46] The force of Lamer J.'s analysis is that this property right must also be protected under section 7, presumably within the guarantee of 'security of the person,' and that invasion of this property interest in the absence of reasonable grounds amounts to a violation of some substantive 'principle of fundamental justice.' In sum, if Lamer J.'s analysis is correct, one is driven to conclude that the guarantee of 'security of the person' in section 7 provides corporations with substantive protection from governmental interference with their property.

Similarly, if the rights guaranteed in section 11 of the *Charter* are merely 'illustrative of deprivations of those rights to life, liberty and security of the person in breach of the principles of fundamental justice,'[47] it follows that being charged with any offence, even an offence leading to the imposition of a fine,[48] amounts to a denial of 'security of the person' under section 7. If this is so, then all absolute liability offences, not merely those requiring imprisonment, must violate the substantive principle of fundamental justice identified in *Motor Vehicle Reference*. Indeed, Lamer J. hints at this result later in his judgment:

I would not want us to be taken by this conclusion as having inferentially decided that absolute liability may not offend s. 7 as long as imprisonment or probation orders are not available as a sentence. The answer to that question is dependant upon the content given to the words 'security of the person.' That issue was and is a live one.[49]

What Lamer J. does not seem to realize is that his reasoning concerning the relationship between sections 7 and 11 requires him to conclude that the words 'security of the person' would necessarily apply to such offences. Furthermore, though he suggests at one point in his decision that section 7 might not extend to corporations,[50] his own analysis concerning the relationship between sections 7 and 8 (which the Supreme Court held in *Southam* did apply to a corporation) would require him to conclude that corporate security is protected within the guarantee of 'security of the person.'

Thus the effect of Lamer J.'s reasoning is not only to give effect to substantive due process, but to do so in a way that also extends substantive protection to corporate security and property. If this reasoning were taken seriously, it would inhibit the ability of the state to use economic penalties as a means of allocating social costs[51] and would open the door to the inclusion in section 7 of further substantive economic rights along the lines developed in the United States in the first third of this century.

(3) Meaning of 'The Principles of Fundamental Justice'

If 'the principles of fundamental justice' in section 7 of the *Charter* are substantive as well as procedural, thus extending beyond the requirements of natural justice, the question that must be addressed is: What is the content of these principles? To invoke Lamer J.'s own words: What are the '"objective and manageable standards" for the operation of the section within such a framework?'[52] Lamer J.'s answer is far from satisfactory:

Sections 8 to 14 ... are ... illustrative of the meaning, in criminal or penal law, of 'principles of fundamental justice'; they represent principles that have been recognized by the common law, international conventions and by the very fact of entrenchment in the *Charter* as essential elements of a system for the administration of justice founded upon a belief in the dignity and worth of the human person and the rule of law.

Consequently, the principles of fundamental justice are to be found in the basic tenets and principles, not only of our judicial process, but also of the other components of our legal system.

We should not be surprised to find that many of the principles of fundamental justice are procedural in nature. Our common law has largely been a law of remedies and procedures ... This is not to say, however, that the principles of fundamental justice are limited solely to procedural guarantees. Rather, the proper approach to the determination of the principles of fundamental justice is quite simply one in which, as Professor L. Tremblay has written, 'future growth will be based on historical roots' ...

Whether any given principle may be said to be a principle of fundamental justice within the meaning of s. 7 will rest upon an analysis of the nature, sources, rationale and essential role of that principle within the judicial process and in our legal system, as it evolves.

Consequently, those words cannot be given any exhaustive content or simple enumerative definition, but will take on concrete meaning as the courts address alleged violations of s. 7.[53]

In other words, while the standards that represent 'the principles of fundamental justice' may be 'objective and manageable,' they defy definition. They represent those values that the Court identifies as essential elements of the system for the administration of justice. They are, in short, whatever the Court says that they are. If this is not Laskin's 'bog of legislative policy-making,' then no such bogs exist.

Furthermore, there is nothing in Lamer J.'s formulation, or in the text of section 7, to indicate that the principles of fundamental justice are confined to principles of criminal or penal law. On the contrary, his suggestion that sections 8 to 14 serve as illustrations of such principles 'in criminal or penal law' suggests that they extend beyond this realm.[54] Nor is there anything limiting in Lamer J.'s reference to principles of the common law. Beyond the confines of criminal law, the substantive principles that animate the common law are, for the most part, centred around the protection of private property and are at odds with the redistributive policies of the modern welfare state. If 'security of the person' now includes the right to privacy in one's property and the right to be free from financial penalties, as Lamer J.'s earlier analysis seems to suggest, then his approach here places in the hands of the judiciary the power to raise to constitutional status such common law principles as those against confiscation of private property and in support of unbridled freedom of contract.

The Principle of Moral Innocence

According to Lamer J., section 94(2) violates 'the principles of fundamental justice' because it offends the common law postulate against the
punishment of the 'morally innocent':

> It has from time immemorial been part of our system of laws that the inno-
> cent not be punished. This principle has long been recognized as an essen-
> tial element of a system for the administration of justice which is founded
> upon a belief in the dignity and worth of the human person and on the
> rule of law.[55]

Later, he states:

> Indeed, as I said, in penal law, absolute liability always offends the prin-
> ciples of fundamental justice irrespective of the nature of the offence; it
> offends s. 7 of the *Charter* if as a result, anyone is deprived of his life,
> liberty or security of the person, irrespective of the requirement of public
> interest. In such cases it might only be salvaged for reasons of public inter-
> est under s. 1.[56]

(1) Moral Innocence and Social Responsibility

The notion that it is always contrary to 'fundamental justice' to impose
penalties upon persons who lack a 'guilty mind' reflects a narrow and
anachronistic view of the function of penal law and of the relationship
between individuals and the state. First, it assumes that deterrence
and punishment are the only legitimate purposes entitling the state to
impose penalties. This view might have been prevalent in the heyday
of the common law, but it does not reflect current societal norms. Today
it is widely accepted that legislatures may create offences and impose
penalties not only as means of deterring and punishing, but also as a
means of allocating social costs and of redefining social responsibilities. Consider, for example, legislation that imposes heavy fines for discharging toxins into waterways. One purpose of such legislation may
be to deter persons from discharging toxins and to punish those who
do so; but another may simply be to require polluters to bear the costs
that such discharges impose upon society. If the purpose of the legislation is to allocate social costs, then it makes good sense to establish the
offence as one of absolute liability.

Another purpose that a legislature may have in making such an offence one of absolute liability is to redefine the nature and scope of social responsibilities assumed by individuals in an increasingly interdependent society. What the legislature may, in effect, be saying is that persons who choose to engage in activities involving the use of toxins must bear complete responsibility for ensuring that those toxins do not end up in waterways. In other words, the stipulation of an absolute liability offence may be a means of creating a form of 'social contract' with persons who choose to engage in dangerous activities – a 'contract' under which such persons agree to accept a predetermined measure of responsibility if any social harm results from their activities.

Similarly, in the case of motor vehicle legislation, one could characterize a provision like section 94(2) as forming part of a 'social contract' between the state and persons who drive. The terms of that 'contract' require those who continue to drive after being convicted of a serious driving offence[57] to bear responsibilities and liabilities that far exceed those imposed by common law principles of criminal responsibility. But, where persons choose to place society at risk by engaging in potentially dangerous activities, why should government not be permitted to require them to bear such extraordinary burdens?

Lamer J. never addresses these issues. While he expresses concern regarding the impact of his decision upon environmental protection legislation,[58] he remains steadfast in his belief that 'irrespective of the nature of the offence' the common law principle of moral innocence is a prerequisite to 'fundamental justice.' According to his view, any absolute liability offence whose impact is to deprive one of 'life, liberty and security of the person' constitutes a *prima facie* violation of section 7, regardless of its underlying purpose. Such an offence will be upheld only if it can be 'demonstrably justified' to be a 'reasonable limit' within the meaning of section 1.

Thus, assuming that section 7 applies to economic penalties, as Lamer J.'s earlier reasoning seems to dictate, the effects of this holding are (a) to create a strong presumption against the state using penal laws to allocate social costs, and (b) to limit the state's use of such laws to redefine individuals' social responsibilities. With respect to (b), the degree of limitation will depend upon whether the Court rejects strict liability offences, together with those of absolute liability, as violating the prohibition against punishing the 'morally innocent' (or, for that matter, as violating the 'presumption of innocence'). As things stand following *Motor Vehicle Reference*, it is contrary to 'the principles of fundamental justice' for the state to impose penalties upon individuals for harm that results without their knowledge. The question that remains to be addressed is whether the state violates those same principles when it imposes penalties on those who fail to show 'due diligence' in anticipating and preventing such harm.[59]

(2) Moral Innocence: A Principle of Convenience

The Court's adoption of 'moral innocence' as a touchstone of fundamental justice would perhaps be more persuasive if the common law prohibition against punishing the morally innocent were itself based upon some coherent principle that was consistently applied by the courts. Yet this is not the case. While the courts recoil at the thought of punishing someone who lacks knowledge of the factual components of an offence, they have no hesitation whatsoever in punishing someone who lacks the requisite legal knowledge. In other words, the courts have arbitrarily chosen to define moral innocence in a way that places upon citizens an absolute social responsibility to acquaint themselves with law, but little or no responsibility to acquaint themselves with facts.

Moreover, the dividing line between errors of law and errors of fact is a controversial one that can easily be manipulated by the courts to transform moral culpability into moral innocence, or *vice versa*. Nowhere is this better illustrated than in an examination of the legislative and judicial history surrounding section 94(2). What prompted the British Columbia government to enact such a seemingly draconian provision? The answer lies not in the mind of some mean-spirited mandarin but, surprisingly, in an earlier decision of the Supreme Court of Canada.

Prior to 1979, there was no specific offence in British Columbia legislation of driving while one's licence was suspended. There was no need for one because section 238 of the *Criminal Code* provided that persons driving while prohibited from doing so under provincial law were guilty of either an indictable offence or an offence punishable on summary conviction. In 1979, however, section 238 was gutted of much of its force by the decision of the Supreme Court in *R. v. Prue; R. v. Baril.*[60] That case concerned two accused who were convicted under section 238 after their licences had been suspended automatically under the British Columbia *Motor-vehicle Act.*[61] The accused claimed that they were unaware of the suspensions, but the Crown contended that, because the suspensions occurred by operation of law, their mistake was one of law and provided them with no defence. Chief Justice Laskin, writing for the majority, disagreed, holding that, for the purposes of a *Criminal Code* offence, ignorance of a suspension automatically imposed by operation of provincial law was ignorance of fact, not law. The implication of the decision was to enable an accused to deny knowledge of an automatic suspension, placing upon the Crown the almost insurmountable burden of proving that the accused had such knowledge. This, in turn, threatened to make provincial driving suspensions virtually unenforceable.[62]

Prue and Baril was a British Columbia case, and the government in that province moved quickly to plug the gap created by the Supreme Court decision. Within six months of the ruling, legislation was enacted and proclaimed making driving while one's licence was suspended a provincial offence.[63] Furthermore, because the government feared that the Supreme Court's ruling could be extended to allow persons to plead ignorance of automatic driving suspensions as a defence to provincial charges, a provision was included making the provincial offence one of absolute liability. The purpose of this provision, the forerunner of section 94(2), was to enable the province to enforce automatic licence suspensions in the wake of a Supreme Court ruling that threatened to make them unenforceable. Its effect was to require the courts to treat ignorance of automatic driving suspensions in the same way that they treated ignorance of law. Where the province perhaps went too far was in failing to limit the impact of the absolute liability clause to suspensions that occurred by operation of law; the clause also applied to discretionary suspensions ordered by the courts and by the superintendent of motor vehicles.

But the story does not end there. On 23 November 1982, six days before *Motor Vehicle Reference* was to be argued before the British Columbia Court of Appeal, the Supreme Court handed down its decision in *R. v. MacDougall*.[64] In that case, the Court unanimously held that its decision in *Prue and Baril* did not apply to provincial licence suspension offences. Ritchie J., who dissented in the earlier case, held that, where charges were brought under provincial legislation, ignorance of a suspension imposed by automatic operation of provincial law was a mistake of law, not fact, and did not provide a defence to an accused.[65]

In short, by manipulating the distinction between errors of law and errors of fact, the Court in *MacDougall* achieved precisely the same result with respect to automatic suspensions that had been sought by the legislature in section 94(2). Ignorance of such suspensions was now to be regarded as a mistake of law that afforded no defence to an accused.

Because concern for the enforceability of automatic suspensions precipitated the inclusion of the absolute liability clause, the government at this point should simply have abandoned its reference. The absolute liability clause was no longer needed to protect the government's ability to prosecute breaches of automatic suspensions; and with respect to breaches of discretionary suspensions, amendments had already been passed ensuring that these would be imposed only in circumstances where knowledge on the part of an accused was assured and could easily be proved. Given these circumstances, the explicitness of the absolute liability clause, and the significance of the issues at stake, the government's decision to press ahead can only be attributed to poor judgment – judgment that may forever have changed the face of Canadian constitutional law.

There are, however, a number of important things to be learned from this brief survey of the history surrounding section 94(2). First, the absolute liability clause was placed in the British Columbia legislation in direct response to a Supreme Court of Canada ruling that treated ignorance of an automatic licence suspension as ignorance of fact, thereby placing upon the Crown the almost impossible burden of having to prove that an accused had knowledge of such a suspension. Second, while the Supreme Court treated ignorance of an automatic suspension as 'moral innocence' for the purpose of criminal charges, it was not prepared to do so for the purpose of provincial charges. Third, the Court was able to accomplish this quantum shift simply by manipulating the distinction between ignorance of the law and ignorance of fact: the same lack of knowledge regarded in *Prue and Baril* as morally innocent ignorance of fact was transformed in *MacDougall* into morally culpable ignorance of law.

All of this casts considerable light, and considerable doubt, on the principle of 'moral innocence.' Far from being an immutable principle of the common law, it turns out to be a principle of convenience that can be discarded by the courts through a simple shift in characterization. By manipulating the murky line between ignorance of fact and ignorance of law, a court is free to cast social responsibility wherever it whims: upon the state as in the case of *Prue and Baril*, or upon the accused as in the case of *MacDougall*. Yet when the legislature sought to do openly in section 94(2) what the judiciary accomplished covertly in *MacDougall,* the Court apparently felt no compunction about conjuring up the principle of moral innocence as an immutable touchstone of substantive *Charter* justice. For those in the British Columbia government who were aware of the history of section 94(2) and of the Court's involvement with provincial motor vehicle legislation, the irony must have been excruciating.

The Section 12 Solution

Section 12 of the *Charter* creates a specific substantive guarantee against 'cruel and unusual treatment or punishment.' The section invites the courts to review the proportionality between a punishment and an offence, such as whether mandatory imprisonment is an excessive penalty to impose for an absolute liability offence. For this reason, the Attorney General for Ontario, in his written submission to the Court in *Motor Vehicle Reference,* argued that 'the constitutionality of the penalty provision should be determined by reference to s. 12, not s. 7.'[66] Though he fell short of urging that the legislation be struck down under section 12, the Court could easily have taken its cue from his submission and founded its decision upon section 12. This would have permitted the Court to reach the same result on the basis of a narrower *Charter* standard and one that was clearly intended to have substantive effect.

The fact that the Court chose to strike down the legislation on the basis of section 7 rather than section 12 suggests that the decision to infuse section 7 with substantive content was one that was taken willingly and deliberately. What this further suggests is that the current Supreme Court is a very different Court from that of ten or even three years ago.[67] Judicial activism is now the order of the day. Any interpretation is possible provided it can be described as 'broad,' 'liberal,' and 'purposive.' The Court feels unconstrained not only by its own prior rulings, but also by the intentions of the *Charter*'s framers.

Conclusion

Motor Vehicle Reference marks the first attempt by the Supreme Court of Canada to confront openly questions relating to the nature of the adjudicative process and the scope of judicial power under the *Charter*. If the *Charter* permits the courts to articulate the content of such amorphous ideas as 'liberty,' 'security,' and 'fundamental justice' in a way that conflicts with the intention of the framers, what limits are there to the judicial function? And if there are no identifiable limits, how can the role of judges under the *Charter* be reconciled with the principle of democracy?

Unfortunately, the Court's answers to these questions are as superficial as they are unconvincing. According to the Court, *Charter* standards are 'objective and manageable' and therefore do not require the courts to assume a policy role. For this reason, concerns about democracy and the legitimacy of *Charter* review are without foundation. The trouble with this position is that it is contrary to history and common sense. Ideas such as 'liberty,' 'security,' and 'fundamental justice' are contested concepts whose content has been the ongoing preoccupation of political debate. Furthermore, even if these concepts had 'objective and manageable' meanings, this would not end the legitimacy debate. On the contrary, it would give it focus, since any departure from those meanings would have to be characterized as illegitimate.

What the decision in *Motor Vehicle Reference* amounts to is an attempt by the Court to have its *Charter* cake and eat it. On the one hand, the Court wishes to give the impression that the *Charter* does not require it to engage in political decision making. On the other, the Court maintains that the question of legitimacy is a dead letter: that it is free to adopt any interpretation of the *Charter* text free from 'lingering doubts' about legitimacy.

The troubling thing about this is not simply that the Court misconceives its task. It is that, in disavowing the subjectivity of *Charter* adjudication and concerns about its legitimacy, the Court prevents itself from openly confronting the political dynamics of the issues before it and from defining a role for itself that is sensitive to those dynamics. Rather than acknowledging the normative nature of its task, the Court relegates itself to parading about in the fictitious garb of objective meanings and purposive interpretations. Like the Emperor, it shuns clothes that fit in favour of finery that does not exist.

The result is a decision that removes all judicial inhibitions from *Charter* adjudication and that opens the door to political involvement by the judiciary on a scale never envisioned by the *Charter*'s framers. Moreover, even if the Supreme Court itself plans to tread lightly through the political minefield of substantive due process, the interim impact of *Motor Vehicle Reference* in lower courts will be to encourage some heavy judicial slogging through all manner of social and economic regulation, from environmental protection legislation to abortion laws to legislation banning extra-billing.

NOTES

1 The words 'due process' do not appear in section 7 of the *Charter*, but the section was clearly inspired by the 'due process' clauses of the Fifth and Fourteenth Amendments to the United States Constitution.

2 *Reference Re s. 94(2) of Motor Vehicle Act (British Columbia)*, [1985] 2 S.C.R. 486 [*Motor Vehicle Reference*].

3 *Motor Vehicle Act*, R.S.B.C. 1979, c. 288, as amended by the *Motor Vehicle Amendment Act, 1982*, S.B.C. 1982, c. 36. The case arose in response to the judgment of Paradis Prov. Ct. J. in *R. v. Campagna* (1982), 141 D.L.R. (3d) 485 (B.C. Prov. Ct.), striking down the predecessor to section 94(2). Because of the cloud of uncertainty that this decision cast over section 94(2), the B.C. government referred the question of the subsection's constitutionality under the *Charter* to the Court of Appeal. The Court of Appeal held that section 94(2) violated section 7 of the *Charter*: (1983), 42 B.C.L.R. 364 (C.A.). The province then appealed this decision to the Supreme Court of Canada.

4 The name is derived from the decision of the United States Supreme Court in *Lochner v. New York*, 198 U.S. 45 (1905).

5 See J. Cameron, 'The Motor Vehicle Reference and the Relevance of American Doctrine in Charter Adjudication' in R.J. Sharpe, ed., *Charter Litigation* (Toronto: Butterworths, 1987) at 69.

6 Special Joint Committee of the Senate and of the House of Commons on the Constitution of Canada, 1st Sess., 32nd Parl. (27 January 1981) at 46:32–46:43.

7 *Ibid.* at 46:39.

8 *R. v. Duke*, [1972] S.C.R. 917.

9 *Ibid.* at 923.

10 See P.W. Hogg, *Constitutional Law of Canada*, 2nd ed. (Toronto: Carswell, 1985) at 746.

11 Special Joint Committee, *supra* note 6 at 46:32.

12 *R. v. Curr*, [1972] S.C.R. 899 [*Curr*].

13 *Ibid.* at 899–900.

14 *Ibid.* at 902.

15 Dickson C.J., and Beetz, Chouinard, and Le Dain JJ. concurred with Lamer J.

16 Wilson J. appears to go even further in the direction of substantive due process. Unlike the majority, she interprets the second half of section 7 as augmenting rather than qualifying the first. According to this view, section 7 embodies two rights: a right to 'life, liberty and security of the person' and a separate right 'not to be deprived thereof except in accordance with

the principles of fundamental justice.' The consequence of this 'two rights'
approach is to treat the right to 'life, liberty and security of the person' as
a freestanding, substantive right, qualified only by the limits in section 1.
What is perplexing about this interpretation is that it seems at odds with
the views expressed by Wilson J. in *Operation Dismantle Inc. v. R.*, [1985] 1
S.C.R. 441 at 487. Equally perplexing is the fact that, while Wilson J.'s 'two
rights' approach is irreconcilable with Lamer J.'s holding that the second
part of section 7 qualifies the first, Lamer J. nevertheless purports to leave
open the possibility that the right to life, liberty, and security of the person
could be invoked 'absent a breach of the principles of fundamental justice':
Motor Vehicle Reference, supra note 2 at 500.

17 *Motor Vehicle Reference, ibid.* at 496.
18 *Ibid.*
19 *Ibid.* at 497.
20 *Ibid.* at 497–9.
21 *Ibid.* at 497.
22 *Ibid.* at 496.
23 *Hunter v. Southam*, [1984] 2 S.C.R. 145.
24 See Hogg, *supra* note 10 at 652–7.
25 See British Columbia, Legislative Assembly, 4th Sess., 32nd Parl. (3 June
    1982) at 7974–5; British Columbia, Legislative Assembly, 4th Sess., 32nd
    Parl. (7 June 1982) at 8022–32. See also British Columbia, Legislative
    Assembly, 3rd Sess., 32nd Parl. (30 June 1981) at 6521–2.
26 See British Columbia, *Motor Vehicle Task Force Interim Report* (Victoria: Task
    Force, 1979) at 17–18. See also the discussion of moral innocence, *infra*.
27 *Motor Vehicle Reference, supra* note 2 at 521 [emphasis added].
28 *Curr, supra* note 12 at 902.
29 *Motor Vehicle Reference, supra* note 2 at 498.
30 *Ibid.*
31 *Ibid.*
32 *Ibid.*
33 *Ibid.*
34 It is worth noting, however, that section 52 bears a striking resemblance to
    the supremacy clause found in Article VI of the United States Constitution.
    Both provisions recognize the constitution as 'supreme law,' while neither
    explicitly confers upon the courts the role of enforcing that law. See Cam-
    eron, *supra* note 5 at 78–81.
35 *Marbury v. Madison*, 5 U.S. (1 Cranch) 137 (1803).
36 *Motor Vehicle Reference, supra* note 2 at 501.
37 *Ibid.* at 504–5.

38 *Ibid.* at 508.
39 *Ibid.* at 509.
40 J.D. Whyte, 'Annotation' (1986) 48 C.R. (3d) 291 at 294.
41 *Motor Vehicle Reference, supra* note 2 at 502,
42 *Ibid.*
43 *Ibid.*
44 As noted by Wilson J. in her concurring judgment, *ibid.* at 530: 'Unlike my colleague, I do not think that ss. 8 to 14 of the *Charter* shed much light on the interpretation of the phrase "in accordance with the principles of fundamental justice" as used in s. 7 ... I prefer, therefore, to treat these sections as self-standing provisions, as indeed they are.'
45 Section 14 of the *Charter* provides: 'A party or witness in any proceedings who does not understand or speak the language in which the proceedings are conducted or who is deaf has the right to the assistance of an interpreter.'
46 See chapter 1, 'The Politics of the *Charter*,' at 29–31.
47 *Motor Vehicle Reference, supra* note 2 at 502.
48 Section 11 confers rights upon '[a]ny person charged with an offence,' not just offences leading to imprisonment.
49 *Motor Vehicle Reference, supra* note 2 at 516.
50 *Ibid.* at 518.
51 The implications of this are further examined in the context of the discussion on moral innocence, *infra.*
52 *Motor Vehicle Reference, supra* note 2 at 499, quoting Laskin J. in *Curr, supra* note 12 at 899.
53 *Ibid.* at 512–13.
54 Besides, many of the guarantees encompassed within sections 8 to 14 themselves extend beyond the criminal context. For example, the right to be free from unreasonable search and seizure presumably applies to all searches and seizures by the state, whether or not they are conducted in the course of a criminal investigation.
55 *Motor Vehicle Reference, supra* note 2 at 513.
56 *Ibid.* at 517.
57 The prohibitions and suspensions that could give rise to an offence under section 94(1), as it stood at the time of the reference, were all conditioned upon conviction for a serious driving offence.
58 *Motor Vehicle Reference, supra* note 2 at 518.
59 Though strict liability offences would seem to offend the common law notion of moral innocence that Lamer J. identifies as 'a principle of fundamental justice,' he makes a point on two occasions of distinguishing

between the impact of strict liability and absolute liability offences: *ibid.*
at 519, 521. Elsewhere, he goes out of his way to state that he need not
address the question of strict liability in this judgment: *ibid.* at 515. This
suggests that the Court may be prepared to view strict liability offences
differently under section 7.

60 *R. v. Prue; R. v. Baril*, [1979] 2 S.C.R. 547 [*Prue and Baril*].
61 *Motor-vehicle Act*, R.S.B.C. 1960, c. 253, as amended by S.B.C. 1976, c. 35, a.
20 and S.B.C. 1977, c. 41, s. 3.
62 Theoretically, it might have been possible for the government to have
established a system for providing notice of each and every suspension
that occurred by operation of law, but the large number of such suspensions made such a solution impracticable. In any event, the offence in section 238 was declared constitutionally invalid in *R. v. Boggs*, [1981] 1 S.C.R.
49.
63 *Miscellaneous Statutes Amendment Act, 1979*, S.B.C. 1979, c. 22, s. 31.
64 *R. v. MacDougall*, [1982] 2 S.C.R. 605.
65 Except, perhaps, where the mistake arose from an 'officially induced
error': *ibid.* at 613.
66 Factum of the Attorney General for Ontario [unpublished] at 69.
67 It is significant to note that during the course of oral argument in *R. v.
Westendorp*, [1983] 1 S.C.R. 43, Laskin C.J. persuaded counsel to abandon
its *Charter* argument by commenting that section 7 did not protect substantive justice: see J.D. Whyte, 'Developments in Constitutional Law: The
1982–83 Term' (1984) 6 Sup. Ct. L. Rev. 49 at 53.

3 Private Rights/Public Wrongs: The Liberal Lie of the *Charter**

Beware then the heathen gods; have no confidence in principles that come to us in the trappings of the eternal. Meet them with gentle irony, friendly skepticism and an open soul.

Learned Hand[1]

I

Doctor Arbuthnot was not far short of the mark: 'Law is a bottom-less pit.'[2] It is capable of accommodating all manner of philosophical insight, ideological choice, and hermeneutical possibility. In the three centuries following his observation, liberal theorists have railed against this existential reality. With hubris worthy of the pharaohs, they have sought to shape the legal pit in their own philosophical image. Their goal has been to construct, or to discover, a solid jurisprudential foundation on which to erect their legal edifices. Sometimes they claim to have succeeded. But inevitably the foundation collapses, like a false bottom, disclosing the political chasms beneath.

In this country, the enactment of the *Charter of Rights and Freedoms* has given new impetus to the liberal quest. Urged on by the courts, liberal academics are busily engaged in the construction of yet another foundation, 'a theoretical framework of constitutional principles,' to give meaning and stability to the *Charter* enterprise.[3] While judges have followed the time-honoured traditions of the common law and worked

* With Allan C. Hutchinson. Originally published in (1988) 38 U.T.L.J. 278-97. Copyright © 1988 by University of Toronto Press Inc. Reprinted by permission of Allan C. Hutchinson and University of Toronto Press Inc.

in a piecemeal and pragmatic way, it has been left to the academics to draw up the construction plans and to insist that, whatever the judges may believe they are doing, they are really following some immanent blueprint.[4] Of course, there is disagreement about the precise contours of the judicial artefacts and the details of the architectural design. Nevertheless, all agree that the foundation can be built. Some even insist that it has always been there – it is simply a matter of finding it.

Our position is different from that of most commentators – we remain unrepentant Arbuthnotians. We do not deny that the *Charter* reflects a particular vision of society and social justice; to do so would flout reality and would be both naive and dangerous. What we do maintain, however, is that the coherence of the *Charter* vision is grounded solely upon the ideological assumptions of its framers and interpreters. These liberals mistake their own creations for the hard rock of hermeneutical necessity. The platform on which the *Charter* is built is attached to nothing; it hurtles through the Arbuthnotian void, giving the appearance of support only to those who are perched precariously upon it and falling at the same rate of speed.

Because of this, it might be tempting to dismiss the *Charter* enterprise as 'nonsense without stilts.'[5] To do so, however, would be to miss the major point. The construction project undertaken by the courts and the liberal commentators may be without foundation, but it carries political clout. The *Charter* is a potent political weapon, one that is being used to benefit vested interests in society and to weaken the relative power of the disadvantaged and underprivileged.[6] Moreover, it is not simply that the particular decisions reached are regressive in result; the problem runs much deeper. Decisions are made in the context of, and are the product of, a partial vision of social life and political justice. As Benjamin Cardozo put it over half a century ago, 'the chief lawmakers … may be, and often are, the judges, because they are the final seat of authority. Every time they interpret contract, property, vested rights, due process of law, liberty, they necessarily enact into law parts of a system of social philosophy.'[7]

These ideological assumptions are by no means determinative in each and every case; they do not demand or sanction a particular set of detailed outcomes. However, they do energize and inform the interpretation of the *Charter* and push its enforcement towards certain types of conclusions. As imagined normative bottom lines, these deep-seated premises allow the legal community to maintain institutional legitimacy by pretending to be exercising its considerable power in accordance with ostensibly neutral and formal directives. By so doing, lawyers and judges are able to duck the real and difficult issues of substantive justice that underlie and are hidden by their professional commitments. The result is power without responsibility or accountability. This is not the apotheosis of democratic politics but its nemesis.

In this essay we intend to identify and criticize the discredited vision of social life and political justice that judges and lawyers rely upon in their routine practices. More often implicit than explicit, this vision is part of the institutional architecture of *Charter* jurisprudence. In the recent case of *Dolphin Delivery*,[8] however, these ideological commitments and their frailties were revealed in stark detail for all to see. The Supreme Court of Canada delivered a judgment that let the political cat out of the constitutional bag and into the critical light. Though welcomed in some quarters, the decision has received almost universal criticism, in whole or in part, from the academic community. Yet for all the apparent force and heat of their words, these critics manage to operate within and actually reinforce the ideological paradigm in which the courts work; they are both the critics and the conservers of the liberal credo. To appropriate Noam Chomsky's wisdom:

> The great achievement of the critics is to prevent the realization that what is happening today is not some departure from our historical ideals and practice, to be attributed to the personal failings of this or that individual. Rather, it is the systematic expression of the way our institutions function and will continue to function unless impeded by an aroused public that comes to understand their nature and their true history – exactly what our [judicial] institutions must prevent if they are to fulfill their function, namely, to serve power and privilege.[9]

In the first part of this essay, we introduce the facts and the decision in *Dolphin Delivery* and describe the dilemma facing the Court. Next, we address the basic outline of liberal theory that powers the Court's work and informs its troubled response to the demands of *Charter* adjudication. Though academics make enlightened noises about the character of the judicial role, they remain deeply committed to the assumptions and attachments of liberalism. In the closing sections of the essay we illustrate the ideological course of the *Charter* drama to date and the liberal colouring of its thematic structure. By way of conclusion, we suggest an alternative and better way of thinking about and changing the conditions of social justice.[10]

II

Dolphin Delivery was destined to be an important and troubling case. It was the first major decision by the Supreme Court of Canada that directly concerned the rights of labour under the *Charter*. Moreover, it raised a fundamental political dilemma in the context of an ostensibly technical question of legal interpretation. The case concerned an industrial dispute between the Retail, Wholesale, and Department Store Union and Purolator Courier Inc. The union, which represented the locked-out employees of the company, believed that Dolphin Delivery Ltd., another courier company, was acting as a business ally of Purolator. The union decided to picket Dolphin's premises. Before it could do so, however, Dolphin sought and obtained from the British Columbia Supreme Court an injunction preventing the picketing from going ahead.[11] The granting of the injunction was based on the court's finding that the alleged relationship between Dolphin and Purolator was unproved and that the union's proposed 'secondary picketing' comprised the common law tort of inducing breach of contract between Dolphin and its employees. The matter had to be resolved under common law because Purolator, an interprovincial undertaking, was subject to federal labour law, and the federal legislation was silent on the legal status of secondary picketing.

The issue raised by the case was whether secondary picketing was a protected activity under the *Charter*'s guarantee of freedom of expression. Because of the factual context, this issue in turn raised major questions about the reach of the *Charter* – in particular whether it applied to private litigation and/or the common law. In appealing the decision to grant the injunction, the union was unsuccessful before the Court of Appeal[12] and the Supreme Court of Canada.[13] In the Supreme Court, the seven-member bench unanimously held that both the granting of the injunction and the common law on which it was based were beyond the scope of *Charter* scrutiny.[14]

The leading judgment of the Court was given by McIntyre J. The reasoning he offered in support of the holding can be summarized in the form of seven sequential propositions:

1 The *Charter* applies to the common law.[15]
2 The *Charter* does not apply to 'private litigation divorced completely from any connection with Government.'[16]
3 The *Charter* applies to the executive and legislative branches of government but not to the judicial branch.[17]

4 The *Charter* applies to the common law 'only in so far as the common law is the basis of some governmental action'; thus the *Charter* does not apply to the common law in its regulation of relationships among private actors.[18]
5 The *Charter* does not apply to court orders issued pursuant to the common law.[19]
6 The *Charter* applies to legislation in its regulation of relationships among private actors.[20]
7 Where the *Charter* does not apply to the common law, 'the judiciary ought to apply and develop the principles of the common law in a manner consistent with the fundamental values enshrined in the Constitution.'[21]

It takes little critical capacity to realize that there are obvious inconsistencies between and among these propositions. The giveaway is the Court's holding that, while the *Charter* applies to legislation regulating private relationships, it does not apply to common law rules that do the same. Consequently, while the Court begins by maintaining that the *Charter* applies to the common law, its conclusion is completely at odds with this assertion. By the end of the judgment it is clear that the *Charter* does not apply to the common law; rather, there must be some additional governmental presence or involvement to attract *Charter* scrutiny.[22]

Though it is tempting to write off this internal contradiction as evidence of a confused and incompetent judiciary, such an assessment is both too harsh and too kind. It is too harsh because the contradiction is not one of the Court's own making; it is a reflection of the inherent contradiction of liberal ideology in a positivist age. It is too kind because the political implications of the contradiction are more pervasive and pernicious than if it had been a product of mere confusion or incompetence. Like its marine namesake, *Dolphin* shows that, beneath the surface, there is a whole world of action and agony.

III

The *Charter* is, at root, a liberal document. Its enactment was a constitutional affirmation of liberal faith. The framework and tenor of the *Charter* reflect traditional liberal values: it arms individuals with a negative set of formal rights to repel attempts at government interference.[23] This fact is confirmed by section 32(1), which limits *Charter* application to 'the Parliament and government of Canada' and to 'the legislatures and government of each province.' Thus, in *Hunter v. Southam Inc.*, Dickson J. was able to say that the purpose of the *Charter* is 'to constrain governmental action inconsistent with those rights and freedoms [enshrined within it]; it is not in itself an authorization for government action.'[24] In the *Charter* vision, the main enemy of freedom is not disparity in wealth or concentration of private power, but the state. It is the state whose tendency to abuse power and hamper the heroic individual must be kept in constant check lest we begin the irresistible slide down the totalitarian slope.

Though such fears are not groundless, their exaggeration makes liberals blind to the threat of unchecked private power and to the role of government as a promoter of liberty, particularly for the disadvantaged and oppressed. The *Charter*'s incorporation of liberal legalism as the dominant Canadian ethos is mistaken. It is neither descriptively accurate of existing social and political conditions nor prescriptively desirable as a future model for social and political life.

Derived from the writings of John Locke and Thomas Hobbes, and developed in modified form by Robert Nozick and John Rawls, the liberal theory of rights and political justice is premised on the belief that individuals possess a pre-political sphere of pure autonomy and freedom that does not depend upon the state for its existence: individuals are independent and complete entities who interact with others out of a grudging necessity to better satisfy their self-regarding wants and preferences. Accordingly, the major function of a liberal charter is to police the boundary that separates the political and the collective from the pre-political and the individual – to contain the state so as to prevent it from intruding, in its utilitarian zeal, upon the 'natural' realm of individual liberty. The major difficulty confronting adherents of liberalism lies in identifying the line that separates the domain of individual liberty from the domain of state action. This problem is less daunting for proponents of natural law, who can at least claim that the boundary is a product of the natural order of social life and justice.[25] For positivists, however, the task of determining where the public sphere ends and the private sphere begins is an intractable one. Because they have no natural authority on which to rely,[26] the distinction between the public and the private seems beyond objective assessment; thus positivists are driven to depend on the unreliable pointers of prevailing mores and consensus. While naturalists seek to 'find' that elusive line, positivists struggle over where to 'draw' the line. The line drawers may be a more advanced and sophisticated lot than the line finders, but they are part of the same intellectual heritage and political tradition. Moreover, the line drawers tend to hide rather than dispense with their naturalist affiliations; they draw their lines in accordance with an undisclosed map of ideological commitments.

In the nineteenth century, jurists of a positivist persuasion thought that they could finesse this difficulty by relying upon the distinction between the market and the state. The political orthodoxy of the day enabled them to assume that the bounds of private action were drawn by the invisible hand of the market, whose operation was in turn directed by the strong arm of the common law. An abuse of power occurred when the state, or someone acting through or on behalf of the state, interfered with or failed to protect such common law entitlements. There was no empirical analysis of the actual quality of those rights and their exercise. Instead, the courts engaged in an analytical inquiry as to whether the state was involved or not. If it was, remedial intervention through the courts was warranted; if not, those affected had to lobby for political reparations through the legislature. The emphasis throughout was upon whether the impugned act could be identified with the formal attributes of governmental authority, not upon whether it had actually inhibited or damaged the interests of particular citizens. Pedigree and form rather than effect and substance were the standards for evaluating impermissible behaviour.

The difficulty with this view is that it contained the seeds of its own destruction. Absent some theory of natural rights, the labelling of market activity as 'private' and regulatory activity as 'public' can be exposed as wholly arbitrary. Without an acknowledged 'natural order,' the market is simply one choice among many. This means that the state is implicated in the market in the same way it is implicated in any other political choice made within its territorial jurisdiction. Its claim to sovereignty implies that a decision not to intervene and regulate, or mere inaction, is as much a governmental responsibility as a decision to do so. Thus the attempt to limit state activity to efforts directed at changing the status quo is misconceived; the state is equally implicated in the *retention* of the status quo. Acquiescence and action are merely opposite sides of the same governmental coin.

Moreover, from a positivist perspective, common law protection of private property and freedom to contract must itself be characterized as a form of state activity.[27] The plea of free marketeers and their ilk that government stay out of our lives – their credo that the state which governs least governs best – is as contradictory as it is disingenuous.

Judicial enforcement of private property and of contractual rights is as coercive to those who do not share in their benefits as confiscation is coercive to those who do share. In other words, the relevant issue is not whether the state ought to 'intervene': the state is already there. The only question is on whose behalf state power should be exercised. As Duncan Kennedy puts it:

> The private owner's 'freedom' to exclude others from his possessions has as its corollary his 'power' to control the lives of those who cannot live without access to the means of production. Admission to use of the property is the carrot, exclusion the stick that orders our lives. It is a familiar notion that, through the definition and enforcement of legal rights in things, the state is deeply implicated in the particular order that emerges from the interaction of private individuals.[28]

The public/private distinction is not an indifferent structure that provides a convenient framework for debating and deciding the distribution of political power. Rather, it skews that debate and prods its resulting decisions in particular directions. The entitlements of private property owners exist only insofar as the state is prepared to recognize and lend support to those entitlements in the face of competing claims. What is referred to as 'private power' is in reality public power that has been delegated to certain individuals and that can be wielded in a largely unchecked and democratically unaccountable way.[29] This exposure of the illusory nature of the public/private distinction also lays bare the underlying fallacy of liberalism. If the distinction between the public and the private is without substance, the liberal enterprise of seeking to police the boundary between the two spheres is at best futile and at worst covertly ideological. Whether it is a question of line finding or line drawing, it is a formal fraud that perpetuates a substantive injustice.

IV

The liberal vision of social life and justice not only is intellectually discredited, but also fails to present even a rudimentary picture of the contemporary workings of Canadian society and government. The welfare state has long since come of age in Canada. However, the tragedy of Canadian jurisprudence is that the liberal vision still holds the legal imagination and intellect in its inequitable grip. The Supreme Court of Canada's judgment in *Dolphin Delivery* is the clear product of such impoverished thinking. Moreover, though the academic response to the decision was one of widespread criticism, it shares the same ideological assumptions and standards. The pre- and post-*Dolphin* commentary on the reach of the *Charter*, the line between public and private action, is all of a piece. It speaks in the elite and anachronistic language of nineteenth-century liberalism, though it often adopts a more modern and sophisticated accent.

A claque of academics welcomes the attempt to draw a line between the public and private sectors of social life and to confine the *Charter*'s application to the former.[30] For them, it is simply a matter of drawing the line in the right place according to the *Charter* map's textual coordinates. For instance, in his comment on *Dolphin*, Peter Hogg contends that McIntyre J.'s cartographical interpretation is mistaken and that his line drawing is therefore inaccurate. Hogg agrees with McIntyre J. that 'the best reading' of the *Charter* is to restrict it to government action so that 'there is a private realm in which people are not obliged to subscribe to "state" virtues and into which constitutional norms ought not to intrude.'[31] Hogg also states, however, that since the courts are part of government, the *Charter* applies to the granting of injunctions. This assertion is consistent with his earlier view that the *Charter* ought to apply to the common law 'only when it crystallises into a rule that can be enforced by the courts.'[32] Though these two statements are logically entailed by his major axiom, they are little more than an attempt to preserve the discredited public/private dichotomy by obscuring the line beneath a new, but equally arbitrary, distinction.

Given that the state is implicated in virtually all forms of so-called private activity, the question whether that involvement manifests itself as a crystallized 'rule,' a court injunction, or some less obvious form is completely beside the point. This can be illustrated by considering the facts in *Blainey v. Ontario Hockey Association*.[33] In that case, the Ontario Hockey Association (OHA), a 'private' body, denied Justine Blainey the opportunity to play hockey in a male league. Was the decision of the OHA an activity authorized by government? According to the test enunciated by Hogg, a negative answer is required: there was no common law 'rule' and no court injunction specifically authorizing the OHA to deny women access to its leagues. Yet this conclusion is misleading. Whether the OHA's legal authority to deny Blainey the right to use its facilities flowed from the complex tapestry of common law property rights or from a single thread, it was a power conferred upon the OHA by the state.

The arbitrary nature of Hogg's distinction is further evidenced by its indeterminacy. What may appear as private activity in one factual context can be transformed into state action in another. All that is required is for the actors to position themselves so that the underlying presence of the state is driven to the surface and forced to reveal itself. Suppose, for example, that Justine Blainey decided to flout the OHA's decision by chaining herself to the boards of the rink whenever an OHA game was scheduled. Further, suppose that, in order to enforce its decision, the OHA sought an injunction to have her removed for trespass. According to Hogg, Blainey could then invoke the *Charter* to resist the OHA's action. Yet the only difference here is that, by challenging the OHA's assertion of its property entitlement, Blainey would force the state's support of that entitlement into the light of day.

Recognizing some of these difficulties, a less traditional group of liberal scholars eschew such dubious distinctions and reject the public/private dichotomy.[34] They acknowledge that any attempt to draw a coherent and principled line between the public and private realms of life is ill-fated. The nexus between the state and the challenged action is never sufficiently close to rule out any private behaviour and is always too loose to catch only public activity: best to be rid of the distinction altogether. Moreover, they argue that even if a line could be drawn, there is no convincing political justification for doing so. For instance, in a particularly trenchant criticism of *Dolphin*, David Beatty concludes that McIntyre J.'s effort to characterize the courts and common law as outside government not only is conceptually confused, but also places the courts above the *Charter*: it is 'élitist and anti-democratic' and 'will act as a cancer on the moral authority on which the very life of the judiciary depends.'[35]

The constructive consequence of this critique is the recommendation that constitutional norms ought to apply to and inform all facets of Canadian life and that *Charter* justice should be available in both the private and the public realms. Yet for all their apparent perspicacity, these scholars are unwilling or unable to see the full implications of their critique. Without some notional sphere of private autonomy to be preserved from the intrusions of others, whether it be the state or other individuals, the knit of liberal rights and freedoms starts to unravel. If the state is implicated in all forms of societal activity, *Charter* claims cease to be about the protection from state interference of some preordained realm of individual autonomy; rather, they become claims about the appropriate allocation of state powers and social resources.

The negative notion of liberty – a freedom to be let alone to enjoy one's assets without government interference – becomes incoherent. The question of whose entitlements are to be protected from whose interference becomes a matter of contested political choice rather than the correct application of abstract principle. Accordingly, if there is to be any genuine constitutional sense or meaning, the role of the state must be completely revised, and people's understanding of and relation to it must be transformed.

The liberal revisionists have thrown themselves on the horns of a painful dilemma. Unless they are prepared to develop a substantive vision of distributive justice, they have no metewand against which to measure the social value of any particular act or state of affairs. If they do develop such a vision, however, it will enjoy no prior claim over competing visions of a liberal or any other persuasion. Moreover, any move in this direction obliges them to accept the impossibility of a neutral or apolitical mode of *Charter* adjudication: a conclusion that no stripe of liberal, naturalist or positivist, can countenance.

The practical implications of this theoretical shambles are devastating for courts and for liberal theory generally. Relying on early-nineteenth-century ideas to tackle and resolve late-twentieth-century problems is like trying to repair a computer with a hammer and chisel: it will do much more harm than good. Working from a positivist tradition in a post-realist age, Canadian judges struggle to make sense of a liberal *Charter* of rights. Without clearly defined realms of public and private activity, 'constitutional rights become affirmative rights which impose affirmative duties on governments to intervene to redress deprivations in civil society.'[36] Neutrality ceases to be a plausible characteristic or attainable goal of judicial review. For instance, imagine the archetypal dispute between the person who wants to take property to satisfy life-sustaining needs and the property owner who claims a right to dispose of it as he or she wishes. Liberals seek to resolve such disputes by resort to the spurious rhetoric of rights. Yet in the absence of the mythical support of a public/private distinction, it is impossible to reach coherent solutions without addressing the deep normative assumptions that rights talk masks and seeks to finesse.[37]

V

In light of these difficulties, it is not hard to see that the Supreme Court of Canada in *Dolphin Delivery* was faced with an unenviable task. On the one hand, the Court had to accept that it would be stretching things too far to pretend that the common law was 'non-law' or 'found law.' Even the most formalistic of contemporary lawyers must acknowledge that the common law is a creation of courts, not a product of providence. Of course, judges still want to cling to the myth that the act of creation was and continues to be neutral and distinct from politics. Judges see themselves as passive referees who develop the law in an even-handed and impartial manner.[38] Yet even this view must have posed difficulties for a court dealing with a case involving industrial torts in the *Dolphin* context. The invention in the nineteenth century of the tort of induc- ing contractual breach is a notoriously crude example of judicial power being mobilized to further the interests of employers at the expense of the labour movement.[39] Perhaps for this reason, McIntyre J., while insisting that judges act as 'neutral arbiters' when they *apply* the law, was strangely silent on the question of how that law was created in the first place.[40]

On the other hand, the Court could not have interpreted the *Charter* in a way that would have required it to abandon liberal conceptions of the state and of the judicial role. To have done so would have com- pelled the Court to confront the complicity of the state, *including the courts*, in all forms of social activity. This in turn would have required the Court to embrace an overtly political role for itself. It would have had to acknowledge constitutional responsibility for the social state of affairs that resulted when its ostensibly neutral decisions combined and reacted with 'private' activity. Existing distributions of property, wealth, and power would be up for grabs in an ideological battle over the content of such guarantees as 'liberty,' 'security,' and 'equality.' Moreover, without the reassuring disguise and rhetorical trappings of liberal legalism, the courts' participation in the ideological debate would be naked and an affront to liberal sensibilities.

The Court in *Dolphin* found itself between a rock and a hard place. The rock was the incoherence of the public/private dichotomy in a post-realist age; the hard place the overtly political character of *Char- ter* adjudication in the absence of a public/private cushion. Given this uncomfortable state of affairs, the Court's only choice was to produce a judgment as contradictory and incoherent as liberalism itself. The prod- uct was a decision that appeared to recognize the positivist nature of the common law but at the same time sought to preserve the semblance of a public/private distinction by excluding that law from *Charter* scru- tiny. What has so bitterly offended liberal critics is the transparency of the exercise. Instead of obscuring the liberal dilemma beneath layers of pseudo-profound abstraction about the distinction between laws that crystallize into enforceable rules and those that do not,[41] or between agencies that perform public roles and those that do not,[42] or between laws that authorize unconstitutional conduct and those that merely permit it,[43] the Court ensured that the incoherence of the public/private distinction was laid bare for all to behold.

As if this were not enough, the Court highlighted that incoherence through its invocation of the Ontario Court of Appeal's decision in *Blainey*. One aspect of that case concerned the constitutionality of section 19(2) of the *Ontario Human Rights Code*, which provides that 'the right ... to equal treatment [with respect to services, goods, and facilities] ... is not infringed where membership in an athletic organization or participation in an athletic activity is restricted to persons of the same sex.'[44] The Court of Appeal held that this section contravened the *Charter*'s guarantee of sexual equality. In *Dolphin*, McIntyre J. referred to this aspect of *Blainey* as an example of a sufficiently 'direct and close connection' between the claim advanced and some 'element of government action' to warrant *Charter* scrutiny.[45]

The difficulty with this view is that the effect of section 19(2) of the *Ontario Human Rights Code*, when studied closely, is merely to preserve the common law. The provision does not itself discriminate on the basis of sex; all it does is exempt from statutory prohibition sex-based distinctions made by athletic organizations. In other words, the legislature could have achieved the same result by drafting a provision that read: 'Notwithstanding the right to equal treatment, the common law shall continue to apply where membership in an athletic organization or participation in an athletic activity is restricted to persons of the same sex.' Alternatively, the legislature could have specified those organizations that were bound by the statutory prohibition on sexual discrimination and omitted athletic organizations from the list. Thus the government's 'direct and close' involvement with the conduct complained of in *Blainey* in fact went no further than permitting the common law regime and its political morality to continue. Yet if this is sufficient government involvement to attract *Charter* scrutiny, it is difficult to see why the federal government's failure to alter the common law rules at work in *Dolphin* did not also provide the necessary 'element of government action.' Indeed, it is difficult to see why the failure of government to proscribe any conduct that violates constitutional norms would be beyond the scope of the *Charter*.[46]

VI

The public/private distinction may be theoretically incoherent, but that does not mean it lacks political purpose. On the contrary, the distinction gives a discernible ideological direction to the courts' work. The effect of limiting *Charter* application to actions of the legislative and executive branches of government is to exclude from *Charter* scrutiny the major source of inequality in our society: the maldistribution of property entitlements amongst individuals. When confronted with questions of *Charter* justice, the courts, like Lord Nelson, turn a blind eye to underlying disparities in wealth and power. If both eyes were permanently denied constitutional sight, this might not be so bad; a judiciary deprived completely of *Charter* vision is not an uninviting prospect. However, the courts' selective blindness to 'private' inequities is offset by an acuity of vision in cases of 'public' denials of individual rights. The result is a judiciary that disregards primary causes of social injustice in its determination to restrain the arm of the state best equipped to redress those causes – the democratic limb represented by the legislature and the executive. Put simply, the *Charter* can be invoked to challenge the *Combines Investigation Act*,[47] but not the combine.

The presumption underlying the public/private dichotomy is that existing distributions of wealth and power are a product of individual initiative, not state action. Conveniently overlooked is the fact that such distributions and accumulations of wealth generally depend for their very existence and legitimacy upon a panoply of state-supported laws and institutions. Moreover, it is not just that existing distributions of wealth and power are removed from *Charter* scrutiny; such distributions form the baseline, or 'natural foundation,' upon which *Charter* rights are grounded and against which the constitutionality of state action is to be judged. For example, the right to equality promises not substantive social equality in the liberal scheme of things, but equal treatment by the legislative and executive arms of the state. For this reason, section 15 of the *Charter* does not place affirmative duties upon the state; it is satisfied by 'equal' legislative inaction as much as it is by 'equal' legislative action. Provided that everyone is disentitled to benefits 'equally,' the requirements of section 15 are met. Thus a recent decision of the Nova Scotia Court of Appeal remedied the failure of provincial legislation to provide welfare benefits to single fathers by striking down the provision that bestowed such benefits on single mothers.[48] Equality is reduced to a matter of hollow form rather than being elevated to a commitment to substantive justice.[49] Similarly, the right to freedom of expression, in the words of the Federal Court of Appeal, 'is a freedom to express and communicate ideas without restraint … It is not a freedom to use someone else's property to do so.'[50] The implication is obvious: property is the foundation upon which *Charter* rights are conferred, protected, and enhanced. The less property one has, the less one can exercise and enjoy one's rights. There is a strong correlation between finance and franchise. In our technological society, wealth is a precondition of one's being able to speak broadly and effectively. Though anyone can stand on the street corner, only the rich can have direct access to our homes through the costly channels of the media. When the rights of property owners and speakers collide, speakers stand dumb before the claims of property. While the courts invalidate legislation that seeks to restrict the exaggerated impact of the wealthy on electoral campaigning,[51] they uphold manufacturers' claims that their freedom of speech is infringed by legislation that restricts television advertising for children.[52]

Anyone who doubts the foundational nature of common law property rights after the decision in *Dolphin Delivery* need only consider the following example. Suppose that the common law prohibition on secondary picketing considered in *Dolphin* had been embodied in legislation. Further suppose that the Court had decided that this legislative prohibition violated the *Charter* and should therefore be struck down.[53] Where would the Court then have looked to determine the legal rights and obligations of the parties? Presumably, the common law would fill the constitutional void. It will come as no surprise to those with a knowledge of the history of labour relations that the common law treats secondary picketing as a tortious and unlawful act. On the basis of the Court's decision in *Dolphin*, the perverse outcome would be that the same prohibition would now be deemed acceptable because it was directed by the providential common law. Whatever its fate elsewhere, the common law has been reinstated by the *Charter* as 'the brooding omnipresence in the [Canadian] sky.'[54]

The public/private distinction also permits the judiciary subtly to influence the results of the *Charter* game in accordance with judicial values. In particular, it enables courts to decide whether certain entities ought to be subjected to or exempted from *Charter* scrutiny on the basis of an ostensibly neutral determination as to whether they are 'public' or 'private' in nature. Indeed, the consequences go further. The decision that an entity is 'private' not only permits it to act without fear of breaching the moral imperatives contained in the *Charter,* but also makes more likely that the entity will be permitted to mobilize the *Charter* as a weapon to resist government regulation and to insulate itself from popular scrutiny and control.

The courts' treatment of corporations under the *Charter* provides an excellent example. It takes little legal imagination to construct an argument showing how the activities of modern corporations can be attributed to the state. Corporations, after all, are creatures of statute; their existence and the extraordinary powers they wield are a product of legislation.[55] Yet despite this, the Supreme Court has simply assumed that corporations are 'private' entities; as such, they have been granted *Charter* protection and at the same time have effectively been excluded from *Charter* scrutiny. In *Hunter v. Southam Inc.*, for example, the Court interpreted section 8 of the *Charter* as conferring a privacy right upon corporations.[56] In *R. v. Big M Drug Mart*, the Court, while speaking of 'the inviolable rights of the human person,' permitted a corporation to invoke the right to freedom of religion to challenge a law that was deleterious to its economic interests.[57]

The approach of the Supreme Court to corporate power in these cases can be contrasted with its approach to trade union power in the round of freedom-of-association cases decided after *Dolphin Delivery*. Continuing a long tradition of judicial antipathy to the labour movement, the Court refused to grant constitutional protection to the very core of union activities: collective bargaining and striking.[58] Not surprisingly, one of the reasons offered by the Court to support its decision was the 'public' nature of union power. Speaking for the majority in *Alberta Reference*, LeDain J. stated that such union rights 'are not fundamental rights or freedoms' because '[t]hey are the creation of legislation, involving a balance of competing interests in a field which has been recognized by the courts as requiring specialized expertise.'[59] Thus, while 'private' corporate teams get a chance to score on every *Charter* shot, 'public' union teams have trouble even getting onto the ice. Of course, if the Court follows through on its suggestion that union power is 'public,' labour may yet get its chance to enjoy some *Charter* action – playing defence.[60]

VII

Liberalism is a failure; it cannot pass conceptual, social, legal, or political muster. A continued reliance on its intellectual assumptions and ideological prescriptions is indefensible.[61] The challenge is to replace it with a substantive vision of social justice that is capable of responding to the vast inequalities of economic and political power that liberalism and its disciples permit and, through their theoretical intransigence, condone. The immediate need is to conceive of individuals, relations with others, and freedom in different ways. People are not isolated, self-contained units that stand ontologically free of their social settings. The contemporary image of the individual as a self-interested competitor in the human race is a product of existing social structures and their supporting liberal ethos. Yet whatever the rhetoric, the reality is that society comprises a thick web of interdependent relations.[62] Though liberal theorists seem bent on destroying our interconnectedness, the fate of each person is intimately and inexorably tied to that of others. Rather than allowing this dependency to be abused in circumstances of social inequality, our task is to establish the best conditions in which to nurture a more cooperative ethic and a greater sense of responsibility for the lives of others. Social justice must look to the lived concerns of everyone, not only to the abstract claims of the few.

The platform of liberal legalism on which the *Charter* is built impoverishes politics and ensures that any attempt to challenge its individualistic structure is effectively defused. The courts' response to the claims of constitutional protection for unions and their political activities is illustrative of this attitude. In *Dolphin*, for instance, the Supreme Court insisted on treating picketing as a 'speech' activity by individual workers.[63] While this classification is necessary under *Charter* thinking, it fails to recognize that picketing is intended to be a group act of industrial resistance. To characterize picketing as an exercise of individual speech rights robs it of its broader and more radical political significance as a challenge to prevailing social conditions and thinking. Similarly, in the freedom of association cases, the Court based its refusal to grant constitutional status to the right to strike on the view that people cannot obtain more rights by joining a group than they could possess as individuals.[64] Yet the whole idea and purpose of a union is to foster social solidarity and to establish a collective presence that can overcome workers' vulnerability to the greater power of employers. To limit union rights to those that can be exercised by members individually is to subvert the whole *raison d'être* of unions. The refusal to recognize such rights is a punishing betrayal of the hopes and opportunities of working people for an improved life. Unions are reduced to one more interest group in the ethical bazaar of pluralistic politics, where all are welcome provided that they are liberal.

The *Charter* forces us to cram the rich complexities of social life into an abstract and simplistic framework. Distinctions like those developed in *Dolphin* provide formal paraphernalia behind which private power thrives relatively unchecked and substantive issues are arbitrarily and unjustly resolved. Liberal rights talk constrains our choices and makes us look at the world in the absolutist and static terms of a black-and-white photograph. The courts reinforce this monochromatic impoverishment of democratic politics and its vivid possibilities. They contribute to the failure to see and participate in the world as an iridescent and dynamic experience in which each person can play an active role in constructing an egalitarian society. By abandoning liberal individualism and engendering a more open-ended form of social democracy, it might be possible not only to comprehend the world in its many drab shades of existential grey, but also, as Frances Olsen suggests, to envision it in bright blues, yellows, and reds.[65]

NOTES

1 L. Hand, *The Spirit of Liberty and Other Writings* (New York: Alfred A. Knopf, 1953) at 101.
2 J. Arbuthnot, *The History of John Bull* [1712], Alan W. Bower & Robert A. Erickson, eds. (Oxford: Clarendon Press, 1976) at ch. 24.
3 B. Dickson C.J., 'Address to the Mid-Winter Meeting of the Canadian Bar Association' (2 February 1985) N.A.C. 139:10 at 14.
4 See A.C. Hutchinson, *Dwelling on the Threshold: Critical Essays on Modern Legal Thought* (Toronto: Carswell, 1988) at 247–60.
5 In our view, Bentham conceded too much when he suggested that such nonsense could be supported even by stilts (though 'stilted' it undoubtedly is). See J. Bentham, 'Anarchical Fallacies' in *The Works of Jeremy Bentham* (London: Simpkin Marshall & Co., 1843) at 501.
6 See ch. 1, 'The Politics of the *Charter*'; and Hutchinson, *supra* note 4 at 223–46.
7 B.N. Cardozo, *The Nature of the Judicial Process* (New Haven: Yale University Press, 1949) at 171.
8 *Dolphin Delivery Ltd. v. Retail, Wholesale and Department Store Union, Local 580*, [1986] 2 S.C.R. 573 [*Dolphin Delivery*].
9 N. Chomsky, 'The Manufacture of Consent' (1985) 17 Our Generation 83 at 90–1.
10 This essay owes much to the earlier work of Paul Brest; see P. Brest, 'State

Action and Liberal Theory: A Casenote on *Flagg Brothers v. Brooks'* (1983)
130 U. Pa. L. Rev. 1296. Though the American state-action doctrine is
universally condemned, it still plays a major role in contemporary judicial
review; see *e.g. Lugar v. Edmondson Oil Co.*, 457 U.S. 922 (1982). For a thorough survey of the law and the literature, see E. Chemerinsky, 'Rethinking
State Action' (1985) 80 Nw. U. L. Rev. 503.

11 *Dolphin Delivery Ltd. v. Retail, Wholesale and Department Store Union, Local
   580*, [1983] B.C.W.L.D. 100 (S.C.).

12 *Dolphin Delivery Ltd. v. Retail, Wholesale and Department Store Union, Local
   580* (1984), 52 B.C.L.R. 1 (C.A.).

13 *Dolphin Delivery, supra* note 8.

14 Presumably by way of sop, the majority also held that picketing is a form
   of expression protected by the *Charter*. However, this view was qualified by the further holding that, had the *Charter* applied, the restriction in
   Dolphin would have constituted a 'reasonable limit' within the meaning of
   section 1.

15 *Dolphin Delivery, supra* note 8 at 592.

16 *Ibid.* at 593.

17 *Ibid.* at 598–9. McIntyre J. tried to suggest that though the *Charter* does
   not apply to the judiciary, the courts are 'bound by the *Charter* as they are
   bound by all law.' Here, however, he was using the word 'bound' in a
   particular sense to refer to the fact that the courts must apply the *Charter* in
   their judicial capacity as 'neutral arbiters': *ibid.* at 600.

18 *Ibid.* at 599, 603.

19 *Ibid.* at 600.

20 *Ibid.* at 600–3.

21 *Ibid.* at 603.

22 McIntyre J. seems to have reached these contradictory conclusions by
   basing his first assertion (that the *Charter* applies to the common law) on
   an interpretation of section 52 of the *Constitution Act, 1982*, and his second
   assertion (that there must be some additional governmental presence) on
   an interpretation of section 32(1) of the *Charter*. Though this helps explain
   his reasoning, it does not alter the fact that the two assertions ultimately
   cannot be reconciled with each other.

23 This is not to deny that the *Charter* contains traces of a more positive and
   communitarian strand of politics. Guarantees of language rights, the
   reasonable limits clause, protection for affirmative action programs, and
   references to the preservation of aboriginal and denominational school
   rights are evidence of such thinking. See P.J. Monahan, *Politics and the Constitution: The Charter, Federalism, and the Supreme Court of Canada* (Toronto:

Carswell, 1987). The important thing to note, however, is that, with the exception of language rights, these communitarian concerns find voice only in the qualifications of and limitations on *Charter* guarantees. Thus, they may occasionally serve as brakes on the full expression of *Charter* rights, but they do not alter the fact that liberal individualism is the engine that drives the *Charter* carriage. Moreover, in keeping with the *Charter's* liberal thrust, the Supreme Court has indicated that it regards the language guarantees as 'political' rights deserving of a lower level of constitutional protection than the 'principled' rights found elsewhere in the *Charter*. See P.J. Monahan & A. Petter, 'Developments in Constitutional Law: The 1985–86 Term' (1987) 9 Sup. Ct. L. Rev. 69 at 125–43.

24 *Hunter v. Southam Inc.*, [1984] 2 S.C.R. 145 at 156 [*Southam*]. See also *R. v. Big M Drug Mart*, [1985] 1 S.C.R. 195 at 336 [*Big M Drug Mart*], Dickson C.J.: 'freedom can primarily be characterized by the absence of coercion or constraint.'

25 See J. Finnis, *Natural Law and Natural Rights* (Oxford: Clarendon Press, 1980).

26 See H.L.A. Hart, *The Concept of Law* (Oxford: Clarendon Press, 1961).

27 See R.L. Hale, 'Coercion and Distribution in a Supposedly Non-Coercive State' (1923) 38 Pol. Sci. Q. 470; and M.R. Cohen, 'Property and Sovereignty' (1927) 13 C.L.Q. 8.

28 D. Kennedy, 'The Structure of Blackstone's Commentaries' (1979) 28 Buff. L. Rev. 205 at 334.

29 See M.J. Horwitz, 'The History of the Public/Private Distinction' (1982) 130 U. Pa. L. Rev. 1423 at 1426.

30 See *e.g.* P.W. Hogg, *Constitutional Law of Canada*, 2nd ed. (Toronto: Carswell, 1985) at 670–8; K. Swinton, 'Application of the Canadian Charter of Rights and Freedoms' in W.S. Tarnopolsky & G.A. Beaudoin, eds., *The Canadian Charter of Rights and Freedoms: Commentary* (Toronto: Carswell, 1982) at 41; J.D. Whyte, 'Is the Private Sector Affected by the Charter?' in L. Smith, ed., *Righting the Balance: Canada's New Equality Rights* (Saskatoon: Canadian Human Rights Reporter, 1986) at 145.

31 P.W. Hogg, 'The Dolphin Delivery Case: The Application of the Charter to Private Action' (1987) 51 Sask. L. Rev. 273 at 274.

32 Hogg, *Constitutional Law of Canada, supra* note 30 at 678.

33 *Blainey v. Ontario Hockey Association* (1986), 54 O.R. (2d) 513 (C.A.) [*Blainey*], leave to appeal to S.C.C. refused, [1986] 1 S.C.R. xii.

34 See *e.g.* D. Gibson, *The Law of the Charter: General Principles* (Toronto: Carswell, 1986) at 1–24; Y. de Montigny, 'Section 32 and Equality Rights' in A.F. Bayefsky & M. Eberts, eds., *Equality Rights and the Canadian Charter of*

Rights and Freedoms (Toronto: Carswell, 1985); and B. Slattery, 'Charter of Rights and Freedoms – Does It Bind Private Persons?' (1985) 63 Can. Bar Rev. 148.

35 D. Beatty, 'Constitutional Conceits: The Coercive Authority of Courts' (1987) 37 U.T.L.J. 83 at 190–1.

36 H. Lessard, 'The Idea of the "Private": A Discussion of State Action and Separate Sphere Ideology' (1986) 10 Dalhousie L.J. 107 at 120.

37 See P.J. Monahan, 'Dialogue' (1987) 21 U.B.C.L. Rev. 177 at 204–5.

38 For an extended critique of modern formalism, see Hutchinson, *supra* note 4 at 23–55.

39 See *Lumley v. Gye* (1853), 2 E. & B. 216, 118 E.R. 749. For a thorough account of the circumstances surrounding this case and its subsequent history, see F.B. Sayre, 'Inducing Breach of Contract' (1923) 36 Harv. L. Rev. 663; H.J. Glasbeek, 'Lumley v. Gye – The Aftermath: An Inducement to Judicial Reform?' (1974–5) 1 Mon. U. L. Rev. 187; and J.A.G. Griffith, *The Politics of the Judiciary*, 3rd ed. (London: Fontana Press, 1985) at 53–82.

40 *Dolphin Delivery, supra* note 8 at 600.

41 See Hogg, *Constitutional Law of Canada, supra* note 30 at 677–8.

42 See Whyte, *supra* note 30.

43 See Slattery, *supra* note 34 at 157.

44 *Supra* note 33 at para. 14.

45 *Dolphin Delivery, supra* note 8 at paras. 43–4.

46 The incoherence of *Dolphin* is further highlighted by the decision of the Supreme Court of Canada five months later in *Rahey v. R.,* [1987] 1 S.C.R. 588. In that case the Court simply assumed that the *Charter* could be invoked against the actions of a trial judge for failing to decide a motion on a directed verdict within a reasonable time. Yet this assumption is completely at odds with McIntyre J.'s holding that courts act as 'neutral arbiters' and fall outside the scope of section 32 of the *Charter*.

47 See *Southam, supra* note 24.

48 See *Phillips v. Nova Scotia (Social Assistance Appeal Board)* (1986), 76 N.S.R. (2d) 240 (C.A.), aff'g (1986), 73 N.S.R. (2d) 415 (S.C.T.D.).

49 Moreover, this would be true even if the Nova Scotia court had chosen the alternative remedy of extending benefits to single fathers. It still would have been open to the legislature to have lowered or eliminated the benefits paid to all recipients. Indeed, this is precisely what happened after a British Columbia ruling struck down regulations providing lower welfare rates for those under twenty-six: see *Silano v. B.C.* (1987), 16 B.C.L.R. (2d) 113 (S.C.). The response of the provincial government was to offset increased payments to younger claimants by reducing general welfare

rates: 'B.C. cuts welfare by $6 a month' *Globe and Mail* (14 August 1987) at A9. In other words, equality was achieved by lowering benefits for those over twenty-six – a group that makes up the bulk of welfare recipients.

50 *New Brunswick Broadcasting Co. v. Canada (C.R.T.C.),* [1984] 2 F.C. 410 (C.A.) at 413, Thurlow C.J.

51 *National Citizens' Coalition Inc. v. Canada (Attorney General)* (1984), 32 Alta. L.R. (2d) 249 (Q.B.).

52 *Irwin Toy Ltd. v. Quebec (Attorney General)* (1986), 3 Q.A.C. 285 [subsequently rev'd in [1989] 1 S.C.R. 927].

53 Such a statutory prohibition would clearly be subject to *Charter* scrutiny. As McIntyre J. noted in *Dolphin Delivery,* if there had been a statutory provision specifically outlawing secondary picketing, 'the case … would be on all fours with *Blainey* and, subject to s. 1 of the *Charter,* the statutory provision could be struck down': *supra* note 8 at 603.

54 *Southern Pacific Co. v. Jensen,* 244 U.S. 205 at 222 (1917), Holmes J.

55 See A.A. Berle Jr, 'Constitutional Limitations on Corporate Activity: Protection of Personal Rights from Invasion through Economic Power' (1952) 100 U. Pa. L. Rev. 933.

56 *Southam, supra* note 24.

57 *Big M Drug Mart, supra* note 24.

58 *Reference Re Public Service Employee Relations Act (Alberta),* [1987] 1 S.C.R. 313 [*Alberta Reference*]; *Public Service Alliance of Canada v. Canada,* [1987] 1 S.C.R. 424; and *Retail, Wholesale and Department Store Union, Locals 544, 496, 635 and 955 v. Saskatchewan,* [1987] 1 S.C.R. 460.

59 *Alberta Reference, ibid.* at 391 [emphasis added].

60 For an example of how the *Charter* can be used to undermine labour interests, see *Lavigne v. O.P.S.E.U.* (1986), 55 O.R. (2d) 449 (H.C.); and *Lavigne v. O.P.S.E.U.* (No. 2) (1987), 60 O.R. (2d) 486 (H.C.), White J. [subsequently rev'd in (1989), 67 O.R. (2d) 536 (C.A.) and in [1991] 2 S.C.R. 211].

61 For a thorough critique of liberalism see *e.g.* R.P. Wolff, *The Poverty of Liberalism* (Boston: Beacon Press, 1968); R.M. Unger, *Knowledge and Politics* (New York: Free Press, 1975); and T.A. Spragens Jr, *The Irony of Liberal Reason* (Chicago: University of Chicago Press, 1981).

62 For an extended attempt to explain and defend this view and its prescriptive consequences, see Hutchinson, *supra* note 4 at 281–7.

63 *Dolphin Delivery, supra* note 8 at 588.

64 *Alberta Reference, supra* note 58 at 397, McIntyre J.

65 See F. Olsen, 'The Family and the Market: A Study of Ideology and Legal Reform' (1983) 96 Harv. L. Rev. 1497 at 1578.

4 Canada's *Charter* Flight: Soaring Backwards into the Future*

> I often wonder whether we do not rest our hopes too much upon constitutions, upon laws and upon courts. These are false hopes; believe me, these are false hopes. Liberty lies in the hearts of men and women; when it dies there, no constitution, no law, no court can save it; no constitution, no law, no court can even do much to help it. While it lies there it needs no constitution, no law, no court to save it.
>
> Learned Hand[1]

When legal intellectuals become disillusioned with the sordid world of politics, their thoughts frequently turn to the alluring realm of rights. It should come as no surprise, therefore, that after a decade of Thatcher Conservatism a growing number of reform-minded lawyers in Britain are voicing support for a constitutional bill of rights. This proposal appears to offer a civilized alternative to the crude practices of parliamentary government. According to its proponents, a bill of rights would provide a mechanism for evaluating social policy on the basis of reason and principle rather than partisanship and ideology. Moreover, the bill could serve as an important instrument for protecting the rights of trade unionists, women, racial minorities, and other casualties of the Thatcher revolution.

Bill of rights supporters in Britain have recently cast their gaze westward. The *Canadian Charter of Rights and Freedoms*,[2] proclaimed into law on 17 April 1982, has been held out as a working model of how a constitutional bill of rights can function successfully within a system of

---

* Originally published in (1989) 16 Brit. J. Law & Soc. 151–65. Copyright © 1989 by Basil Blackwell. Reprinted by permission of Blackwell Publishing.

government 'similar in principle to that of the United Kingdom.'[3] Canadian judges, lawyers, and academics have been enlisted to champion the virtues of the *Charter* to their British counterparts. For example, in the past two years the British journal *Public Law* has run five major articles on the *Charter*, four of them written by Canadians, all of them strongly sympathetic to the *Charter* record.[4]

My purpose in this essay is to throw some cold water on the fires of infatuation that have started burning in Britain for the Canadian *Charter*. While it was sold to the public as part of a 'people's package,' the *Charter* is a regressive instrument more likely to undermine than to advance the cause of ordinary and disadvantaged Canadians. Seven years of litigation have shown that, except in criminal cases, the major beneficiaries of *Charter* rights are corporations, professionals, and other privileged interests. The reasons for this lie partly in the nature of the rights and partly in the nature of the judicial system that is charged with their interpretation and enforcement.

The Nature of *Charter* Rights

In order to understand the nature of the rights contained within the *Charter* it is necessary to understand the framework in which they operate. The *Charter* is regarded as 'fundamental law' because it is entrenched in Canada's written constitution. For this reason it is more difficult to amend than regularly enacted laws and takes priority over those laws. As a broad-ranging document, it sets out a variety of rights, such as liberty, equality, and freedom of association, which it guarantees to citizens in their relations with government. While these rights are fundamental, they are not absolute. They are almost always subject to limitation, either implied within the right or imposed upon it by means of the 'reasonable limits' clause set out in section 1.[5] The task of interpreting the rights and their limits rests ultimately with the courts. Yet judges do not have a roving commission. The agenda is set on a case-by-case basis in response to claims brought before the courts, for the most part by private litigants at their own expense.

Like the American and many Western European bills of rights, the *Charter* derives its coherence and legitimacy from the values and assumptions of classical liberal thought. The rights set out in the *Charter* are founded upon the belief that the main enemies of freedom are not disparities in wealth, nor concentrations of private power, but the state.[6] Thus one finds in the *Charter* little reference to positive economic or social entitlements, such as rights to employment, shelter, or social services. Rather, *Charter* rights are predominantly negative in nature, aimed at protecting individuals from state interference or control with respect to this matter or that.[7] In the words of Mr Justice Dickson, the *Charter* 'is intended to constrain governmental action inconsistent with those rights and freedoms [enshrined within it]; it is not in itself an authorization for governmental action.'[8]

Consider, for example, the right to equality in section 15. That right does not impose upon the state any positive obligation to undertake measures aimed at eliminating societal disparities in wealth and power. Section 15 may be invoked only negatively to challenge those dispari-ties that can be attributed to some action of government.[9] For this rea-son the right is satisfied by 'equal' governmental inaction as much as it is by 'equal' governmental action. Provided that everyone is disentitled to social and economic benefits 'equally,' the requirements of section 15 are met.[10]

The negative nature of the rights embodied in the *Charter* reflects what John Hart Ely refers to as a 'systematic bias' in favour of the inter-ests of the 'upper-middle, professional class from which most lawyers and judges, and for that matter most moral philosophers, are drawn.'[11] These people perceive their social and economic status as most threat-ened by the regulatory and redistributive powers of the modern state. It is not surprising, therefore, that they regard as 'fundamental' those values that afford them protection from such state powers. But, as Ely observes, 'watch most fundamental-rights theorists start edging toward the door when someone mentions jobs, food, or housing: those are important, sure, but they aren't *fundamental*.'[12]

This 'systematic bias' is reinforced by a highly selective view of what constitutes the state. The presumption underlying the *Charter* is that existing distributions of wealth and power are products of private ini-tiative as opposed to state action. Never mind that these distributions depend for their existence and legitimacy upon a panoply of state-sponsored laws and institutions. They are nevertheless viewed as pre-political and beyond the scope of *Charter* scrutiny. Thus, far from being subject to *Charter* challenge, such distributions comprise the 'natural' foundation upon which *Charter* rights are conferred and against which the constitutionality of 'state action' is judged.[13]

Any attempt to use the *Charter* right to freedom of expression, for example, to challenge a property owner's refusal to allow picketing on its premises would be doomed from the start. As stated by Thurlow J. in the Federal Court of Appeal:

> The freedom [of expression] guaranteed by the *Charter* is a freedom to express and communicate ideas without restraint, whether orally or in print or by other means of communication. It is not a freedom to use some-one else's property to do so. It gives no right to anyone to use someone else's land or platform to make a speech, or someone else's printing press to publish his ideas.[14]

Nor could one invoke the *Charter* to challenge the common law of trespass that legitimizes the property owner's refusal. Common law rules governing the property entitlements of private parties are seen as pre-political norms not subject to *Charter* scrutiny.[15] Similarly, one could not rely upon the *Charter* to avoid common law damages for the trespass, nor the injunction that the courts might issue to prohibit one from continuing to trespass, nor the police powers that would be used against one for failing to observe the injunction. When courts, police, and, presumably, jailers use their powers to enforce common law norms, they are functioning not as state actors but as 'neutral arbiters.'[16]

The negative nature of *Charter* rights combined with this selective view of state action remove from *Charter* scrutiny the major source of inequality in our society: the unequal distribution of property entitlements among private parties. At the same time, they direct the restraining force of the *Charter* against the arm of the state best equipped to redress fundamental economic inequalities: the democratic arm, consisting of the legislature and the executive.

The irony of this will not be lost on those with a sense of history. The victories that have been won in this century on behalf of workers, the unemployed, women, and other socially and economically disadvantaged persons have been achieved, for the most part, through democratic action. They are victories that have been won by harnessing the powers of the state to redistribute wealth and to place limits on the exercise of 'private' economic power. Thus workers have been granted the collective bargaining rights they now enjoy by virtue of legislation overriding common law rules that protected employers' liberty and privity of contract and that treated trade unions as illegal conspiracies. The economic benefits guaranteed to the unemployed flow from redistributive policies of the welfare state. The lot of women has been advanced, to the degree that it has, by means of legislative intervention in the form of labour standards legislation, minimum wage laws, and human rights codes.

I am not suggesting that these responses have been comprehensive or adequate. In my view they have not been. Nor do I wish to imply that, once such reforms have been put in place, legislators cannot take them away. The recent experience in Britain shows all too clearly that legislators can. My point is simply that, where there has been progress, that progress, with few exceptions, has been realized in the democratic rather than the judicial arena. Such progress has been achieved through political action aimed at displacing the common law vision of unbridled individual autonomy with a legislative counter-vision of collective social responsibility. Put simply, the negative conception of liberty imposed by the courts to protect the interests of the 'haves' has been partly supplanted by a positive conception of liberty imposed by the legislatures to further the interests of the 'have-nots.'

Yet the *Charter* now threatens to undermine political capacity to institute such reform. The rights and freedoms in the *Charter* are predicated on the same hostility to legislative action and the same reverence for individual autonomy that animated the common law. This does not mean that the current legislative regime of social and economic regulation will suddenly be eliminated under the *Charter*. The political costs of doing so are thankfully too great for most courts to contemplate. What the *Charter* is more likely to do is enable the judiciary to chisel away at certain aspects of that regime and to erect barriers to future innovation.

Evidence of this process may already be found in numerous *Charter* decisions. For example, (1) the Alberta Court of Appeal has held that the right to freedom of association prohibits governments from interfering with the formation of business partnerships;[17] (2) legislation granting combines officers the power to search corporate records for evidence of anti-competitive behaviour has been struck down by the Supreme Court of Canada as denying a right to privacy;[18] (3) the Nova Scotia Court of Appeal has invoked mobility rights to strike down legislation requiring door-to-door sellers to be permanent residents of the province in which they do business;[19] (4) the right to liberty has been interpreted by the British Columbia Court of Appeal as prohibiting provincial governments from controlling the number and location of doctors who practise medicine in the province;[20] and (5) the Supreme Court of Canada has interpreted the right to freedom of expression as protecting commercial speech, including the posting of commercial signs,

from government regulation.[21] I will have more to say about some of
these decisions later in this essay. I refer to them now simply as evidence of how the *Charter* will be used to chip away at the regulatory
framework of the modern state.

This does not mean that there will be no 'progressive' *Charter* decisions. Undoubtedly there will be some, particularly in the area of criminal law, where police powers continue to be directed against the poorer
and weaker classes. Here the liberal thrust of the *Charter* is more likely
to coincide with the interests of some socially disadvantaged persons,
enabling them to protect their personal autonomy from unwelcome
intrusions by government.[22] An obvious example is the *Morgentaler*
case,[23] in which a majority of the Supreme Court of Canada struck
down a criminal law restricting women's access to abortion services.

Beyond the confines of the criminal law, however, the 'progressive'
Charter decisions are likely to be those in which the courts uphold legislation – in other words, do nothing.[24] Of course, there will be instances
in which the *Charter* is used to expand the protection afforded by a particular regulatory scheme (subject to the right of legislatures to dismantle the scheme altogether).[25] Yet these cases will be the exception rather
than the rule.[26] Indeed, the very notion of looking to courts to enhance
social and economic legislation is somewhat perverse. Legislation of
this kind was enacted to counteract the *laissez-faire* individualism of
court-made common law. Courts, even today, remain hostile to, or at
best suspicious of, the 'eccentric principles of socialist philanthropy'
upon which the welfare state is founded.[27] Thus, looking to the courts
to repair flaws in the existing regulatory regime is rather like taking
one's car to be fixed by an auto wrecker.

The Nature of the Judicial System

The regressive impact of the *Charter* is exacerbated by the nature of the
judicial system that is charged with its interpretation and enforcement.
There are two features of this system that make it particularly inappropriate as a forum for advancing the interests of the disadvantaged. One
is the cost of gaining access to the system; the other is the character of
the system itself.

(1) Access to the Judicial System

It will come as no surprise to those familiar with the process of litigation to discover that the cost of mounting a *Charter* challenge is extremely high. A newspaper report in 1985 estimated that the cost of taking a criminal case to the Supreme Court of Canada 'can be more than $34,500,' while those bringing non-criminal cases under the *Charter* 'should be prepared to spend at least $200,000.'[28] The operative words are 'at least.' A woman from Ontario recently reported spending $200,000 on a *Charter* case that had not yet reached the Ontario Court of Appeal.[29] A challenge brought by college instructor Merv Lavigne against the use of union dues for political causes cost the National Citizens Coalition, the right-wing lobby funding the case, $400,000 before the trial judge ever rendered a decision.[30]

Costs like these represent a formidable obstacle to disadvantaged and even middle-income Canadians who wish to pursue their *Charter* rights in the courts.[31] This reality is reflected in the breakdown of equality rights cases to date.[32] Most such cases have been based upon grounds of discrimination (such as province of residence) that have little or nothing to do with underlying social disadvantage.[33] The claimants in such cases have not been the poor, but rather professionals, business people, and persons charged with drunk driving. Even in cases involving sex and age discrimination, those initiating equality claims have tended to represent socially dominant groups. For example, of the first thirty-five sex discrimination claims made under the *Charter*, twenty-five, more than 70 per cent, were raised by males.[34]

Besides serving as a barrier to the disadvantaged, the costs of *Charter* litigation will produce two important second-order effects. First, they will siphon scarce political resources from the democratic to the judicial arena. Women's groups, for example, are raising millions of dollars to engage in *Charter* litigation, a considerable portion of which is being used to defend legislation that is beneficial to women.[35] A similar process is occurring with trade unions. Having thrown away millions of dollars on fruitless *Charter* challenges, unions are now having to spend millions more to defend themselves from *Charter* attacks levelled against them. The Ontario Public Service Employees Union, for example, has already spent $400,000 defending its interests just in the union dues case referred to above.[36] The resources that groups such as these devote to *Charter* litigation are resources that are taken away from lobbying, campaigning, and other forms of political action. The unsuccessful challenge against cruise missile testing brought by Operation Dismantle, a Canadian peace coalition, provides a graphic illustration.[37] As Michael Mandel has shown, the human and financial resources that were required to sustain the legal battle sapped the organization of time, energy, and money, weakening its ability to pursue and publicize more fruitful political initiatives.[38]

Second, by making it difficult for all but the economically powerful to bring *Charter* claims to court, litigation costs will influence the interpretation of *Charter* guarantees. Consider, for example, the *Charter* right to freedom of expression. Opportunities to raise a claim concerning this right are restricted to those who can command sufficient resources to bring an action in court and who consider it economically or politically worthwhile to do so. Litigation concerning this right is thus more likely to be brought by economically powerful interests in society, such as business interests, for whom the costs of litigation are small in relation to the potential economic gains. As a consequence, the jurisprudence surrounding freedom of expression will, of necessity, respond to and reflect business concerns.[39] I am not suggesting that all such cases will be decided in favour of business interests. What I *am* suggesting, however, is that over time the legitimacy of business claims in relation to freedom of expression will be heightened. Furthermore, the exposure of the courts to arguments made on behalf of business interests will give judges a greater awareness of business concerns. This, in turn, is likely to work to the advantage of these interests, particularly in cases in which the rights and entitlements of business owners are pitted against those of consumers, employees, and other groups in society whose concerns have been less well represented in the courts. As John Stuart Mill once observed, 'in the absence of its natural defenders, the interest of the excluded is always in danger of being overlooked; and, when looked at, is seen with very different eyes from those of the person whom it directly concerns.'[40]

(2) Character of the Judicial System

The political influence of the cost of gaining access to the judicial system is exacerbated by the political influence of the system itself. There is little about the composition or structure of Canadian courts to suggest that they have the disposition or capacity to resolve *Charter* claims in ways that protect, let alone promote, the interests of the economically and socially disadvantaged. Few public institutions are less representative of, or less conversant with, the interests of underprivileged Canadians. Moreover, in Canada as in Britain there exists deep in the judicial ethos a special reverence and concern for private property rights[41] – a concern and reverence that will inevitably guide and constrain judicial decision making in *Charter* cases.

Evidence of this influence may already be found in the failure of judges to distinguish between the interests of human beings and those of corporations. This failure was graphically displayed by the Supreme Court of Canada in *Hunter v. Southam*.[42] In that case, Dickson J. identified the right 'to be secure against unreasonable search and seizure' in section 8 of the *Charter* as a 'privacy right' enjoyed by 'individuals.' Yet he then proceeded to confer this right upon a corporation without giving any consideration to the possibility that the privacy interests of corporations might differ from those of human beings.[43]

The Supreme Court's willingness to entertain corporate *Charter* claims stands in stark contrast to its attitude towards claims brought by trade unions. In a trilogy of labour cases the Supreme Court refused to interpret the *Charter* right to 'freedom of association' as protecting the very core of union activities: collective bargaining and striking.[44] Among the reasons given by the majority were that: union powers are 'the creation of legislation';[45] to accept the unions' claim would be to grant a collective entity constitutional rights greater than those enjoyed by its individual members;[46] and the *Charter* 'does not concern itself with economic rights.'[47] The irony, of course, is that these reasons would appear to provide an equally compelling rationale for denying corporate claims such as the one raised in *Southam:* the status and powers of modern corporations derive from legislation; the effect of recognizing corporate claims is to bestow upon collective entities *Charter* rights that go beyond those of their individual members; and, due to the economic function of corporations, such claims are necessarily preoccupied with economic interests.

This suggests that the Supreme Court has treated union powers differently under the *Charter* not because they are legislative, collective, or economic, but because they offend underlying judicial attitudes concerning property and contract. While corporations are regarded as market actors whose 'private' personalities qualify them for full *Charter* protection, unions are treated as statutory interlopers whose 'public' status diminishes their claim to *Charter* rights. Moreover, the perception that union powers are public makes them more vulnerable to *Charter* scrutiny. Thus, while courts would dismiss out of hand a *Charter* challenge against a corporation's power to use shareholders' monies for political purposes, judges agonize over whether the *Charter* limits the power of unions to use workers' dues in precisely the same way.[48]

Further evidence of the judiciary's underlying concern for the preservation of property rights may be found in the propensity of judges to interpret section 2 of the *Charter*, the 'fundamental rights' section, as protecting market activity. In *R. v. Big M Drug Mart Ltd.*[49] the Supreme Court of Canada permitted a corporation to invoke the right to freedom of religion to escape legislative penalties under the *Lord's Day Act* for transacting business on a Sunday. In *Ford v. Quebec*[50] the Supreme Court held that the right to freedom of expression encompasses commercial speech, including the right to post business signs in the language of one's choice. In *Black v. Law Society of Alberta*[51] the Alberta Court of Appeal decided that freedom of association guarantees lawyers the right to form business partnerships 'with the object of the earning of a livelihood.' The effect of these rulings has been to afford persons (including corporations) constitutional rights to engage in a wide range of entrepreneurial activity. The protection of commercial speech paves the way for *Charter* challenges to all manner of labelling and advertising restrictions.[52] The protection of economic association has broader implications still. If freedom of association includes the right to form business partnerships, it is difficult to see why it would not also include the right to form business contracts. What is contracting if not association 'with the object of the earning of a livelihood'? Yet to provide constitutional protection to contracting would subject to *Charter* scrutiny a vast array of economic regulation, from consumer protection legislation to minimum wage laws.

As significant as property rights themselves is the shared judicial assumption that such rights flow from a 'natural' system of private ordering. This assumption reinforces the dichotomy between private and state action that underlies the *Charter*, making it more difficult for individuals to mobilize the *Charter* against underlying social disparities. Judges conceive their role under the *Charter* as not one of interest balancing, which they view as the preserve of politics, but rather as one of policing the boundary between the 'natural' zone of individual autonomy (represented by the market) and the 'unnatural' activities of the state (represented by the regulatory and redistributive instruments of modern government).[53] Thus the bias that judges bring to their task reinforces the bias of the *Charter* itself: 'liberty' is represented by those things that expand the zone of individual autonomy by limiting the ability of the state to 'interfere' in the lives of individual Canadians. The task of judges is to interpret the *Charter* generously so as to 'secur[e] for individuals the full benefit of the *Charter*'s protection.'[54] Hence, narrow *Charter* interpretations are 'bad' while expansive interpretations are 'good.'

What is conveniently forgotten in this equation is that liberty is a relative value: the power the market confers upon those who hold property enhances the liberty of owners at the expense of others who must yield to their rights of ownership. From the point of view of those who lack market power, therefore, liberty is a value more likely to be advanced by increasing, not diminishing, the regulatory and redistributive functions of the state (assuming 'liberty' includes the liberty to be clothed, housed, and fed, and the liberty not to be preyed upon by those who command economic power). This is a point that most judges have been unable to see or unwilling to acknowledge. In *Southam*, for example, the Supreme Court of Canada decided it was 'unreasonable' for combines officers to use search powers as a means of monitoring and regulating corporate behaviour without once considering the impact of this decision on the interests of consumers, small entrepreneurs, and others who depend upon combines legislation to protect them from coercion at the hands of large corporate interests.[55]

This same anti-regulatory bias reflects itself in the judicial assumption that the role of the courts is to strike down legislation that contravenes the *Charter* rather than to repair it. As Dickson J. stated in *Southam*:

> While the courts are the guardians of the Constitution and of individuals' rights under it, it is the legislature's responsibility to enact legislation that embodies appropriate safeguards to comply with the Constitution's requirements. It should not fall to the courts to fill in the details that will render legislative lacunae constitutional.[56]

This attitude makes sense only if one assumes that striking down legislation is less of a political act than preserving that legislation in a modified form. Yet this, of course, is precisely the assumption that courts do make. Striking down legislation is seen as being consistent with the judicial task of expanding liberty, whereas repairing legislation is seen as involving courts in the political task of regulating. Thus in *Southam* the Supreme Court struck down the search and seizure provision of the combines legislation instead of permitting searches to continue in accordance with the specific safeguards set forth in the Court's decision. Similarly, in *Re Phillips and Lynch*[57] the Nova Scotia Court of Appeal struck down welfare benefits for single mothers instead of extending those benefits to single fathers. Equality of no welfare benefits was more consistent with judicial conceptions of liberty than equality of some welfare benefits.

Conclusion

The nature of *Charter* rights and of the judicial system charged with their interpretation and enforcement suggests that, beyond the confines of criminal law, the *Charter* will tend to serve the interests of the economically privileged over those of ordinary and disadvantaged Canadians. At best, the *Charter* will divert progressive energies, inhibit market regulation, and legitimize prevailing inequalities in wealth and power. At worst, it will undermine existing programs and block future reform.

More generally, the Canadian experience with the *Charter* shows the danger of relying upon elite institutions to serve popular ends. The assumption underlying bills of rights is that courts possess a unique ability to provide principled, non-ideological solutions to persistent social problems. Yet this assumption is as untenable as it is undemocratic. If seven years of *Charter* cases have demonstrated anything, it is that social prescriptions remain ideological whether or not they are adorned in the rhetoric of rights. What *Charter* proponents describe as an alternative to politics is, in reality, the entrenchment of one particular political vision. Moreover, it is a vision that looks backward rather than forward: the fresh new ideas promised by the *Charter* exude the stale stench of nineteenth-century thinking.

But perhaps the argument thus far has been needlessly complex. To understand the political significance of Canada's *Charter*, one need only close one's eyes for a moment and consider the following proposal. Suppose tomorrow it were announced that a Political Entitlements Tribunal would be established; that the tribunal would be given sweeping powers to curtail the activities of modern government in the name of protecting such vaguely defined entitlements as 'liberty,' 'equality,' and 'freedom of association'; that the tribunal would be composed of nine white affluent lawyers, the majority of whom would be men, all of whom would be of or beyond middle age; that members of the tribunal would be able to remain in office until the age of seventy-five and would be accountable only to themselves; and that the cost of bringing a claim before the tribunal would amount to more than five times the average annual income of a Canadian family. What would one's reaction to such a proposal be?[58]

Once stripped of the mystique that surrounds courts and constitutionalism, questions concerning the political nature of the *Charter* and other bills of rights become almost rhetorical.

NOTES

1 L. Hand, *The Spirit of Liberty and Other Writings* (New York: Alfred A. Knopf, 1953) at 144.
2 Part I of the *Constitution Act, 1982*, being Schedule B of the *Canada Act, 1982* (U.K.), 1982, c. 11.
3 These words are contained in the preamble to the *British North America Act 1867*, 30 & 31 Vict. (U.K.) c. 3, now renamed the *Constitution Act, 1867* by the *Canada Act 1982* (U.K.), 1982, c. 11, Schedule B, s. 53.
4 These articles are R.J. Sharpe, 'The Charter of Rights and Freedoms and the Supreme Court of Canada: The First Four Years' (1987) Public Law 48; G. Marshall, 'Liberty, Abortion, and Constitutional Review in Canada' (1988) Public Law 199; B.L. Strayer, 'Life under the Canadian Charter: Adjusting the Balance between Legislatures and Courts' (1988) Public Law 347; B. Wilson, 'The Making of a Constitution: Approaches to Judicial Interpretation' (1988) Public Law 370; P.H. Russell, 'Canada's Charter of Rights and Freedoms: A Political Report' (1988) Public Law 385. It is worth noting that, of the four articles written by Canadians, two were authored by judges and one by an academic who now serves as an executive officer to the Chief Justice of Canada.
5 Section 1 provides that the rights in the *Charter* are subject to 'such reasonable limits prescribed by law as can be demonstrably justified in a free and democratic society.'
6 Any doubts in this regard were laid to rest in *Dolphin Delivery Ltd. v. Retail, Whole-sale and Department Store Union, Local 580*, [1986] 2 S.C.R. 573 [*Dolphin Delivery*], in which the Supreme Court of Canada held that section 32(1) restricts *Charter* application to the executive and legislative arms of government.
7 While the *Charter* contains traces of a more positive and communitarian strand of politics, these traces with the exception of language rights are found only in the qualifications and limitations to *Charter* guarantees. Moreover, the Supreme Court has already held that language guarantees are 'political' rights deserving of a lower level of constitutional protection than the 'principled' rights found elsewhere in the *Charter*: *Assn. of Parents for Fairness in Education v. Société des Acadiens du Nouveau-Brunswick Inc.*, [1986] 1 S.C.R. 549.
8 *Hunter v. Southam Inc.*, [1984] 2 S.C.R. 145 at 156 [*Southam*].
9 As stated by McIntyre J. in *Andrews v. Law Society (British Columbia)*, [1989] 1 S.C.R. 143 at 163–4 (dissenting, but speaking for the majority on this point), the *Charter* 'does not provide for equality between individuals or

groups within society in a general or abstract sense, nor does it impose
upon individuals an obligation to accord equal treatment to others. It is
concerned with the application of the law.'

10 For a graphic illustration of this point, see *Re Phillips and Lynch* (1986),
73 N.S.R. (2d) 415 (S.C.) [*Phillips and Lynch*], in which the Nova Scotia
Supreme Court corrected the failure of provincial legislation to provide
welfare benefits for single fathers by striking down the provision that
provided such benefits to single mothers. This decision was subsequently
affirmed by the Nova Scotia Court of Appeal: (1986), 76 N.S.R. (2d) 240
(C.A.). Moreover, even if the Court had chosen the alternative remedy of
extending the benefits to single fathers, this would not have converted the
right into a positive one; it still would have been open to the legislature
to have lowered or eliminated the benefits altogether: see *Schachter v.
Canada* (1988), 18 F.T.R. 199 [subsequently aff'd in [1990] 2 F.C. 129 (C.A.)
and rev'd, but not on this point, in [1992] 2 S.C.R. 679].

11 J.H. Ely, *Democracy and Distrust: A Theory of Judicial Review* (Cambridge,
MA: Harvard University Press, 1980) at 59.

12 *Ibid.* [original emphasis].

13 See ch. 3, 'Private Rights/Public Wrongs: The Liberal Lie of the *Charter*.'

14 *New Brunswick Broadcasting Co. Ltd. v. C.R.T.C.*, [1984] 2 F.C. 410 (C.A.) at
413, Thurlow C.J.

15 See *Dolphin Delivery*, *supra* note 6, in which the Supreme Court of Canada
refused to allow the *Charter* to be invoked against a common law injunction aimed at protecting the proprietary interests of contracting parties.
According to the Court, the injunction lacked 'the required element of
government intervention or intrusion' (at 603). In making this assertion,
the Court put the lie to its claim earlier in the same case that the *Charter*
'does apply' to the common law (at 592). See ch. 3, 'Private Rights/Public
Wrongs: The Liberal Lie of the *Charter*.'

16 *Dolphin Delivery, ibid.* at 600.

17 *Black v. Law Society (Alberta)* (1986), 44 Alta. L.R. (2d) 1 (C.A.) [*Black*] [subse-
quently aff'd on other grounds in [1989] 1 S.C.R. 591].

18 *Southam, supra* note 8.

19 *Basile v. Nova Scotia (Attorney General)* (1984), 62 N.S.R. (2d) 410 (C.A.).

20 *Wilson v. British Columbia (Medical Services Commission)* (1988), 30 B.C.L.R.
(2d) 1 (C.A.), leave to appeal to S.C.C. refused, [1988] 2 S.C.R. viii.

21 *Ford v. Quebec*, [1988] 2 S.C.R. 712 [*Ford*].

22 However, it is important not to overstate the case. While it is true that
a disproportionate number of those subjected to criminal sanctions are
poor, it is also true that the victims of criminal activity, particularly crimes

against the person, tend also to be economically underprivileged. Thus a successful *Charter* challenge in criminal cases may advance the interests of some disadvantaged persons at the expense of others who are even more disadvantaged. A good illustration is provided by the numerous *Charter* challenges that have been brought by male defendants seeking to avoid conviction for sexual assault. See *e.g. R. v. Seaboyer; R. v. Gayme*, [1991] 2 S.C.R. 577 and *R. v. LeGallant* (1986), 6 B.C.L.R. (2d) 105 (C.A.).

23 *R. v. Morgentaler*, [1988] 1 S.C.R. 30 [*Morgentaler*].

24 One of the ironies of *Charter* litigation to date is that most of the cases hailed as victories for workers, women, and trade unions are ones in which courts have simply preserved existing legislative benefits. See *e.g. R. v. Edwards Books and Art Ltd.*, [1986] 2 S.C.R. 713 [*Edwards Books*] (upholding a statutory common pause day for retail workers); *Canadian Newspapers Co. v. Canada*, [1988] 2 S.C.R. 122 (upholding a provision of the *Criminal Code* allowing complainants in sexual assault cases to request a ban on publication of their names); *Lavigne v. Ontario Public Service Employees Union* (1989), 67 O.R. (2d) 536 (C.A.) [*Lavigne*] [subsequently aff'd by S.C.C. in [1991] 2 S.C.R. 211] (upholding the power of a trade union to spend compulsory union dues on political causes).

25 See note 10 above.

26 One obvious reason for this is that, due to the negative nature of *Charter* rights, judges feel more comfortable striking legislation down rather than repairing or supplementing it: see note 56 below and accompanying text. The ironic result is that, while courts have been reluctant to expand legislation directly, they have not hesitated to do so indirectly by striking down an exemption in a statutory scheme: see *e.g. Blainey v. Ontario Hockey Association* (1986), 54 O.R. (2d) 513 (C.A.), leave to appeal to S.C.C. refused, [1986] 1 S.C.R. xii, in which the Ontario Court of Appeal struck down an exemption in human rights legislation, thereby extending statutory protection against sexual discrimination to persons seeking membership in athletic organizations.

27 Lord Atkinson in *Roberts v. Hopwood*, [1925] A.C. 578 at 594. See P. Fennell, 'Roberts v. Hopwood: The Rule Against Socialism' (1986) 13 Brit. J. Law & Soc. 401.

28 'Taking case up to Supreme Court can cost $34,500' *Toronto Star* (23 April 1985).

29 'Asserting your rights is easy if you are rich, woman says,' *Globe and Mail* (15 April 1987) at A8.

30 L. Slotnick, 'Top court vetoes using dues for political aims,' *Globe and Mail* (8 July 1986) at A1.

31 The average annual income of a Canadian family in 1985 was $37,368: see
    J. Filion, ed., *The Canadian World Almanac and Book of Facts, 1988* (Toronto:
    Global Press, 1987) at 351. Moreover, except in criminal cases, there is little
    opportunity for *Charter* litigants to obtain legal aid: see ch. 1, 'The Politics
    of the *Charter*,' at 23–4.

32 By virtue of section 32(2) of the *Charter*, the equality guarantee in section
    15 was delayed for three years and did not take effect until 17 April 1985.

33 See F.L. Morton & M.J. Withey, 'Charting the Charter, 1982–1985: A Sta-
    tistical Analysis' in W. Pentney & D. Proulx, eds., *Canadian Human Rights
    Yearbook 1987* (Toronto: Carswell, 1987).

34 See A. Petter, 'Legitimizing Sexual Inequality: Three Early Charter Cases'
    (1989) 34 McGill L.J. 359.

35 See G. Brodsky, *LEAF Case Update* (1986). For example, the Women's Legal
    Education and Action Fund (LEAF) has to date intervened in the following
    cases: *Shewchuk v. Ricard* (1986), 28 D.L.R. (4th) 429 (B.C.C.A.) (to argue that
    child support benefits ought to be extended to men rather than taken away
    from women); *R. v. Seaboyer; R. v. Gayme*, op. cit., n. 22 (to defend provi-
    sions of the Criminal Code limiting the ability of defence counsel in sexual
    assault cases to cross-examine complainants on their sexual histories);
    Canadian Newspapers Co. v. Canada, op. cit., n. 24 (to defend a provision of
    the Criminal Code allowing complainants in sexual assault cases to re-
    quest a ban on publication of their names); *Schachter v. Canada*, op. cit., n.
    10 (to argue that maternity benefits provided to women under Canada's
    unemployment insurance scheme do not violate the equality rights of
    men).

36 L. Slotnik, 'Use of union dues for political causes does not violate Charter,
    court rules,' *Globe and Mail*, 31 January 1989, at A1.

37 See *Operation Dismantle Inc. v. The Queen* (1985) 18 D.L.R. (4th) 481 (S.C.C.).

38 M. Mandel, 'The Rule of Law and the Legalization of Politics in Canada'
    (1985) 13 *International J. of the Sociology of Law* 273 at 281–4.

39 This process is already evident from the growing number of cases in which
    corporations and professionals have invoked the right to freedom of
    expression to protect commercial speech activities: see note 52 below and
    accompanying text.

40 J.S. Mill, 'Considerations on Representative Government,' Book III, in *Utili-
    tarianism, Liberty, and Representative Government*, quoted in W.T.E. Mishler,
    Political Participation in Canada (1979) 133.

41 See J.A.G. Griffith, *The Politics of the Judiciary*, 3rd ed. (London: Fontana
    Press, 1985) at 202–3.

42 *Southam, supra* note 8.

43 For fuller discussion of this case, see ch. 1, 'The Politics of the *Charter*,' at 29–31 and 33–6.
44 *Reference Re Public Service Employee Relations Act (Alberta)*, [1987] 1 S.C.R. 313 [*Alberta Reference*]; *Public Service Alliance of Canada v. R.* [1987] 1 S.C.R. 424; *Retail, Wholesale and Department Store Union, Locals 544, 496, 635 and 955 v. Saskatchewan*, [1987] 1 S.C.R. 460.
45 *Alberta Reference, ibid.* at 391, LeDain J.
46 *Ibid.* at 404, McIntyre J.
47 *Ibid.* at 412, McIntyre J.
48 See *Lavigne, supra* note 24, reversing (1986), 55 O.R. (2d) 449 (H.C.).
49 *R. v. Big M Drug Mart Ltd,* [1985] 1 S.C.R. 295.
50 *Ford, supra* note 21.
51 *Black, supra* note 17.
52 Appellate courts in Alberta and Ontario have already struck down legislation imposing restrictions on advertisements by health professionals: *Grier v. Optometric Assn. (Alberta)* (1987), 53 Alta. L.R. (2d) 289 (C.A.); *Rocket v. Royal College of Dental Surgeons (Ontario)* (1988), 64 O.R. (2d) 353 (C.A.) [subsequently aff'd in [1990] 2 S.C.R. 232]. The Quebec Court of Appeal has struck down legislation prohibiting advertisements directed at young children: *Irwin Toy Ltd. v. Quebec (A.G.)* (1986), 3 Q.A.C. 285 [subsequently rev'd in [1989] 1 S.C.R. 927]. In addition, a major challenge to legislation prohibiting tobacco advertising is currently before the courts. [Sections of the *Tobacco Products Control Act* requiring unattributed health warnings on cigarette packages were subsequently held to abridge tobacco companies' right to freedom of expression in *RJR-MacDonald Inc. v. Canada*, [1995] 3 S.C.R. 199.]
53 The clearest expression of this can be found in the judgment of Wilson J. in *Morgentaler, supra* note 23 at 164: '[T]he rights guaranteed in the *Charter* erect around each individual, metaphorically speaking, an invisible fence over which the state will not be allowed to trespass. The role of the courts is to map out, piece by piece, the parameters of the fence.'
54 *Big M Drug Mart*, [1985] 1 S.C.R. 295 at 344, Dickson C.J.
55 According to Dickson C.J., such powers can be exercised only after officials demonstrate 'reasonable and probable grounds' for believing that an offence had been committed: *Southam, supra* note 8 at 168. There was, however, some indication at the time this essay was written that the Court had started to question the one-sided view of liberty that it embraced in *Southam*, particularly in its application of the 'reasonable limits clause' in section 1. For example, in *Edwards Books, supra* note 24, the majority made explicit reference to the competing interests of retail

workers and consumers in deciding to uphold secular legislation requiring large retail stores to close on Sundays. See generally A. Petter & P.J.
Monahan, 'Developments in Constitutional Law: The 1986–1987 Term'
(1988) 10 Sup. Ct. L. Rev. 61.
56 *Southam, supra* note 8 at 169.
57 *Phillips and Lynch, supra* note 10.
58 This paragraph owes its inspiration to R. Martin, 'The Judges and the
Charter' (1984) 2 Socialist Studies 66 at 78.

5 Rights in Conflict: The Dilemma of *Charter* Legitimacy[*]

All colours will agree in the dark.

Francis Bacon

Introduction

For an aristocrat, Lord Acton had a profound influence on the development of popular democratic theory and practice. His famous aphorism that 'power tends to corrupt and absolute power corrupts absolutely' is regarded today as common wisdom. Some might even regard it as the first principle of democratic government, such that a society must be organized to reduce the corrupting influence of power to an operative minimum.

Despite its popular appeal, this Actonian axiom is too limited in scope and too negative in character to warrant exclusive loyalty. In any organized society, the exercise of power is constant and inevitable. Power does not so much lead to corruption as provide the framework within which corruption, or enlightenment, is achieved.[1] Nevertheless, Lord Acton's principle underscores the need to guard against the accumulation of power and emphasizes the attraction of democracy as a device for ensuring that power is widely shared. In short, he has provided an important, if rudimentary, benchmark against which to measure the organization of bureaucratic power and governmental authority.

In the contemporary Canadian state, democracy is the primary mech-

* With Allan C. Hutchinson. Originally published in (1989) 23 U.B.C.L. Rev. 531–48. Copyright © 1989 by Andrew Petter and Allan C. Hutchinson. Reprinted by permission of Allan C. Hutchinson.

anism used to justify the power and legitimacy of government. Though government exercises vast power, its authority is warranted by the fact that those with ultimate responsibility for governmental action are elected officials. While these representatives may not exactly qualify as the public's alter ego, they are considered to owe a responsibility to Canadian electors and are accountable to them. Whatever the short-comings of the actual practice,[2] the moral authority and political legitimacy of government rests largely on a principle of democratic representation.

For this reason, the enactment in 1982 of the *Canadian Charter of Rights and Freedoms* created something of a dilemma for the theoretical apologists of Canadian politics and democracy. Their task was to demonstrate that, though its function was to withdraw large areas of social regulation from the legislative reach of elected bodies, the *Charter* remained faithful to the ideals of democratic government. This apprehended crisis in legitimacy was heightened by the fact that the *Charter* was to be interpreted and enforced by the judiciary, a small and unrepresentative group of appointed officials. Thus the challenge for supporters of the *Charter* was to explain the seeming paradox that democracy was best promoted by a reduction in popular sovereignty and the transfer of power to a small coterie of unelected bureaucrats. In Actonian terms, why is it that, while power tends to corrupt, the absolute exercise of judicial power not only fails to corrupt but actually guards against the corrupt exercise of legislative power?

In this short essay, we intend to show that the traditional defence of *Charter* adjudication in the name of democracy is more of a contradiction than a paradox. We will comment upon the primary justification offered by the commentators and courts to defend the legitimacy of *Charter* adjudication. The only real difference between scholarly and judicial writings is that the former are more explicit and less superficial than the latter. Though there are many subtle shadings, what unifies the academic literature is its reliance upon a combination of liberal rights theory and conservative resort to conventional morality. Our intention is to demonstrate, by reference to the growing body of court decisions, that this theoretical amalgam fails to provide a satisfactory account of *Charter* legitimacy.

The Defence of *Charter* Legitimacy

In most writings on the *Charter*, the structural framework within which judicial decisions are made is too often taken for granted. The *Charter of Rights and Freedoms* is regarded as 'fundamental law' because it is entrenched in the nation's Constitution. Thus it is more difficult to amend than regularly enacted laws; moreover, it takes priority over those laws. As a broad-ranging document, it sets out certain general rights, such as equality, liberty, and freedom of association, which it guarantees to all citizens. However, while these rights are fundamental, they are not absolute. They are almost always subject to limitations, either implied within the right or imposed upon it by means of the 'reasonable limits' proviso in section 1. The task of interpreting these rights and their limits rests ultimately with the courts. Yet judges do not have a roving commission. The agenda is set on a case-by-case basis in response to claims brought before the courts, for the most part by private litigants at their own expense.

The *Charter* raises special concerns about the interpretive method of judges and the legitimacy of their role. These concerns are made more pressing by the open-ended nature of *Charter* rights and by the invitation to the courts to place 'reasonable limits' upon those rights. Thus the problem is not about who should interpret the *Charter*, but rather about how judges should interpret it.

A variety of answers are offered. The most general and common is that judicial decision making retains an essential degree of functional autonomy. Legal interpretation can and should be performed in a way that distinguishes it from ideological debate. The role of traditional jurists has been to give theoretical substance to these ideas and intuitions. Though this endeavour has assumed a higher profile since the advent of the *Charter*, the task of legitimizing judicial interpretation has been the abiding preoccupation of common law jurisprudence. In the first half of this century the dispute was over the possibility of establishing a mode of judicial activity that was completely separate from politics. In the past couple of decades, however, the jurisprudential focus has shifted subtly but substantially.[3] The contemporary approach is to fashion an interpretive theory that recognizes that judicial decision making does not operate independently of politics, but neither does it reduce entirely to politics. Acknowledging the intimate relation between law and politics, theorists search for an explanation that both unifies and distinguishes legal and political method. Nonetheless the ultimate goal of the enterprise remains the same: to establish a meaningful division between law and politics. Formalism – that is, the belief in a mode of legal justification distinct from open ideological debate that provides a workable scheme of social justice – continues to cast its long shadow over the modern terrain.

While there are as many jurisprudential theories as there are theorists, two general themes emerge from the literature defending the legitimacy of constitutionally entrenched rights. One line of argument suggests that such rights reflect some transcendent set of norms or values, rooted in Nature, God, or some lesser philosophical deity. According to this naturalist vision, the role of the courts is simply to identify and give interpretive effect to these higher norms and values. Another school of thought proceeds from the assumption that such rights reflect the shared values and aspirations of the community from which they arise. According to this positivist perspective, the role of the courts is confined to locating these values and applying them to litigated cases.

Within the Canadian genre of rights jurisprudence, the naturalist and positivist tendencies do not run in competing lines, but weave together in an effort to avoid the shortcomings of each. With characteristic genius for pragmatic compromise, Canadian theorists have recognized that invoking a vision of natural rights, be it John Stuart Mill's, Brian Mulroney's, or Ayatollah Khomeini's, would do little to bolster the *Charter*'s legitimacy unless that vision could be tied to some social consensus concerning the scope and identity of those rights. This recognition has been reinforced by the strong positivist tradition in Anglo-Canadian law. Accordingly, the naturalist impulse in Canadian jurisprudence has been accommodated and subsumed within an indigenous and cultural account of entrenched rights.

As a result of this theoretical merger, Canadian defenders of *Charter* adjudication tend to differ more in emphasis than in kind. For example, Brian Slattery gravitates towards the naturalist pole. He contends that *Charter* rights are 'anchored in a belief in the equal worth of the individual human being, a worth that has a transcendent, and not merely a conventional status.' Yet even Slattery feels compelled to seek refuge in a positivist account of *Charter* interpretation, arguing that 'constitutional adjudication involves contextual decision making within a particular tradition by reference to values and principles that represent aspects of the tradition without exhausting it.'[4] John Whyte and David Beatty are more willing to consolidate their naturalist impulses within a positivist account of rights. Whyte maintains that *Charter* rights embody the enduring principles of liberal politics. According to his argument, such rights are justified 'on the basis of the necessary conditions for representative democracy' and 'on the basis of the ideas of security and autonomy which are the underlying justifications for representative democracy.'[5] Beatty adopts a variation on this theme. In elaborating a constitutional labour code, he suggests that the liberal vision of rights he espouses is found within and has informed Anglo-Canadian law over the past century. Thus the *Charter* has imposed an organic logic upon the future means and ends of legislators, who must now engage in a 'conversation of justification' with the courts.[6] Patrick Monahan pursues a similar idea of 'constitutional conversation,' but his presentation is more overtly positivist. Espousing a form of democratic communitarianism, Monahan contends that a legitimate mode of judicial review must confine itself to nurturing and protecting active participation in public decision making; this is a goal that is integral to the Canadian political tradition.[7] Whereas Slattery, Whyte, and Beatty want to hold the courts to the substantive dictates of an individualist ethic, Monahan seeks to enlist courts in the procedural ambition to maximize openness and revision in community relations.

All of these scholars intend their theories to check and legitimize the potentially limitless and undemocratic authority of judicial review. At the same time, each justifies the vision of *Charter* rights he espouses by reference to values that are said to characterize Canada as a community. At the root of these theories is the notion that *Charter* rights reflect some form of social consensus, whether grounded in conventional norms, community relations, or an evolving tradition.

The Conflicting Nature of Rights Claims

The suggestion, sophisticatedly expressed and elegantly packaged, that the rights expressed in the *Charter* reflect the abiding values and shared aspirations of the Canadian community has an appealing ring to it. Moreover, it is a view that appears, at first glance, to have much to recommend it. Public opinion polls show that the vast majority of Canadians favour the *Charter*. In addition, the rights contained in the *Charter*, such as equality, liberty, and freedom of association, are ones to which most Canadians appear to subscribe.[8] Yet first glances can be deceiving. As attractive and plausible as the suggestion may seem, it does not withstand close scrutiny. What it offers in style, it lacks in substance. The very fact that there is strong disagreement among *Charter* theorists over the source and nature of the community values to which they refer hints at the paper-thin cogency of their jurisprudential strategy.

The fallacy upon which these theorists depend is that the existence of broad public support for *Charter* rights is evidence that those rights reflect a normative consensus. If anything, the opposite is true. Far from representing a consensus, the rights in the *Charter* mask fundamental social and political conflicts. Rights talk is more a medium of dispute than an instrument of discovery. So long as these conflicts remain buried, the appearance of consensus, and thus of legitimacy, is maintained. However, as soon as they are exposed, that appearance quickly evaporates. Once the Pandora's box of *Charter* adjudication is thrown open, pressing its lid back down becomes impossible. The objectivity of *Charter* interpretation ceases to be credible, and the legitimacy of the *Charter* is once again called into question.

In the remainder of this essay we outline the conflicts that arise in rights adjudication and discuss the inability of orthodox theory to account for or respond to these conflicts. While such conflicts are numerous, they can be grouped into three categories: conflicts that occur within rights; conflicts that occur amongst rights; and conflicts that occur between rights and competing social interests. In tracing these conflicts, our purpose is to build upon and extend a democratic critique of liberal jurisprudence and legal practice in a post-*Charter* Canada.[9] While a more thorough embracing of democratic politics cannot resolve these conflicts, the abandonment of rights talk may at least clear the ground for more promising and progressive efforts to achieve a genuine sense of community and common social purpose.

(1) Conflicts within Rights

Though the *Charter* lists clearly the rights to which people are entitled, the content of those entitlements is anything but clear. The rights in the *Charter* are characterized by their indeterminacy: they mean different things to different people at different times. Indeed, the malleable nature of *Charter* rights is one of the reasons why they enjoy such widespread public support. While such malleability may prove an inconvenience in specific disputes, it helps explain the attraction of those rights in general terms.

Consider the rights mentioned earlier: equality, liberty, and freedom of association. These rights are central to the *Charter* and its political appeal, yet they have no definite or uncontroversial meaning. They are contested concepts whose interpretation is a major and elusive preoccupation of political debate. They are like empty sacks that cannot stand up on their own until they have been filled with political content.

'Who fills them' and 'with what' are the key questions for Canadian politics. Nevertheless, *Charter* proponents seem more concerned with finessing than facing these disturbing issues.

The best example of rights indeterminacy is the popular principle of equality. Though this principle receives almost universal approval, there is very little agreement on its scope and meaning. For example, some commentators espouse a formal vision of equality, one requiring that individuals be subject to equal treatment. Others urge a substantive vision of equality, one demanding that individuals be made equal in their condition. These alternative visions of equality are not just distinct but potentially contradictory. It is obvious, for example, that governments cannot assist the poor to become equal in condition to the rich by subjecting both groups to equal treatment. Thus, while women's rights groups invoke substantive equality to support special programs for women, men's rights groups invoke formal equality to attack such programs.

A good illustration of the conflict between formal and substantive equality is provided by *Tomen v. Federation of Women Teachers' Associations of Ontario*.[10] In that case the Ontario Public School Teachers' Federation (OPSTF) – a predominantly male organization – helped Margaret Tomen challenge an Ontario Teachers' Federation regulation requiring women teachers in public elementary schools to belong to the Federation of Women Teachers' Associations of Ontario (FWTAO). The FWTAO had fought long and hard on behalf of women teachers and in doing so had become something of a thorn in the side of the male organization.[11] Tomen and the OPSTF maintained that the regulation contravened the *Charter*'s guarantee of equality in that it subjected teachers to unequal treatment on the basis of their sex. The FWTAO responded that, far from denying sexual equality, the regulation sought to *advance* equality. The membership requirement ensured that the FWTAO would remain an effective instrument for promoting equal conditions for women teachers. Both sides invoked equality: one to attack the regulation, the other to defend it.[12]

Tomen shows how formal and substantive visions of equality can pull in opposite directions. But the problem does not end there. Conflicts arise not only between these alternative visions, but even within them. For instance, proponents of formal equality maintain that the principle of equal treatment applies only to persons who are 'similarly situated.' Those who are differently situated should be dealt with differently. Yet the question of whether one person is similarly situated with another is highly controversial. Thus even formal equality theorists can reach contradictory conclusions depending upon their answer to this prior question.

An example of this form of conflict is provided by *Andrews v. Ontario (Minister of Health).*[13] The issue in that case was whether the Ontario Hospital Insurance Plan (OHIP) contravened the *Charter*'s guarantee of equality by providing medical coverage to couples who were of the opposite sex, but not to those who were of the same sex. Karen Andrews and her partner, Mary Trenholm, argued that the right to equal treatment implied that lesbian couples should be provided the same benefits as heterosexual couples. OHIP disagreed, arguing that, because lesbian couples are not similarly situated to heterosexual couples, the equality guarantee in the *Charter* mandated that each be treated differently. This latter view was the one adopted by the Court.

As *Tomen* and *Andrews* demonstrate, the enduring attraction of the right to equality does not lie in its content, but in its lack of content. In both cases the contending parties – Tomen and the FWTAO, Andrews and OHIP – espoused a common belief in the principle of equality. Yet the meaning they attached to that principle reflected fundamental differences in political outlook. The message of these cases is clear: to become intelligible, the idea of equality must draw upon external political values to determine which visions and categories are to be employed. Once these external values are identified, however, equality itself becomes a superfluous principle that amounts to little more than window dressing. As Marc Gold has succinctly noted: '[A]ny given law can be both defended and attacked in the name of equality ... To choose one conception of equality over another is to choose between competing political or moral theories.'[14]

The right to liberty is similarly indeterminate. Those who subscribe to a negative vision of liberty conceive of it as a right not to be interfered with by others. Those who subscribe to a positive vision of liberty see it as the right to demand from others a greater share of social resources. Again, these visions are not just distinct but mutually contradictory. While property owners claim the liberty to exclude people from their land, others claim the liberty to enter that land. In *R.W.D.S.U. v. Dolphin Delivery,*[15] for example, a trade union invoked the *Charter* to challenge an injunction preventing it from picketing the premises of a courier company. The union claimed that the injunction violated the liberty of its members to engage in peaceful protest, thus affecting their freedom of expression. The company, on the other hand, argued that the Court should uphold the injunction on the basis that the proposed picketing would interfere with its liberty to conduct business, thus affecting its freedom to contract. The validity of these competing assertions cannot be resolved by reference to the right to liberty. Rather, their validity depends entirely upon the background conditions that are seen to support and inform the operation of that right. As with equality, competing liberty claims can be resolved only by reference to extraneous values.

Freedom of association is another *Charter* right that is susceptible to conflicting interpretations. Those who subscribe to an individualistic conception of freedom of association interpret that freedom as conferring upon individuals the right to associate or disassociate as they see fit. According to this conception, the associated individuals have no more rights as a group than they do as individuals acting on their own account. Those who subscribe to a collectivist conception of freedom of association, on the other hand, interpret that freedom as conferring upon groups and organizations the right to act in concert to protect and promote their associational activities. According to this conception, an association's interests are seen as distinct from, and greater than, those of its individual members. Again, these positions can be invoked to support contradictory conclusions. For instance, while trade unionists look to freedom of association to support the power of unions to act on behalf of all employees at a workplace,[16] those who oppose trade unions point to the same freedom to support the right of individual employees to disassociate themselves from unionized activity.[17] In the words of one commentator, freedom of association is a 'double-edged constitutional sword.'[18]

Rights are like tools. The purposes they serve depend upon the hands that are placed upon them and the minds that direct those hands. The veneer of consensus concerning the existence and desirability of rights masks deeper antagonisms concerning their meaning and application. Such tensions represent profound disagreements about the operative assumptions and informing visions of political life and justice. At bottom, they are matters of 'deep-seated preferences.'[19] Thus the contention that *Charter* rights reflect shared assumptions and values ceases to be credible *even at the point of definition.*

Just because rights are indeterminate in theory, however, does not mean that they are indeterminate in practice. On the contrary, given that their meaning is governed by those who have custody over them, it is safe to assume that the interpretation placed upon *Charter* rights will reflect and reinforce the established values of the legal system and of legal elites. With respect to the rights we have discussed, these values pull strongly in the direction of formal equality, negative liberty, and an individualistic conception of associational rights.[20] This is the *Charter*'s hidden agenda. So long as it remains hidden, people of all stations and political persuasions will see in the *Charter* something to soothe them. It is only when groups like women, gays and lesbians, and trade unions experience that agenda first-hand that the illusion of social consensus engendered by the abstract rights becomes threatened. As with all illusions, the determinacy of rights talk is suspended in the minds of citizens rather than grounded in the imperatives of social conditions.

(2) Conflicts amongst Rights

Conflicts arise not solely within rights; there are also tensions *amongst* rights. Here, again, these tensions cannot be resolved by some vague and hopeful appeal to social values or community consensus. The courts can serve only as a venue for ceaseless efforts to negotiate competing claims. The temporary accommodations made are more a result of political expediency than of moral purity. For instance, the tension between the right to liberty and the right to equality represents a fundamental conflict in ideological values, one that has energized an entire tradition of political theory and debate. Under the *Charter*, the courts are entrusted with the thankless task of providing an answer to this conceptual conundrum. The *Charter* text offers no guidance as to how claims framed in the competing rhetoric of 'liberty' and 'equality' are to be resolved. The judges are on a sleeveless errand.

A prime example of this dilemma is provided by the pre-*Charter* decision in *Gay Alliance Toward Equality v. Vancouver Sun*.[21] In this case a gay rights group relied on the British Columbia *Human Rights Code* to attack the *Vancouver Sun*'s policy of denying gay publications access to the classified advertising section of the newspaper. A Board of Inquiry found for the Alliance, holding that the *Sun*'s policy denied gays equal access to a 'service ... customarily available to the public.' When the case reached the courts, the *Sun* argued that the *Code* should be interpreted as not applying to its classified services, since such application would encroach upon its common law right to freedom of the press. The judges were forced to choose between competing rights: the equality of gays versus the liberty of newspaper publishers. In the Supreme Court of Canada, the majority plumbed for liberty, the minority for equality. To talk of shared values or consensus in such circumstances is far-fetched; there was no agreement even among the members of the Court, let alone among the community at large.

The conflict between equality and liberty rights has also arisen in *Charter* cases concerning pornography. For instance, in *R. v. Red Hot Video Ltd.*,[22] the British Columbia Court of Appeal rejected arguments that the obscenity provision of the *Criminal Code* contravened the *Charter* right to freedom of expression. According to the Court, the provision was justified because the form of expression it prohibited was demeaning to women and therefore undermined sexual equality rights. In this case, unlike *Gay Alliance*, the judges opted for equality over liberty.[23]

Both *Gay Alliance* and *Red Hot Video* required the courts to confront a basic tension between competing individual rights. Another tension that has driven debate in political theory is the conflict between the rights of individuals and those of groups. We have already seen how this conflict can be played out in the context of a single right, such as freedom of association; however, it also arises in the interaction amongst competing rights.

The recent controversy concerning Quebec's language laws testifies to the enduring and pervasive irreconcilability of this conflict. In *Ford v. Quebec (Attorney General)*,[24] storeowners challenged the constitutional authority of the Quebec legislature to require that commercial signs in the province be posted in French only. The province defended its law as a measure necessary to protect the linguistic and cultural rights of a francophone collectivity isolated within a predominantly English-speaking North America. The storeowners, on the other hand, resorted to the familiar rhetoric of individual freedom. They contended that the cultural rights of the collectivity were secondary to the speech rights of individuals in the province. The response of the Supreme Court of Canada was to try to effect a compromise between these competing positions. The Court struck down the law as it stood, but held that the legislature could enact a new provision requiring that French be the predominant, though not exclusive, language on commercial signs. Ironically, even this transparent attempt at political accommodation was unsuccessful as an exercise in consensus building. The Court's compromise failed to satisfy the francophone majority in Quebec; furthermore, it outraged at least one of the storeowners who had initiated the court action.

Conflicts occur not only amongst individual rights and amongst individual and group rights; they also arise amongst the rights of competing groups. This form of conflict arose in the Ontario *Reference re Bill*

30, An Act to Amend the Education Act.[25] When the Ontario government extended full public funding to Roman Catholic high schools, it defended its action on the basis that such funding was required by the rights afforded to denominational schools under the original Confederation compact. Other religious groups, however, took a different view. They contended that the *Charter* right to equality prohibited the government from extending funding to one religious organization without providing comparable funding to all religious organizations. It was left to the Supreme Court to choose between these competing group claims. The Court came down on the side of denominational school rights, though the reasons it offered for doing so were more conclusory than explanatory. Certainly, it would take an inspired or desperate imagination to argue that its choice was based upon a consensus of values that the judges were able to detect within the larger Canadian community.

In each of these disputes the Court was presented with an unenviable task. In order to meet the challenge, judges have increasingly fallen back on the interpretive practice of 'balancing.' The major thrust of this rudimentary methodology is to identify different interests, attribute respective values to each, and then weigh them on a constitutional scale. Instead of offering a solution to the dilemma of constitutional legitimacy, however, balancing seems to concede the fundamental incommensurability of constitutional argument. It seeks to make the political best of a bad legal job. For all its open-endedness, balancing is little more than a convenient device enabling the judiciary to place its political thumb upon the illusive constitutional scales of social justice.

(3) Conflicts between Rights and Competing Social Interests

In addition to there being competition within and amongst rights, there is a third category of conflict: conflicts between rights and competing social interests that are not identified as rights. This form of conflict arises in the vast majority of *Charter* cases. It is most explicitly addressed in applying the 'reasonable limits' proviso in section 1, but it also forms an implicit component of the process of ascertaining the scope of the rights themselves.

It might be tempting to think that whenever there is a conflict between a right and some other interest, the competing interest should give way. But even the strongest rights advocates recognize that there are cases in which rights must yield to competing social considerations.[26] While rights are considered fundamental, they are not portrayed as being absolute. For instance, no one would argue that the right to equality entitles a six-year-old to obtain a driver's licence. The question, therefore, is not whether *Charter* rights should yield to competing social interests, but *when* they should yield. Wherever the answer to this puzzle may lie, it certainly will not be found in a prevailing social consensus or evolving social tradition. In all but the most mundane instances of children who wish to drive, such disputes speak to the fractures in community values, not to the availability of such values as a source of normative resolution.

Three examples will suffice to make the point. The first concerns provincial Sunday closing legislation. Such legislation was challenged in *R v. Edwards Books and Art Ltd.*[27] on the basis that it violated the religious freedom of certain Jewish and Seventh-day Adventist storeowners. These proprietors were being forced to close on Sunday in addition to their regular Saturday sabbath. This placed them at an economic disadvantage in relation to Christian storeowners, who were obliged to close on only one day of the week. The majority of Supreme Court of Canada judges agreed that the legislation denied religious rights, yet they upheld the law. In their view, the violation of religious rights was reasonable in light of the conflicting value of preserving a common day of rest.

The second example concerns the decision of the Supreme Court in *R. v. Morgentaler.*[28] In that case the Court was called upon to decide whether the *Criminal Code* prohibition on abortion violated the right of women to security of the person within the meaning of section 7 of the *Charter*. The majority held that it did. However, that was not the end of the matter. Before striking the provision down, these judges were forced to consider submissions that the conflicting value of preserving fetuses' lives justified the encroachment on women's rights. This they did, rejecting them, though they differed in their explanations as to why.

The third example concerns section 195.1(1)(c) of the *Criminal Code,* which makes it an offence to communicate in a public place for the purposes of prostitution. Two provincial courts of appeal have held that this provision violates the *Charter* guarantee of freedom of expression. In both courts, however, governments argued that the violation was reasonable in order to guard against the public nuisance created by street prostitution. In *R. v. Jahelka,*[29] the Alberta Court of Appeal accepted this argument; in *R. v. Skinner,*[30] the Nova Scotia Court of Appeal did not.

All of these decisions forced the courts to make difficult trade-offs between *Charter* rights and competing social interests. In *Edwards Books* the competing interest won out; in *Morgentaler* the right prevailed; and *Jahelka* and *Skinner* produced split decisions. The key question, however, is not 'who won,' but 'on what basis did they win.' Is it credible to suggest that the choices made were simply a reflection of deep-rooted community norms? Surely it is not, for it is hard to think of three issues on which there are deeper normative divisions in Canada than Sunday closing, abortion, and prostitution. Even the judges in these cases could not agree. Here, as before, the appeal to community consensus provides a convenient blind that hides the informing values and visions of social justice that drive and determine the controversial choices that have to be made.

The Failure of Consensus Theory

Charter adjudication is not about the dispassionate application of constitutional rules to given sets of social facts. Instead, the courts' unavoidable task is to confront and resolve fundamental social and political conflicts, whether they are conflicts within rights, amongst rights, or between rights and competing social interests. Once this is understood, the justification for the *Charter* and, in particular, the courts' role in interpreting and enforcing *Charter* rights on the basis of community values or on the basis of evolving social tradition becomes profoundly unconvincing. Issues like affirmative action, union rights, language policy, and abortion lie at the heart of political controversy in Canada. Whatever the explanation for handing decision-making power over these crucial issues to the courts, it cannot be that of social consensus. If there is any consensus at work in these decisions, it is a consensus manufactured by the community of legal elites.[31]

The irony, of course, is that if there were a true consensus of community values on issues such as these, there would be no need for a *Charter of Rights and Freedoms*. Under the *Charter*, community consensus runs out at the very time that it is most needed – that is, when disputes arise because of a breakdown, gap, or shortfall in the extant body of conventional norms. It is not that there is no sense of shared values in Canada, but rather that there is always one too many sets of such values. Canada is a mosaic of different communities – Aboriginal peoples, Québécois, women, Westerners, WASPs, workers, ethnic minorities, Catholics, Acadians, gays, lesbians, and so on. For instance, in the abortion debate, it is not that there is no sense of social solidarity, but that there are two very strong and largely irreconcilable communities that draw upon, and are energized by, different visions of individual responsibility and social justice.

One of the unanswerable questions for those who seek to justify the *Charter* on the basis of community consensus is why the community cannot be trusted with its own consensus. If the *Charter* is truly about protecting community values, why can those values not be identified and given voice through democratic means? Recognizing that any consensus is organic and protean, it is difficult to understand why it should be entrenched in a document that is practically impossible to change and enforced by a group of citizens who are unrepresentative of and unaccountable to the community at large. If there is a detailed and uncontroversial body of extant norms, there will be no need for judicial review. But if there is no such consensus – and surely there is not – the defence of judicial review in terms of such a consensus is futile.

It seems that, inspired rather than disabused by the tribulations of their American counterparts, Canadian jurists are intent on banging their heads against the proverbial brick wall of constitutional legitimacy. How is it, and how could it ever be, possible to appeal to an idea of community, consensus, or tradition to resolve a division of opinion, when that division arises from the inadequacy, indeterminacy, or contentiousness of the very idea that is being invoked? The only benefit of such an exercise is that it might belatedly knock some political sense into those who go through its motions. Unfortunately, the effect to date seems to have been to encourage even more outrageous hallucinatory reveries of theoretical excess.

The point we are making is certainly not new, nor is it particularly radical. Indeed, it is little more than an elaboration on an observation made over a dozen years ago in a case that involved much the same conflict between picketing and property rights as arose in *Dolphin Delivery*:

> The submission that this Court should weigh and determine the respective values to society of the right to property and the right to picket raises important and difficult political and socio-economic issues, the resolution of which must, by their very nature, be arbitrary and embody personal economic and social beliefs. It also raises fundamental questions as to the role of this Court under the Constitution ... I do not for a moment doubt the power of the Court to act creatively – it has done so on countless occasions; but manifestly one must ask – what are the limits of the judicial function?[32]

Who was this outspoken sceptic of judicial review? Remarkably, it was none other than the Right Honourable Brian Dickson, before he was appointed Chief Justice of Canada. Has the enactment of the *Charter* transformed the 'arbitrary' and 'personal' opinions of Dickson J. and his colleagues into 'principled' and 'objective' pronouncements based upon community values or an evolving tradition? Lord Acton would not be satisfied by that explanation. Nor should we.

Conclusion

Many seem disheartened by the thought that there may be no principled or non-ideological answers to contentious social issues.[33] Yet there is no warrant for cynicism or despair. Acknowledging people as the makers of decisions, rather than the beneficiaries of received wisdom, marks the first step in the long march towards broadening social responsibility and dispersing political power in Canada. Democracy is not about servitude to academic scribblers or imperial judges; it is about personal participation and social solidarity. Power can never be abolished; it can only be entrusted to those whose lives it most directly affects and affirms.

In a world of incorrigible indeterminacy, the sane response is not to collapse in frustration. It is to move forward confidently in the knowledge that decision making is no more mysterious and no less complex than the rest of life. The present failings of democracy can be overcome not by less popular participation, but by more. People must think, decide, and act in the same way in law as they aspire to do in the rest of their lives – that is, through concrete and constitutive action. This recognition and aspiration means that political practice must be given priority over constitutional conversation. Acknowledging the limits of the rule of law in a society in which it is too often invoked to justify rule by lawyers, is a development to be lamented. Democracy is about ourselves; not some of us, but all of us.

NOTES

1 See A. Hutchinson, *Dwelling on the Threshold: Critical Essays on Modern Legal Thought* (Toronto: Carswell, 1988) at 261–93.
2 For a critique, see A. Hutchinson & P.J. Monahan, 'Democracy and the Rule of Law,' in A. Hutchinson & P.J. Monahan, eds., *The Rule of Law: Ideal or Ideology* (Toronto: Carswell, 1987) at 97–123.

3 See A. Hutchinson & P.J. Monahan, 'The Unfolding Drama of American Legal Thought: Law, Politics, and Critical Legal Scholars' (1984) 34 Stan. L. Rev. 199 at 202–8; and M. Tushnet, *Red, White, and Blue: A Critical Analysis of Constitutional Law* (Cambridge, MA: Harvard University Press, 1988).
4 B. Slattery, 'Are Constitutional Cases Political?' (1989) 11 Sup. Ct. L. Rev. 507 at 527.
5 J. Whyte, 'Legality and Legitimacy: The Problem of Judicial Review of Legislation' (1987) 12 Queen's L.J. 1 at 9.
6 D. Beatty, *Putting the Charter to Work* (Montreal: McGill-Queen's University Press, 1987) at 53.
7 P.J. Monahan, *Politics and the Constitution: The Charter, Federalism, and the Supreme Court of Canada* (Toronto: Carswell, 1987).
8 See P. Sniderman *et al.*, 'Liberty, Authority, and Community: Civil Liberties and the Canadian Political Community' (paper presented to the annual meeting of the Canadian Political Science Association, 9 June 1988) (unpublished).
9 See ch. 1, 'The Politics of the *Charter*'; ch. 3, 'Private Rights/Public Wrongs: The Liberal Lie of the *Charter*'; ch. 4, 'Canada's *Charter* Flight: Soaring Backwards into the Future'; and A. Petter, 'Legitimizing Sexual Inequality: Three Early Charter Cases' (1989) 34 McGill L.J. 358.
10 *Tomen v. Federation of Women Teachers' Associations of Ontario* (1987), 61 O.R. (2d) 489 (H.C.) [*Tomen*] [subsequently aff'd in (1989), 70 O.R. (2d) 48 (C.A.), leave to appeal to S.C.C. refused, [1991] 1 S.C.R. xv].
11 See M. Landsberg, 'The Charter: herald of fairness or weapon against women?' *Globe and Mail* (30 May 1987) at 2.
12 Rather than confronting this conflict, the Court sidestepped the issue, holding that the *Charter* did not apply to the bylaw in question because the Ontario Teacher's Federation, though regulated by statute, was a private rather than a governmental body.
13 *Andrews v. Ontario (Minister of Health)* (1988), 64 O.R. (2d) 258 (H.C.) [*Andrews*].
14 M. Gold, 'Moral and Political Theories in Equalities Rights Adjudication,' in J. Weiler & R. Elliot, eds., *Litigating the Values of a Nation: The Canadian Charter of Rights and Freedoms* (Toronto: Carswell, 1986) 85 at 88–9.
15 *R.W.D.S.U. v. Dolphin Delivery*, [1986] 2 S.C.R. 573 [*Dolphin Delivery*].
16 *Reference re Public Service Employee Relations Act (Alberta)*, [1987] 1 S.C.R. 313.
17 See *Lavigne v. Ontario Public Service Employees Union* (1989), 67 O.R. (2d) 536 (C.A.), [subsequently aff'd in [1991] 2 S.C.R. 211].
18 P. Gall, 'Freedom of Association and Trade Unions: A Double-Edged Constitutional Sword,' in J. Weiler & R. Elliot, *supra* note 14 at 245.

19 O.W. Holmes, *Collected Legal Papers* (New York: Harcourt, Brace & Howe, 1920) at 312.

20 See note 9, *supra*.

21 *Gay Alliance toward Equality v. Vancouver Sun*, [1979] 2 S.C.R. 435 [*Gay Alliance*].

22 *R. v. Red Hot Video Ltd*. (1985), 18 C.C.C. (3d) 1 (B.C.C.A.) [*Red Hot Video*], leave to appeal to S.C.C. refused (1985), 46 C.R. (3d) xxv (S.C.C.).

23 The same tension underlies *Charter* cases concerning hate propaganda. For example, in *R. v. Keegstra* (1988), 60 Alta. L.R. (2d) 1 (C.A.) [subsequently rev'd in [1990] 3 S.C.R. 697], the Alberta Court of Appeal struck down the *Criminal Code* provision making it an offence to wilfully promote hatred against an identifiable group. According to the Court, the provision violated the *Charter*'s right to freedom of expression. However, in *R. v. Andrews* (1988), 65 O.R. (2d) 161 (C.A.) [subsequently aff'd in [1990] 3 S.C.R. 870], the Ontario Court of Appeal ruled that the *Charter* provided no protection for hate propaganda. According to the majority, such propaganda 'is entirely antithetical to our very notion of freedom.'

24 *Ford v. Quebec (Attorney General)*, [1988] 2 S.C.R. 712.

25 *Reference re Bill 30, An Act to Amend the Education Act*, [1987] 1 S.C.R. 1148.

26 See R. Dworkin, *Taking Rights Seriously* (Cambridge, MA: Harvard University Press, 1977); and *idem*, *A Matter of Principle* (Cambridge, MA: Harvard University Press, 1985).

27 *R v. Edwards Books and Art Ltd.*, [1986] 2 S.C.R. 713 [*Edwards Books*].

28 *R. v. Morgentaler*, [1988] 1 S.C.R. 30 [*Morgentaler*].

29 *R. v. Jahelka* (1987), 54 Alta. L.R. (2d) 1 (C.A.) [*Jahelka*] [subsequently aff'd in [1990] 1 S.C.R. 1226].

30 *R. v. Skinner* (1987), 79 N.S.R. (2d) 8 (C.A.) [*Skinner*] [subsequently rev'd in [1990] 1 S.C.R. 1235].

31 See J. Bakan, 'Constitutional Argument: Interpretation and Legitimacy in Canadian Constitutional Thought' (1989) 27 Osgoode Hall L.J. 123.

32 *Harrison v. Carswell*, [1976] 2 S.C.R. 200 at 218.

33 See A. Hutchinson, 'Democracy and Determinacy: An Essay on Legal Interpretation' (1989) 43 U. Miami L. Rev. 541.

6 Rip Van Winkle in *Charterland**

Return from the Wild

In which the author leaves a brutal land and comes home to a brutal class

This story is about the experiences and observations of an intrepid constitutional law professor upon returning to *Charterland* after a decade wandering through the political wilds of Canada's West Coast.

As some may recall, I wrote a thing or two about the *Charter* in the decade following its inception in 1982. Early in the 1990s, however, I left *Charterland* to explore British Columbia's political wilderness, where I battled orcs and struggled to survive in this harsh and unforgiving environment.[1] Many of my academic colleagues gave me up for dead; but miraculously, after ten years, I managed to drag my way across treacherous terrain back to *Charterland*, arriving home to the more hospitable climes of the University of Victoria in the summer of 2001.

While this experience took its toll, both physically and mentally, it also provided me with a 'Rip Van Winkle-like' perspective on changes that have occurred in *Charterland* over the past decade. And a lot has changed. This was brought home to me most clearly when I resumed teaching an upper-year seminar entitled 'Civil Liberties and the *Charter*.'

Having spent many an hour since my return catching up on the multitude of constitutional judgments released during my absence, I decided that the one class in which I could safely rely on old materials was in my first session on the nature and legitimacy of judicial review.

* Originally published in *The Advocate* 63, no. 3 (2005): 337–46. Copyright © 2005 by Vancouver Bar Association. Reprinted by permission of *The Advocate*.

So I wiped the dust from my ten-year-old notes and boldly headed off to the seminar room.

'The first thing you need to understand about judicial review,' I began, 'is that it is represented by the courts and its proponents as a principled process that operates autonomously from politics. That is the view of the Supreme Court of Canada in cases like *Morgentaler*[2] and *Motor Vehicle Reference*,[3] and it is a view that is shared in large measure by academics like David Beatty[4] and Lorraine Weinrib.'[5]

No sooner were the words out of mouth than up shot the hand of a disturbingly bright-looking student seated directly across the table from me.

'Actually, Professor Petter,' she said, 'that isn't consistent with current thinking on *Charter* dialogue.'

'*Charter* dialogue?' I replied.

'Yes. Professor Hogg says that, given the degree of discretion exercised by the courts in interpreting the *Charter*, judicial review is best understood as part of an interactive dialogue between courts and legislatures.'[6]

'Peter said that?' I responded, trying to make it sound more like a statement than a question.

'Yes,' she said. 'And the Supreme Court in cases like *Vriend*[7] and *Mills*[8] appears to agree with him.'

'Well in any event,' I went on, returning to my ten-year-old notes, 'clearly the most salient feature of judicial review under the *Charter* is that it has given the courts the dominant role and the final say in enunciating our fundamental rights and freedoms in Canada.'

Up shot the hand of a young man seated to my left.

'Perhaps you haven't seen the Symposium Edition of the *Canadian Bar Review*,' he waxed. 'In it, Professor Monahan employs a Coasian analysis to argue that legislatures can usually bargain around court decisions under the *Charter*.'[9]

'Oh he does, does he?' I sputtered, making a mental note to congratulate Patrick for having squeezed another article out of Robert Coase's 'The Problem of Social Cost,'[10] and reassuring myself that some things at least had not changed.[11]

'Along the same lines,' added the first student, 'Professor Hogg advances the view that, in *Charter* dialogues, it is the legislature that usually gets the last say.'[12]

'Indeed,' I replied, shaking my head in a manner that I hoped might be mistaken as knowingly. (It occurred to me at this stage that my only chance of maintaining any credibility with my students was to have them interpret my approach as a postmodern variant on Socratic teaching – one in which I offered erroneous answers and they responded with corrective questions. Nurturing this thought, I ploughed ahead.)

'One of the main difficulties for *Charter* adherents,' I continued, 'is reconciling the role of the courts under the *Charter* with the requirements of section 1, which, by placing "reasonable limits" on *Charter* rights, requires judges to engage in an explicitly subjective exercise of interest balancing.'

Emboldened by her classmates, a third student entered the fray.

'In his recent book, Professor Kent Roach relies on section 1 to justify judicial review. He says it facilitates *Charter* dialogue by allowing legislatures a "vehicle to respond to judicial decisions."'[13]

'This line of argument has currency at the University of Toronto?' I blathered.

'Ditto Professor Monahan,'[14] the second student nodded.

'And Professor Hogg,'[15] the first student offered helpfully.

'Well, let's turn to section 33,' I soldiered on. 'Surely there can be no dispute that section 33, a provision that permits legislatures to override Canadians' fundamental rights and freedoms, is an embarrassment that *Charter* adherents would like to see repealed at the earliest opportunity.'

The first student's hand was up again.

'Actually, section 33 is key to Professor Hogg's dialogue theory in that it provides legislatures a meaningful opportunity to respond to court decisions.'[16]

'Is that a fact?' I whimpered.

'Yes,' she said. 'And the Supreme Court itself has pointed to the availability of section 33 in justifying its decision in the *Vriend* case.'[17]

'Same with Professor Roach,' the third student chimed in. 'In fact, Professor Roach maintains that, when a legislature is directly opposed to a court decision, section 33 provides it a more palatable alternative to other forms of legislative response.'[18]

Changes in *Charterland*

In which the author confronts how things are not as they once were and wonders what it all means

After a few days of recuperation, and numerous failed attempts to erase the memory of my classroom experience, I decided to turn my attention to what my students had told me. If nothing else, their statements confirmed (albeit painfully) that theories propounding the immutable nature of *Charter* rights are far from immutable. In the space of a decade, the dominant defence of *Charter* review in Canada had shifted from one based upon assertions of objective reasoning and judicial autonomy *from* the political process, to one based upon acceptance of subjective interpretation and judicial engagement *with* the political process.

Attitudes towards key provisions of the *Charter* had shifted as well. Section 1, which had been viewed with suspicion by *Charter* adherents because of its capacity to weaken the *Charter*'s commitment to liberal values, was now embraced for its tendency to strengthen the *Charter*'s commitment to democratic dialogue.[19] Section 33, which had been shunned by *Charter* adherents as a provision that undermined judicial authority to protect fundamental rights and freedoms, was now welcomed as a provision that fortified the legitimacy of judicial decisions enforcing those rights and freedoms.

Moreover, as I studied the matter more carefully in the ensuing months, it became clear to me that these shifts were linked to further changes in judicial attitudes and approaches to *Charter* interpretation. The most fundamental of these was a change in judges' explanations of their own *Charter* role. In the 1980s, Supreme Court of Canada judges had insisted that, by employing a 'purposive analysis,' they could 'measure the content of legislation against the constitutional requirements of the *Charter*,' derive 'objective and manageable standards' for its operation, and thereby 'avoid adjudication of the merits of public policy.'[20] By the 1990s, judges were prepared to recognize that the *Charter* imposed upon them significant policy-making powers. The most explicit acknowledgment of this came from Madame Justice McLachlin, who, in a lecture delivered in 1990, spoke of 'the impossibility of avoiding value judgments in *Charter* decision-making,' and who referred to such judgments as 'essentially arbitrary.'[21]

But not only had the courts abandoned the ideal of judicial objectivity, they had also dispensed with many of the formal liberal trappings previously relied upon to bolster that ideal. In early *Charter* cases, for example, Supreme Court judges had portrayed the section 1 'proportionality test' set out in *Oakes* as a neutral framework for objective decision making.[22] By the early 1990s, these judges were prepared to concede that the *Oakes* test did not enable them to avoid difficult policy choices and were arguing publicly about how those choices should best be made.[23]

Another liberal shibboleth that had been embraced by the Supreme Court in early *Charter* cases was the view that the purpose of the *Charter* was to constrain governmental action, not to authorize or compel it.[24] This view had been reinforced by the portrayal of judges as 'neutral arbiters' whose conduct (except when associated with conduct of the legislative or executive branches) was non-governmental and beyond the scope of *Charter* scrutiny.[25] In the 1990s the Court shifted ground on these positions as well, holding that the *Charter*, in certain circumstances, may require as well as constrain governmental action,[26] and that judicial decisions cannot be insulated from *Charter* norms.[27]

A related belief espoused by judges in early *Charter* cases was that, because their role was adjudicative rather than legislative, they were limited to striking down legislation found to be inconsistent with the *Charter*, rather than repairing or extending it.[28] In subsequent cases this belief was dispensed with along with the rest, as the Court embraced new remedies – including severance,[29] declarations of temporary validity,[30] and the reading in of statutory exclusions[31] and extensions[32] – in order to reshape legislation in creative ways.

In short, what had occurred in the space of ten years was a wholesale shift, not only in the justification for *Charter* decision making, but also in judges' understanding of the scope and nature of the *Charter*, and of their role in its enforcement. Viewed in this light, the Court's embrace of 'democratic dialogue' as the dominant justificatory theory for judicial review under the *Charter* took on new significance. Far from being an isolated or haphazard occurrence, this change could be seen as a necessary development to enable the Court to explain to itself and others its new approach to *Charter* decision making – an approach that could no longer be justified on the basis of judicial objectivity and purposive reasoning. Like a snake that outgrows and sheds its skin, the Court had shed one theory of judicial review to take on another that better met its requirements.

Monologuing on Dialogue

In which the author surveys the dimensions of dialogue theory to see how it measures up

Armed with these new insights, I decided to examine more carefully the dialogue theory espoused by Professors Hogg, Monahan, and Roach, and embraced by the Supreme Court of Canada. Does this theory, which gained so much favour in academic and judicial circles during my absence, present a more convincing account of judicial review under the *Charter* than its 'purposive' predecessor?

In some respects I have come to believe it does. Most obviously, dialogue theory better explains and accommodates key provisions of the *Charter*, especially sections 1 and 33. These provisions, by creating space for legislatures to enact laws that impose reasonable limits on or that override *Charter* rights, sit more easily with a theory that provides a positive role for legislatures in *Charter* decision making.

Dialogue theory is also more credible in its rejection of what Kent Roach refers to as 'the myths of right answers' – arguments that any one theory of judicial review will reliably produce the 'right answer' in difficult constitutional cases[33] – and in the willingness of its adherents to acknowledge that judicial review is a subjective process. As Peter Hogg and Alison Bushell state in their seminal article on *Charter* dialogue, 'judges have a great deal of discretion in "interpreting" the law of the constitution, and the process of interpretation inevitably remakes the constitution into the likeness favoured by the judges.'[34]

Finally, dialogue theory has some capacity to encourage courts to produce *Charter* decisions that are more socially progressive. Because the theory is less dependent on nineteenth-century liberal assumptions about the role of judges and the relationship between the individual and the state, it provides courts greater scope to impose positive obligations, to protect collective interests, and to fashion creative remedies.

The ideology of liberal legalism that captured the courts in the first ten years of *Charter* litigation cut in a decidedly regressive direction. It prevented courts from using the *Charter* to confront private abuses of power and the common law entitlements that supported them. It inhibited the courts from recognizing positive or collective rights. And it discouraged the courts from modifying or expanding legislation that was seen as deficient or underinclusive.[35]

Dialogue theory provides support to judges who wish to edge away from these assumptions. This is most clearly evident in the *Vriend* case, in which the Supreme Court of Canada invoked the theory to support its decision to extend the reach of Alberta human rights legislation to prohibit private-sector employment discrimination against gays and lesbians.[36] And the theory may have informed other recent developments, such as the Court's decision in *Pepsi-Cola* to abandon the common law prohibition on secondary picketing (in which the Court noted that its decision did not forestall subsequent legislative action),[37] and its decision in *Dunmore* to declare unconstitutional legislation excluding agricultural workers from Ontario's labour relations regime (in which the Court justified its remedy by referencing the legislature's ability to further amend the legislation),[38]

It would be a mistake, however, to exaggerate the significance of these decisions. While dialogue theory may provide some comfort to judges who wish to modify law on the margins, liberal legalism will continue to exert a powerful guiding influence at the core of the *Charter* enterprise. There is no clearer confirmation of this than the Court's judgment in *Gosselin*, in which the majority held that section 7 of the *Charter* did not place on government any positive obligation to protect the life, liberty, or security of the person of a Quebec resident whose welfare benefits had been reduced as a result of changes to that province's social assistance scheme.[39]

In other respects, it seems to me that dialogue theory is seriously deficient. While represented by its proponents as a justification for judicial review under the *Charter*, dialogue theory mitigates more than it legitimates. By acknowledging that *Charter* decision making is not justified on the basis of 'right answers,' dialogue theory undercuts the legitimacy of judicial review as it seeks to explain why legislatures should be allowed to trump judicial decisions. And in arguing that court decisions under the *Charter* are ultimately less influential than is sometimes supposed, dialogue theory calls into question why courts should be allowed to make such decisions in the first place.

This is particularly so given that dialogue theory lacks normative content and exerts no moral claim to support judges' involvement in *Charter* decision making.[40] I do not mean to suggest that individual dialogue theorists do not have strong moral views; but these views, while they may be accommodated within dialogue theory, are clearly grounded somewhere else. Evidence of this can be found in judicial opinions and academic writings that expound the theory. In recent cases, judges have taken to arguing amongst themselves as to whether particular *Charter* decisions are consistent with or contrary to the theory.[41] Academic proponents of dialogue theory disagree on whether it cuts in favour of judicial activism or restraint.[42] And the Supreme Court of Canada has relied upon the theory to support decisions that are both narrow and expansive.[43]

Another deficiency of dialogue theory is its tendency to discount the extent to which judicial decision making under the *Charter* influences public policy. This happens in three ways. First, dialogue theorists tend to exaggerate the influence of legislatures in responding to judicial decisions. As others have pointed out, not all legislative responses are evidence of genuine dialogue,[44] and many are better characterized as reflections of, rather than responses to, judicial norms.[45]

Second, dialogue theorists play down the privileged position that courts occupy in *Charter* dialogues. While courts get to speak in the rhetoric of rights, legislatures are left to mouth the language of limits. Moreover, it is the judges whose interpretations govern the meanings of *Charter* rights and, absent a section 33 override, who decide what limits on those rights can be justified.[46]

Third, and perhaps most importantly, dialogue theory ignores the extent to which *Charter* rights shape public discourse and influence public policy independently of any dialogue taking place.[47] One thing that I can confidently report from my ten years in the political wilderness is that the *Charter*, and judicially conditioned assumptions about its interpretation, permeate and influence every aspect of political life, from deciding how best to regulate the use of tobacco, to debating election finance reform, to determining the standards for legal liability in environmental offences.

Through a Dialogue Darkly

In which the author sees a darker side to dialogue theory and its implications for democracy

So, after my travels and travails, where does this modern day Rip Van Winkle come down on the merits of dialogue theory? Having lived with the theory for several years now, my feelings are somewhat divided.

Some aspects of dialogue theory strike me as an improvement over other attempts to legitimize judicial review under the *Charter*. I applaud the willingness of dialogue theorists to acknowledge the subjective nature of *Charter* decisions. By doing so, they help to demystify judicial decisions and to encourage a fuller and franker debate about judicial review and its consequences. And while they exaggerate the capacity of legislatures to counter judicially imposed *Charter* values, I welcome their efforts to legitimize democratic engagement on rights issues. I also see benefit in the capacity of dialogue theory to encourage courts to ease their attachment to liberal legalism and – on the margins at least – to discard some of the regressive assumptions that animated *Charter* jurisprudence in the 1980s.

Other aspects of the theory, however, I find much less convincing. The argument advanced by dialogue theorists to justify judicial review, for example, essentially boils down to a claim that, under the *Charter*, legislatures can have the final say. The reason we should accept the legitimacy of judicial review, dialogue theorists want us to believe, is because the institution being reviewed can escape its consequences. Not only is the claim upon which this proposition is based questionable (for reasons I have explained above), but the proposition itself is devoid of logic. The fact that one institution can escape the consequences of another's actions may say something about the latter's efficacy, but it says nothing about its legitimacy.

At a deeper level, I also see a darker side to dialogue theory. In the past, theorists who acknowledge the subjective nature of judicial review have felt compelled by that insight to question its legitimacy or, at minimum, to urge judicial deference to democratic institutions. Dialogue theory is different. While some of its proponents are less activist than others, none of them regard the theory as raising fundamental questions about the legitimacy of judicial review or the privileged position afforded courts in defining *Charter* values.

In this way, dialogue theory carries with it a disturbing message about the state of Canadian democracy. Say what you will about conventional liberal theory, its tolerance for judicial interference with democratic decisions is based on an assurance that judicial review yields 'right answers.' That is why conventional liberal theorists have laboured so mightily to show that judicial review is distinct from politics – a product of principled reasoning, aimed at protecting transcendent truths or embedded social norms. By accepting judicial interference with democratic decisions in the absence of such an assurance, dialogue theory shows itself more willing to compromise democracy than its critical or conventional predecessors.

The fact that a theory of this kind has found such ready acceptance among courts and commentators lends credence to those who argue that support for democracy is on the wane in Canada.[48] I am not suggesting that judicial review is the main cause of this phenomenon. On the contrary, my political experiences have persuaded me that the major threats to Canadian democracy lie in the undemocratic character of our 'democratic' institutions and their inability to withstand the pressures of globalization. Unlike dialogue theorists, I do not believe that these institutions, as currently structured, can claim legitimacy for themselves, let alone for judicial review. Nor do I see how the interplay between unaccountable legislatures and unelected judges qualifies as 'democratic dialogue.'

Surely we can do better than this. We live in an era in which governments seem increasingly unable to respond to the needs of ordinary Canadians, political participation rates are falling, and Canada is suffering from what the Law Commission describes as a 'democratic malaise.'[49] For those of us concerned for the future of Canadian democracy, there is much work to be done. Rather than directing our energies to what Lawrence Tribe has called 'the futile search for legitimacy,'[50] or looking for democracy where it does not reside, we would do better to try resuscitating it where it does, by seeking ways to reform and revitalize the faltering institutions of the democratic state.[51] A strong and effective democracy – one that is more representative of and responsive to the needs of all citizens – would better demonstrate to Canadians that their rights are being taken seriously than the most compelling theory of judicial review.

NOTES

1 From 1991 to 2001, I served as a Member of the Legislative Assembly of British Columbia and held numerous cabinet portfolios. See Introduction at 10–11.
2 *R. v. Morgentaler*, [1988] 1 S.C.R. 30 at 45–6, 136–41 [*Morgentaler*].
3 *Reference Re s. 94(2) of Motor Vehicle Act (British Columbia)*, [1985] 2 S.C.R. 486 at 495–500 [*Motor Vehicle Reference*].
4 See D.M. Beatty, *Putting the Charter to Work: Designing a Constitutional Labour Code* (Montreal: McGill-Queen's University Press, 1987) at 181.
5 See L.E. Weinrib, 'The Supreme Court of Canada and Section One of the Charter' (1988) 10 Sup. Ct. L. Rev. 469 at 506.
6 P.W. Hogg & A.A. Bushell, 'The *Charter* Dialogue between Courts and Legislatures (or Perhaps the *Charter of Rights* Isn't Such a Bad Thing After All)' (1997) 35 Osgoode Hall L.J. 75.
7 *Vriend v. Alberta*, [1998] 1 S.C.R. 493 at para. 138 [*Vriend*].
8 *R. v. Mills*, [1999] 3 S.C.R. 668 at para. 57 [*Mills*].
9 P.J. Monahan, 'The Supreme Court of Canada in the 21st Century' (2001) 80 Can. Bar Rev. 374 at 389.
10 R. Coase, 'The Problem of Social Cost' (1961) 3 J.L. & Econ. 1.
11 In the 1980s, Monahan relied on Coase to support his views on the opera-

tion of Canadian federalism: see P.J. Monahan, *Politics and the Constitution: The Charter, Federalism, and the Supreme Court of Canada* (Toronto: Carswell, 1987) at ch. 10.

12 Hogg & Bushell, *supra* note 6 at 96–8.

13 K. Roach, *The Supreme Court on Trial: Judicial Activism or Democratic Dialogue* (Toronto: Irwin Law, 2001) at 6–7.

14 Monahan, *supra* note 9 at 394–5.

15 Hogg & Bushell, *supra* note 6 at 84–7.

16 *Ibid.* at 83–4.

17 *Vriend, supra* note 7 at para. 139.

18 Roach, *supra* note 13 at 281–2.

19 This it does, according to dialogue theorists, not only by allowing governments to defend legislative provisions as being 'reasonable limits' on *Charter* rights, but also by providing them opportunities to respond to adverse judicial decisions with legislative changes that propose more proportionate means to achieve the same objectives. See Hogg & Bushell, *supra* note 6 at 84–7.

20 *Motor Vehicle Reference, supra* note 3 at 495–500.

21 B. McLachlin, 'The *Charter*: A New Role for the Judiciary?' (1991) 29 Alta. L. Rev. 540 at 545–6.

22 *R. v. Oakes*, [1986] 1 S.C.R. 103.

23 See *e.g.* G. LaForest, 'The Balancing of Interests under the Charter' (1992) 2 N.J.C.L. 133; and B. Wilson, 'Constitutional Advocacy' (1992) 24 Ottawa L. Rev. 265.

24 See *Hunter v. Southam Inc.*, [1984] 2 S.C.R. 145 at 156 [*Southam*].

25 See *Dolphin Delivery Ltd. v. Retail, Wholesale and Department Store Union, Local 580*, [1986] 2 S.C.R. 573 at 600–1.

26 See *Dunmore v. Ontario (A.G.)*, [2001] 3 S.C.R. 1016 at paras. 19–29 [*Dunmore*].

27 As Hogg points out, the Court implicitly shifted position on this in the late 1980s in *Rahey v. R.*, [1987] 1 S.C.R. 588 and *B.C.G.E.U. v. B.C.*, [1988] 2 S.C.R. 214: see P.W. Hogg, *Constitutional Law of Canada*, student ed. (Toronto: Thomson Carswell, 2000) at 706–9. Moreover, the Court has lately been far more willing to modify the common law to take account of *Charter* values: see *Pepsi-Cola Canada Beverages (West) Ltd. v. R.W.D.S.U., Local 558*, [2002] 1 S.C.R. 156 [*Pepsi-Cola*], in which the Court effectively reversed its decision in *Dolphin Delivery*, holding that the common law rule rendering secondary picketing *per se* illegal should be modified in light of the *Charter* guarantee of freedom of expression.

28 See *Southam, supra* note 24 at 168–9; *Singh v. Canada (Minister of Employment & Immigration)*, [1985] 1 S.C.R. 177 at 235–6.

29 See *R. v. Hess*, [1990] 2 S.C.R. 906; *Tétreault-Gadoury v. Canada (Employment & Immigration Commission)*, [1991] 2 S.C.R. 22.

30 See *Schachter v. Canada*, [1992] 2 S.C.R. 679 at 715–17; *Dunmore, supra* note 26 at paras. 19–29, 66.

31 See *R. v. Sharpe*, [2001] 1 S.C.R. 45 at 111–27.

32 *Vriend, supra* note 7 at paras. 144–79.

33 Roach, *supra* note 13 at 225–38.

34 Hogg & Bushell, *supra* note 6 at 77. Monahan makes no bones about the fact that the 'complex and multidimensional nature of balancing required in Charter cases' requires 'the application of subjective judgment': P.J. Monahan, *Constitutional Law*, 2nd ed. (Toronto: Irwin Law, 2002) at 421. And while Roach goes to pains to argue that judicial review is constrained by 'both the text and the purposes of the *Charter*,' his thesis ultimately rests on a rejection of the view that 'any theory of judicial review will generate reliably right answers' and an acknowledgment that 'judges exercise creativity as they interpret the vague provisions of the *Charter*': Roach, *supra* note 13 at 140, 116.

35 See ch. 1, 'The Politics of the *Charter*'; ch. 3, 'Private Rights/Public Wrongs: The Liberal Lie of the *Charter*'; and ch. 4, 'Canada's *Charter* Flight: Soaring Backwards into the Future.'

36 *Vriend, supra* note 7.

37 *Pepsi-Cola, supra* note 27 at para. 86.

38 *Dunmore, supra* note 26 at para. 66.

39 *Gosselin v. Quebec (Attorney General)*, [2002] 4 S.C.R. 429.

40 The closest any dialogue theorists come to making a moral claim is Roach's attempt to argue that judicial interpretation is guided by an obligation 'to make good-faith interpretations of the text': Roach, *supra* note 13 at 140–1.

41 See *R. v. Hall*, [2002] 3 S.C.R. 309, in which McLachlin C.J., on behalf of herself and four others, described the interplay between Parliament and the Court with respect to the bail provisions of the *Criminal Code* as 'an excellent example of [constitutional] dialogue' (para. 43); while Iacobucci J., on behalf of himself and three others, claimed that this interaction 'demonstrates how … constitutional dialogue can break down' and accused the Chief Justice of having 'transformed dialogue into abdication' (para. 127). At the same time, Iacobucci J. went out of his way to characterize the Court's decision in *Mills, supra* note 8, as a 'good example' of constitutional dialogue (paras. 124–6), implicitly challenging Roach's suggestion that the decision was misguided and 'may actually inhibit further dialogue': Roach, *supra* note 13 at 281. See also *Sauvé v. Canada (Chief Electoral Officer)*, [2002] 3 S.C.R. 519 [*Sauvé*], in which McLachlin C.J., on behalf of herself

and four others, rejected the view expressed by Gonthier J., on behalf of himself and three others, that respect for constitutional dialogue required the Court to defer to Parliament's response to previous *Charter* rulings concerning prisoners' voting rights.

42 Monahan argues that dialogue theory is best served by the courts producing 'minimalist rulings' in order to leave 'the greatest scope possible for potential responses by the legislative and executive branches': Monahan, *supra* note 9 at 392, while Roach refers to minimalist definitions of rights as 'unfortunate,' arguing that constitutional dialogue permits legislatures to respond to 'even bold and broad judicial rulings': Roach, *supra* note 13 at 154.

43 Contrast *Vriend*, *supra* note 7 at para. 138, where the Court invoked dialogue theory to justify extending the scope of Alberta human rights legislation, with *Bell ExpressVu Limited Partnership v. R*, [2002] 2 S.C.R. 559 at paras. 65–6, in which the Court invoked dialogue theory to justify its refusal to interpret the federal *Radiocommunication Act* to make it conform to the *Charter*. See also *Sauvé*, *supra* note 41, in which McLachlin C.J. rejected the position taken by Gonthier J. that, based on dialogue theory, the Court should show deference to Parliament's response to its previous *Charter* rulings.

44 See C.P. Manfredi & J.B. Kelly, 'Six Degrees of Dialogue: A Response to Hogg and Bushell' (1999) 37 Osgoode Hall L.J. 513.

45 See F.L. Morton & R. Knopff, *The Charter Revolution and the Court Party* (Peterborough: Broadview Press, 2000) at 166.

46 See J. Webber, 'Institutional Dialogue between Courts and Legislatures in the Definition of Fundamental Rights: Lessons from Canada (and Elsewhere)' in W. Sadurski, ed. *Constitutional Justice, East and West: Democratic Legitimacy and Constitutional Courts in Post-Communist Europe in a Comparative Perspective* (The Hague: Kluwer Law International, 2002) 61 at 97: 'The rights [under a constitutional charter] assume a superordinate importance, resistant to balancing. Any attempt by the legislature or the executive to define rights or determine their application is viewed with extreme scepticism, as an illegitimate attempt to impair fundamental liberties. The ability of legislatures to derogate in section 33 becomes virtually unusable.' See also Manfredi & Kelly, *supra* note 44 at 523, pointing out that what Hogg and Bushell call *Charter* dialogues involve legislatures 'subordinating themselves ... to the Court's interpretation of the *Charter*'s language'; and Roach, *supra* note 13 at 241–3, criticizing a doctrine of coordinate construction that would allow legislatures to place their own interpretation on constitutional rights.

47 See J.L. Hiebert, *Charter Conflicts: What Is Parliament's Role?* (Montreal: McGill-Queen's University Press, 2002) at 7–18.

48 See *e.g.* J. Simpson, *The Friendly Dictatorship* (Toronto: McLelland and Stewart, 2001).

49 Law Commission of Canada, *Renewing Democracy: Debating Electoral Reform in Canada* (Ottawa: Law Commission of Canada, 2002) at 11.

50 L.H. Tribe, *Constitutional Choices* (Cambridge, MA: Harvard University Press, 1985) at 3.

51 For one view of what this might entail, see A. Petter, 'Putting the "D" into Social Democracy: The Need for a Re-energized State' (McGill Conference on the Future of Social Democracy, Institute for the Study of Canada, McGill University, 25 May 2001), online: McGill University http://www.misc-iecm.mcgill.ca/socdem/petter.htm.

7 Look Who's Talking Now: Dialogue Theory and the Return to Democracy[*]

Introduction

What is the constitutional role of legislatures in a liberal democratic state? Different scholars provide different answers. Some depict legislatures as objects of constitutional decision making; for them, the primary role of legislatures is to be directed by constitutional norms.[1] Others represent legislatures as instruments of constitutional decision making; for them, legislatures play a significant role in fulfilling constitutional norms.[2] Still others characterize legislatures as sources of constitutional decision making; for them, legislatures play a key role in the generation of constitutional norms.[3]

Canadian adherents of 'dialogue theory' go further. They portray legislatures as playing a crucial role in legitimizing constitutional norms, including norms articulated through judicial decision making. Advanced by leading constitutional scholars and embraced by the Supreme Court of Canada, this theory holds that the purpose of judicial review under the *Canadian Charter of Rights and Freedoms* is to augment democratic decision making. Dialogue theorists maintain that judicial decisions under the *Charter* are not conclusive, but form part of a dialogue with legislatures in which the latter retain the final say. It is this capacity of legislatures to decide the outcome of *Charter* issues that, in the eyes of dialogue theorists, bestows democratic legitimacy upon *Charter* decision making.

[*] Originally published in R.W. Bauman & T. Kahana, eds., *The Least Examined Branch: The Role of Legislatures in the Constitutional State* (Cambridge: Cambridge University Press, 2006) at 519–31. Copyright © 2006 by Cambridge University Press. Reprinted by permission of Cambridge University Press.

The notion that the legitimacy of constitutional decision making rests upon the ability of legislatures to trump judicial decisions is replete with ironies and contradictions; it also raises questions that have both promising and troubling dimensions. Chief among these is whether Canadian legislatures are capable of fulfilling the democratic mandate attributed to them by dialogue theorists. In my view, there are strong reasons for believing that they are not and that dialogue theorists and others who regard democracy as a core constitutional value need to give more urgent attention to the democratic shortcomings of the Canadian state. Before addressing these and other issues, however, it might be helpful to review the developments that have given rise to dialogue theory and to consider some of its implications.

The Demise of Legislative Supremacy

The enactment of the *Canadian Charter of Rights and Freedoms* in 1982 was meant to mark the demise of legislative supremacy in Canada. According to its early adherents, the purpose of the *Charter* was to provide courts with a constitutional mandate to invalidate legislative and governmental actions that were inconsistent with the fundamental rights and freedoms it guaranteed. As a consequence, the doctrine of legislative supremacy was to be replaced with a doctrine of constitutional supremacy. One problem with this view was that, while supremacy of the Constitution was largely uncontroversial, its meaning was not. The open-ended nature of *Charter* rights, combined with the qualification in section 1 subjecting these rights to 'such reasonable limits prescribed by law as can be demonstrably justified in a free and democratic society,' made the *Charter* more a forum for argument than a fount of answers. This, in turn, begged the question as to who bore constitutional responsibility for resolving *Charter* arguments, many of which concerned highly charged and long-standing political issues such as abortion, commercial speech, and religious rights.

The conventional wisdom at the time of the *Charter*'s enactment was that final say over the meaning of constitutional rights and their limitations belonged to the courts.[4] But on what basis would courts exercise their interpretative powers, and how would they justify the legitimacy of their decisions? In a country like Canada, with a positivist legal tradition and a culture of judicial deference to legislatures, these questions were not easily answered. The initial response of the Supreme Court to these issues was to fall back on the familiar assumptions of liberal legalism. These assumptions, grounded in nineteenth-century legal traditions, hold that courts must act as impartial arbiters whose responsibilities do not extend to policy making, but are limited to unbiased adjudication of legal issues and objective interpretation of legal texts. Early *Charter* cases are steeped in language that reflects these assumptions. In the *British Columbia Motor Vehicle Reference*, for example, the Court maintained that by subjecting the *Charter* to a 'purposive analysis,' it could derive 'objective and manageable standards' for its operation, thereby 'avoiding adjudication of the merits of public policy.'[5] And while grappling with the thorny issue of abortion in *R. v. Morgentaler*, the Court insisted that its task was 'not to solve nor seek to solve what might be called the abortion issue, but simply to measure the content of [legislation] against the *Charter*.'[6]

These same assumptions were evident in the Court's approach to the 'reasonable limits' clause in section 1. The amorphous standard created by this section appears to call upon courts to engage in interest balancing, an activity normally associated with political decision making. As such, it represents a threat to liberal legalism and its vision of judges as objective interpreters of the constitutional text. In *R. v. Oakes*, Supreme Court judges responded to this threat by setting out a two-stage 'proportionality test.'[7] By converting the section 1 inquiry from one focused on the 'reasonableness' of legislation to one focused on the 'proportionality' between legislative means and ends, and by stipulating specific criteria and a stringent standard for determining whether the requisite degree of 'proportionality' had been met, the *Oakes* test diminished the subjective appearance of section 1 by providing an ostensibly neutral framework for judicial decision making.

The Court's resort to liberal legalism as the basis for understanding and explaining its new *Charter* role is also reflected in other aspects of its early *Charter* work. One example is the position it articulated in early *Charter* cases that the purpose of *Charter* rights is to constrain governmental action, not to authorize or compel it.[8] This precept is grounded in nineteenth-century liberal assumptions that the division between public and private spheres is clear and uncontested and that state interference with private action represents the greatest threat to individual liberty. According to this view, the role of courts under the *Charter* is simply to police the boundary between these spheres so as to constrain the state from unduly interfering with individual freedoms.[9] Thus the Court in *Dolphin Delivery Ltd. v. R.W.D.S.U.* was able to refer to judges as 'neutral arbiters' whose conduct (except when linked to legislative

or executive actions) was non-governmental and beyond the scope of
Charter scrutiny.[10]

A related view embraced by the Court in early *Charter* cases was its
insistence that, because the role of judges is adjudicative rather than
legislative, they were limited to striking down legislation inconsistent with the *Charter*, rather than repairing or extending it. In *Hunter
v. Southam Inc.*, for example, the Court refused to read provisions into
the *Combines Investigation Act*,[11] stating that it did 'not fall to the courts
to fill in the details that will render legislative lacunae constitutional.'[12]
Similarly, in *Singh v. Canada*, the Court declined to repair deficiencies in
the *Immigration Act*,[13] noting that the *Charter* allowed the courts to perform 'some relatively crude surgery on deficient legislative provisions,
but not plastic or re-constructive surgery.'[14]

The Rebirth of Legislative Supremacy

Drawing on the values of liberal legalism, the Court by the late 1980s
had forged a seemingly coherent set of positions concerning the scope
and nature of *Charter* rights and the role of judges in their enforcement.
Yet, unhappily for the judges, these positions proved unsustainable.
There are a number of reasons for this. First, the Court's attempts to
portray *Charter* decision making as neutral and apolitical were simply
not credible in an age informed by the insights of legal realism. Whatever the Court said, none but a few true believers were willing to accept
that judges' interpretations of contested *Charter* rights, such as liberty
and equality, were the objective outcome of 'purposive reasoning,' or
that grappling with contentious public issues such as abortion and Sunday closing laws did not require judges to make subjective judgments
based on their personal moral values. Second, the paradigm of liberal
legalism, grounded as it was on nineteenth-century assumptions about
the nature of the state, was out of sync with twentieth-century social
norms and realities. The notions that *Charter* rights could constrain
but not compel state action, that judges could strike down legislation
but not repair or extend it, and that courts would apply a stringent
standard against upholding legislation under section 1, gave the *Charter* an ideological slant that was at odds with – and at times hostile
to – political expectations concerning the regulatory and redistributive
functions of the modern state.[15] Third, as the Court was confronted
with increasingly complex and difficult cases, splits started to emerge
among judges, as some, feeling uncomfortable with the consequences

of these assumptions, began to modify them or back away from them altogether. As a result, the number of Supreme Court *Charter* cases that were unanimously decided plummeted from over 85 per cent in the first two years of *Charter* judgments (1984 and 1985) to about 60 per cent in the next four years (1986 to 1989).[16] These growing divisions within the Court further undermined the appearance of judicial objectivity.

By the turn of the decade, Supreme Court judges were openly admitting that the *Charter* imposed upon them significant policy-making powers.[17] As they discarded the myth of judicial objectivity, judges also dispensed with many of the trappings of liberal legalism associated with it. By the early 1990s, some judges not only were conceding that the *Oakes* test required them to make difficult value judgments under section 1, but also were arguing publicly about how those judgments should best be made.[18] The Court also started shifting ground on its approach to state action, acknowledging that judicial decisions should not be insulated from *Charter* norms,[19] and accepting, in certain circumstances, that the *Charter* may compel as well as constrain governmental action.[20] At the same time, the Court abandoned earlier claims that it was limited by its adjudicative role to striking down legislation and began to embrace new *Charter* remedies – including severance,[21] declarations of temporary validity,[22] and the reading in of statutory extensions[23] and exclusions[24] – that allowed it to restructure legislation in a variety of ways.

The effect of these shifts was to destabilize the platform of liberal legalism upon which the Court had built and justified its *Charter* enterprise. This in turn raised a difficult question: if the Court could no longer justify its *Charter* role on the basis that judges' decisions were grounded in objective standards and purposive interpretations, what justification could it offer? Fortunately for the Court, an answer was in the making. While judges had been busy jettisoning key elements of their justificatory theory for judicial review, academic commentators sympathetic to the *Charter* enterprise had been labouring on alternative theories. In 1997, Peter Hogg and Allison Bushell published a paper defending the legitimacy of *Charter* review based on the claim that the *Charter* creates a dialogue between courts and legislatures.[25] According to the authors, *Charter* decisions were seldom determinative of issues, but merely set the stage for legislative responses that, more often than not, achieved the same objective in a different way. Thus the *Charter* did not undermine democratic decision making, but merely encouraged deliberation about rights issues as part of an interactive process

– described by Hogg and Bushell as a 'dialogue' – between courts and legislatures.

The radical nature of this theory is apparent from the fact that the authors proceeded from an assumption that judicial review is a highly subjective enterprise. Noting that 'judges have a great deal of discretion in "interpreting" the law of the constitution,' they conceded that 'the process of interpretation inevitably remakes the constitution into the likeness favoured by judges.'[26] This concession was important not only in accounting for the normative nature of judicial decision making, but also in explaining why legislatures, not courts, should serve as the final arbiters of constitutional norms. According to Hogg and Bushell, democracy alone provides the rationale for public policy making, and *Charter* decisions are merely another contribution to a democratic dialogue in which legislatures, not courts, get the final say.

Supreme Court of Canada judges did not waste any time adopting dialogue theory as their own. Speaking for the majority in the 1998 *Vriend* decision, Mr Justice Iacobucci embraced the concept of dialogue put forward by Hogg and Bushell, emphasizing that 'the final word in our constitutional structure is in fact left to the legislature and not the courts.'[27] He went on to say:

> To my mind, a great value of judicial review and this dialogue among the branches is that each of the branches is made somewhat accountable to the other. The work of the legislature is reviewed by the courts and the work of the court in its decisions can be reacted to by the legislature in the passing of new legislation (or even overarching laws under s. 33 of the *Charter*). This dialogue between and accountability of each of the branches have the effect of enhancing the democratic process, not denying it.[28]

Given the tattered state of the Court's previous efforts to explain judicial review under the *Charter*, the readiness with which it seized upon dialogue theory is perhaps not surprising. The theory provided a convenient justification for the Court's constitutional role and came with the added virtue of malleability. Unlike liberal legalism, which is animated by an established set of norms concerning the character of judicial decision making and the relationship between individuals and the state, dialogue theory is normatively agnostic. Thus, while judges can claim that their role in the dialogue is to make 'reasoned and principled decisions,'[29] the theory does not dictate what the nature of those reasons and principles should be.

Where dialogue theory is *not* malleable, however, is in its claim that the legitimacy of *Charter* decision making is grounded in democracy and, in particular, in the ability of legislatures to exercise final say over judicial decisions. In this way, the Supreme Court's embrace of dialogue theory represents a revival of the doctrine of legislative supremacy as much as it does a repudiation of liberal legalism. Moreover, this reborn version of the doctrine goes further than its predecessor in one important respect: it relies on the democratic character of legislatures to justify political decision making not only by elected governments but also by unelected courts.

Dialogue and Democracy

Despite the support it has received from Canadian scholars and courts, dialogue theory does not in my view provide a compelling justification for judicial review under the *Charter*. First, the theory lacks normative content and provides no moral justification for judges' involvement in *Charter* decision making. Second, the theory is based on the erroneous proposition that a decision is legitimate simply because it is not conclusive. Third, the theory seriously understates the extent to which judicial decision making under the *Charter* drives public policy in Canada.[30] Beyond these objections, the theory suffers from a more fundamental weakness that supporters of *Charter* review have previously attributed to the arguments of *Charter* sceptics – namely, an uncritical acceptance of the democratic nature of political institutions. Dialogue theorists maintain that the *Charter* creates a 'democratic dialogue' between legislatures and courts.[31] This dialogue is said to be democratic, and hence legitimate, insofar as legislatures rather than courts retain the final say. Yet this assumes that legislatures are themselves democratic. If they are not, dialogue theory is reduced to a proposition of two undemocratic wrongs making one democratic right.

There are many reasons to doubt the democratic character of Canadian political institutions. Such institutions remain horribly unrepresentative of the public. Women, for example, make up more than 50 per cent of the Canadian population[32] but only 21 per cent of Members of Parliament.[33] Indigenous people, ethnic minorities, and the poor are similarly underrepresented in Parliament and in provincial legislatures. In addition, our 'first past the post' electoral system produces major distortions in translating voters' preferences into representation. Parties that attract support from a minority of voters regularly get to form majority governments. Voters in federal elections who support smaller parties that are regionally based, such as the Bloc Québécois, are generally overrepresented, while those who support smaller parties that are nationally based, such as the New Democratic Party and the Green Party, are generally underrepresented or get no representation at all.

Federal and provincial governments also lack accountability to their citizens. Within these governments, power is concentrated in the hands of first ministers, who, by virtue of their control over cabinet appointments, government perks, and party structures, exercise enormous sway over elected members of their party, leaving legislatures with little or no capacity to influence government policy. The only significant qualification to this rule arises when there is a minority government. In this circumstance, opposition parties gain some influence from their power to defeat the government, though this influence is usually exercised by way of extra-legislative bargaining and is tempered by the power of first ministers to announce policy, call elections, and otherwise control the levers of government.

At a more basic level, Canadian institutions of parliamentary democracy are artefacts of a nineteenth-century British system[34] that provide citizens with limited means to participate in public policy making. Except when governments consider it in their interest to consult or otherwise engage the public, the only meaningful opportunity that citizens have to influence public policy is to vote in elections, which may occur as infrequently as once every five years.[35] Even this opportunity, precious though it is, has become less relevant as governments have entered trade agreements ceding more and more of their regulatory capacity and transferring decision-making authority to unelected transnational organizations.

It is ironic that, in seeking to defend the legitimacy of judicial review, Canadian constitutional scholars and judges should turn from one set of nineteenth-century assumptions (those associated with liberal legalism) to another (those associated with parliamentary democracy). This irony is made more poignant by the fact that support for this form of democracy, at least as it is currently practised, is on the wane in Canada. Voter participation rates in Canadian elections have been declining dramatically over the past twenty-five years, with turnout in the 2004 federal election the lowest in Canadian history.[36] A majority of Canadians attribute this decline to negative attitudes towards the performance of politicians and political institutions, and to an associated sense that political participation is meaningless.[37] The relationship between growing discontent with political institutions and declining voter turnout is confirmed by public opinion surveys conducted over the past twenty-five years. These surveys show that the number of Canadians with a great deal of confidence in the House of Commons fell 14 percentage points from 1979 to 2001,[38] while those with a great deal of confidence in political parties fell 17 percentage points.[39] In the same timeframe, voter turnout declined nearly 15 percentage points.[40]

Taking Democracy Seriously

The ascendancy of dialogue theory as the prevailing justification for judicial review under the *Charter*, ironic or not, carries with it some important messages. One is that, after two decades of experience with constitutional rights in Canada, democracy has re-emerged as the dominant value supporting Canadian constitutional structures. Another is that, the *Charter* notwithstanding, ultimate responsibility for giving expression to those rights has been recognized to lie with the people rather than with the courts. As a consequence, those who advocate judicial review based on dialogue theory have joined those who remain sceptical of judicial review based on democratic principles in having a significant investment in the democratic nature of the Canadian state. With this investment, however, comes responsibility. Against the backdrop of legislatures that are unrepresentative, governments that are unaccountable, and citizens who are losing faith in political institutions, there is a pressing need for *Charter* enthusiasts and *Charter* sceptics to give more urgent attention to the requirements of democracy. The goal of this enterprise should be to make Canadian political institutions as representative and responsive as possible and to maximize opportunities for citizen participation and deliberation in relation to political decision making.

It is beyond the scope of this essay to set out a detailed agenda of democratic reform, but let me highlight a few areas that deserve to be addressed. One obvious one is electoral reform. I have already described how our current 'first past the post' voting regime produces legislatures that do not represent the views of the electorate, diminishing or denying representation to smaller parties that are ideologically based, and conferring majority powers on parties that are supported by a minority of electors. This regime is an affront to basic principles of democracy and needs to be replaced with a proportional system aimed at producing legislatures that reflect the diversity of public opinion in Canada. Such a system should be accompanied by campaign finance laws that respect the equality of citizens, and ensure that elections are not dominated by those who command money and power. In the context of a proportional system, this means that, in addition to public election financing, campaign contribution limits (including prohibitions on corporate and union donations), disclosure requirements, and spending restrictions, election laws should be reworked to ensure that small parties get adequate funding and a voice in the process.

Based on the experience of other countries, a proportional voting system supported by effective election finance laws is more likely to produce legislatures in which women, Aboriginal people, and ethnic minorities are better represented.[41] Such a system by itself, however, is unlikely to overcome the social and economic barriers that inhibit these groups from achieving their full measure of political representation. For this reason, further educational, fiscal, and structural measures aimed at countering these barriers and promoting equitable representation of these groups ought to be considered.[42]

Electoral reform would also go some distance to fostering parliamentary reform. A proportional voting system will tend to produce minority or coalition governments in which the power of first ministers is constrained by an ongoing need to accommodate the competing views of other parties. In such governments, issues are more likely to be fully and openly debated, and decisions to reflect a broader range of interests. More, however, can and should be done. A range of institutional reforms is needed to give legislatures more sway over first ministers and their executives, to replace or do away with an unelected Senate, to give citizens greater opportunities for input into government decision-making processes, and to ensure that such decision making is conducted in an open and accountable manner.

The changes outlined above speak to the need for legislatures to be more representative and responsive and to operate in a democratic manner. A meaningful commitment to democracy, however, should not be limited to representative institutions and certainly not to legislatures. Much has been written in recent years about the need to pursue new strategies to foster greater participation and deliberation on the part of citizens in relation to decisions that affect their lives.[43] There are a large number of such strategies that merit consideration. I will touch on three examples that I believe hold promise based on my experience in the Government of British Columbia.[44]

One such strategy is to devolve powers to local or regional governments. At a time when globalization has inhibited the ability of national
and provincial governments to pursue social and economic innova-
tions, local and regional governments may be better placed to advance
the public interest in certain policy areas. Such governments enjoy the
benefit of being closer to the people and farther from the reach of international capital. They also have greater capacity than national or provincial governments to be inclusive and responsive and to tailor their
strategies to citizens' needs.[45] To prevent national and provincial governments from using devolution as a means to shirk responsibilities or
download costs, transfers of power must be accompanied by administrative, legislative, and, possibly, constitutional guarantees, in order to
ensure that local and regional governments gain the institutional and
fiscal capacity required to discharge their enlarged responsibilities.

A recent example where this has occurred is in the context of the
Nisga'a Treaty in British Columbia. This treaty enables the Nisga'a people through their 'Lisims Government' to exercise authority on matters of social policy and resource management, guarantees them fiscal
transfers and taxation powers, and sets all this out in a constitutionally
recognized framework.[46] It is still early days, but few would deny that
the Nisga'a government is better positioned to reflect and advance the
needs of its citizens in these areas than was either the federal or provincial government. Thus, far from being a threat to democracy, as some
of its opponents have asserted, the Nisga'a treaty provides a model for
democratic reform that might well be emulated in other Aboriginal and
non-Aboriginal communities.

Another devolutionary strategy, sometimes referred to as 'associative democracy,'[47] would seek to close the gulf between government
and civil society by assigning some matters of public policy to self-
governing associations that can better represent the interests of those
who are most affected. This strategy is nothing new in northern Italy,
where, in the city of Bologna, 85 per cent of social services are delivered
by cooperatives.[48] Similar initiatives have been tried in Canada on a
more limited scale. In British Columbia, for example, experiments were
undertaken in the 1970s and 1990s to give responsibilities as diverse
as delivery of health services and management of forest resources to
community-run boards. Initiatives of this kind could be employed on
a more regular basis to allow citizens greater opportunity to influence
social and economic policy at the local level. And parallel policies could
be contemplated at the provincial or national level in relation to the

governance of certain public utilities and Crown corporations. Transforming such entities into consumer-run cooperatives would preserve their status as civic institutions while enhancing their accountability and providing greater opportunities for public participation in their governance.[49]

A third strategy, which might be called 'deliberative engagement,' involves government charging representative groups of citizens with responsibility for recommending or deciding matters of public policy.[50] This strategy can be particularly productive in generating processes of public deliberation on issues that are polycentric or too complex for popular opinion to be gauged in conventional ways (by polling, for example). A process of this kind was used successfully in British Columbia in the 1990s by the Harcourt government to give representatives of communities and stakeholders responsibility for developing regional and local land use plans. When these representatives were brought into a structured process of public deliberation, deeply held differences were overcome and creative solutions were found to settle land use conflicts that had previously defied resolution.

Another British Columbia experiment in 'deliberative engagement' was launched by the Campbell government in 2003 to review British Columbia's electoral system. A Citizens Assembly of 161 people, composed of one man and one woman chosen by lot from each of the province's 79 constituencies, as well as two Aboriginal members and an independent chair, was formed to study and recommend changes to the province's 'first past the post' electoral system. After months of study, public consultation, and deliberation, the assembly recommended that the province adopt a 'single transferable' voting system that would produce greater proportionality of representation based on multi-member electoral districts.[51] This recommendation was put to voters in a referendum held in conjunction with the 2005 provincial election. The government stipulated that for the proposal to proceed, it would have to gain the approval of 60 per cent of those who voted, as well as a majority of those who voted in 60 per cent of the province's seventy-nine electoral districts. In the result, the assembly's recommendation received the support of over 57 per cent of those who voted, and of a majority in all but two electoral districts. While this degree of support fell just short of the government's first threshold, it nonetheless sent a strong signal about the public's dissatisfaction with the *status quo*.[52] Moreover, while its recommendation was not accepted, the Citizens Assembly was highly successful in generating meaningful citizen engagement on a complex issue of public policy and in producing a proposal that gained significant public interest. The process also broke new ground in ensuring equal representation of women in the deliberative process and in giving citizens direct power to decide the outcome, albeit based on a requirement of support from more than a simple majority of those who voted.

Conclusion

In the early 1980s, when I and other sceptics questioned the *Charter* and its implications for democracy, supporters of judicial review often accused us of romanticizing legislatures and their democratic role. Today, with the benefit of more than twenty years of hindsight – ten of them spent as a member of the British Columbia Legislature – I have come to accept that these accusations had merit. The early preoccupation of *Charter* sceptics with the shortcomings of judicial review diverted our attention from the deficiencies of parliamentary government and caused many of us to take Canadian democracy too much for granted.

During the time that my romance with legislatures has faded, however, many *Charter* enthusiasts have developed a passion for parliamentary government that makes my previous yearnings seem like mild infatuation. I and other *Charter* sceptics regarded legislatures as institutions whose democratic capacity was threatened by *Charter* review; today's dialogue theorists see legislatures as having sufficient democratic capacity not only to withstand *Charter* review but also to legitimize its exercise. Now that's some democratic capacity!

The good news is that, despite other disagreements, *Charter* enthusiasts and *Charter* sceptics now occupy the same boat in viewing democracy as Canada's core constitutional value. The bad news is that this ship is listing badly and taking on water at an alarming rate. Moreover, it is a boat that many Canadians have started to abandon. Rehabilitating this vessel will be no small challenge, but thankfully, work has already begun. Groups calling for changes to the 'first past the post' voting system are mobilizing across Canada, and electoral reform initiatives are under way in a number of provinces.[53] Effective election spending laws have been put in place for national campaigns, parliamentary reforms have been adopted by the federal and some provincial governments, and a deliberative process requiring equal representation for women has been employed in British Columbia. Possibilities for democratizing political decision making through devolution, associative democracy, and other deliberative means abound, and there is a growing body of academic literature on these and other strategies.

What remains is for constitutional scholars who are serious about their democratic commitments to join this enterprise and to direct their knowledge and intellectual energies to helping reclaim and reconstruct Canadian democracy. For those who maintain a sceptical outlook towards the *Charter*, this undertaking requires us to set aside our deconstructive tendencies and to embrace a challenge that may seem as daunting as it does worthwhile. For those who celebrate the *Charter* based on dialogue theory, however, there is additional motivation to partake in the endeavour. Unlike *Charter* sceptics, who must be content with salvaging democracy for its own sake, this new brand of *Charter* enthusiasts can draw sustenance from their remarkable belief that, by salvaging democracy, they are fortifying the legitimacy of *Charter* review.

NOTES

1 See *e.g.* F. Schauer, 'Legislatures as Rule-Followers' in R.W. Bauman & T. Kahana, eds., *The Least Examined Branch: The Role of Legislatures in the Constitutional State* (Cambridge: Cambridge University Press, 2006) at 468.

2 See *e.g.* J. Webber, 'Democratic Decision-Making as the First Principle of Contemporary Constitutionalism' in R.W. Bauman & T. Kahana, eds., *The Least Examined Branch: The Role of Legislatures in the Constitutional State* (Cambridge: Cambridge University Press, 2006) at 411.

3 See *e.g.* W.N. Eskridge, Jr, & J. Ferejohn, 'Super-Statutes: The New American Constitutionalism' in R.W. Bauman & T. Kahana, eds., *The Least Examined Branch: The Role of Legislatures in the Constitutional State* (Cambridge: Cambridge University Press, 2006) at 320.

4 One obvious qualification to this assumption was section 33, which gave legislatures the ability to temporarily override judicial decisions under the *Charter*, but this provision was seen as exceptional, and was regarded with suspicion by *Charter* adherents, many of whom argued that it should never be used and ought to be repealed at the earliest opportunity.

5 *Reference Re s. 94(2) of Motor Vehicle Act (British Columbia)*, [1985] 2 S.C.R. 486 at 495–500.

6 *R. v. Morgentaler*, [1988] 1 S.C.R. 30 at 46, 138.

7 *R. v. Oakes*, [1986] 1 S.C.R. 103 [*Oakes*].

8 See *Hunter v. Southam Inc.*, [1984] 2 S.C.R. 145 at 156 [*Southam*].

 9 See ch. 3, 'Private Rights/Public Wrongs: The Liberal Lie of the *Charter.*'

10 *Dolphin Delivery Ltd. v. Retail, Wholesale and Department Store Union, Local 580,* [1986] 2 S.C.R. 573 at 600–1.

11 *Combines Investigation Act,* R.S.C. 1970, c. C-23.

12 *Southam, supra* note 8 at 168–9.

13 *Immigration Act,* 1976, S.C. 1976–77, c. 52.

14 *Singh v. Canada (Minister of Employment and Immigration),* [1985] 1 S.C.R. 177 at 235–6.

15 See ch. 1, 'The Politics of the *Charter*'; ch. 4, 'Canada's *Charter* Flight: Soaring Backwards into the Future'; and ch. 3, 'Private Rights/Public Wrongs: The Liberal Lie of the *Charter.*'

16 F.L. Morton, P.H. Russell, & M.J. Withey, 'The Supreme Court's First One Hundred Charter of Rights Decisions: A Statistical Analysis' (1992) 30 Osgoode Hall L.J. 1 at 11.

17 The most candid acknowledgment of this came from Madam Justice McLachlin, who, in a lecture delivered in 1990, spoke of 'the impossibility of avoiding value judgments in *Charter* decision-making' and referred to such value judgments as 'essentially arbitrary': B. McLachlin, 'The Charter: A New Role for the Judiciary?' (1991) 29 Alta L. Rev. 540 at 545–6.

18 See *e.g.* G. LaForest, 'The Balancing of Interests under the Charter' (1992) 2 N.J.C.L. 133; and B. Wilson, 'Constitutional Advocacy' (1992) 24 Ottawa L. Rev. 265.

19 As Professor Hogg pointed out, the Court started shifting position on this in the late 1980s in cases such as *B.C.G.E.U. v. B.C. (Attorney General),* [1988] 2 S.C.R. 214: see P.W. Hogg, *Constitutional Law of Canada,* student ed. (Toronto: Carswell, 2000) at 706–9.

20 See *Dunmore v. Ontario (Attorney General),* [2001] 3 S.C.R. 1016 at paras. 19–29.

21 See *R. v. Hess,* [1990] 2 S.C.R. 906; and *Tétreault-Gadoury v. Canada (Employment & Immigration Commission),* [1991] 2 S.C.R. 22.

22 See *Schachter v. Canada,* [1992] 2 S.C.R. 679 at 715–17.

23 *Ibid.* at 695–702. See also *Miron v. Trudel,* [1995] 2 S.C.R. 418 at para. 180.

24 See *R. v. Sharpe,* [2001] 1 S.C.R. 45 at 111–27.

25 P.W. Hogg & A.A. Bushell, 'The *Charter* Dialogue between Courts and Legislatures (or Perhaps the *Charter of Rights* Isn't Such a Bad Thing After All)' (1997) 35 Osgoode Hall L.J. 75.

26 *Ibid.* at 77.

27 *Vriend v. Alberta,* [1998] 1 S.C.R. 493 at para. 137 [*Vriend*].

28 *Ibid.* at para. 139.

29 *Ibid.* at para. 136.

30 For a fuller discussion of these objections, see ch. 6, 'Rip Van Winkle in *Charterland*' at 141–4.

31 K. Roach, *The Supreme Court on Trial: Judicial Activism or Democratic Dialogue* (Toronto: Irwin Law, 2001).

32 Statistics Canada, 'Population by Sex and Age Group' (2003), online: Statistics Canada http://www.statcan.ca/english/Pgdb/demo10a.htm (50.47 per cent in 2007: http://www40.statcan.ca/l01/cst01/famil01-eng.htm).

33 Inter-Parliamentary Union, 'Women in National Parliaments' (31 July 2004), online: Inter-Parliamentary Union http://www.ipu.org/wmn-e/classif.htm. (This number rose to 22.4 per cent in 2008: http://www2.parl.gc.ca/Parlinfo/compilations/parliament/WomenRepresentation.aspx?Language=E&Parliament=8714654b-cdbf-48a2-b1ad-57a3c8ece839.)

34 The British Parliamentary system dates back well before this, but the first serious effort to democratize the system by extending the franchise beyond a narrow set of elites did not occur until passage of the *Representation of the People Act 1832*, 2 & 3 Will. IV, c. 45.

35 As Rousseau observed, the English system of parliamentary democracy is free 'only during the election of members of Parliament. As soon as they are elected, slavery overtakes it, and it is nothing': J.J. Rousseau, *The Social Contract* (New York: Everyman, 1950) at 94.

36 Voter turnout was 60.9 per cent in 2004 compared to 75.7 per cent in 1979: Elections Canada, 'Past Elections' online: Elections Canada On-Line http://www.elections.ca/content.asp?section=pas&document=turnout&lang=e&textonly=false. (Voter turnout further declined to 59.1 per cent in the 2008 federal election: http://www.cbc.ca/news/canadavotes/story/2008/10/15/voter-turnout.html.)

37 J.H. Pammett & L. LeDuc, *Explaining the Turnout Decline in Canadian Federal Elections: A New Survey of Non-Voters* (Ottawa, Elections Canada, March 2003) at 6–18, online: Elections Canada <http://www.elections.ca/loi/tur/tud/TurnoutDecline.pdf.

38 From 38 per cent in 1979 to 24 per cent in 2001: Centre for Research and Information on Canada, *Voter Participation in Canada: Is Canadian Democracy in Crisis?* (Montreal: CRIC, 2001) at 16.

39 From 30 per cent in 1979 to 13 per cent in 2001, *ibid.*

40 From 75.7 per cent in 1979 to 61.2 per cent in 2000, Pammett & LeDuc, *supra* note 37.

41 Law Commission of Canada, *Voting Counts: Electoral Reform for Canada* (Ottawa: Law Commission of Canada, 2004) at 60–2.

42 See *e.g.* M.S. Williams, *Voice, Trust, and Memory: Marginalized Groups and the Failings of Liberal Representation* (Princeton: Princeton University Press, 1998).

43 See *e.g.* B. Barber, *Strong Democracy: Participatory Politics for a New Age* (Berkeley: University of California Press, 1984); J. Fishkin, *The Voice of the People: Public Opinion and Democracy* (New Haven: Yale University Press, 1995); A. Gutman & D. Thompson, *Democracy and Disagreement* (Cambridge: The Belknap Press of Harvard University, 1996); J. Cohen, 'Deliberation and Democratic Legitimacy' in J. Bohman & W. Rehg, eds., *Deliberative Democracy: Essays on Reason and Politics* (Cambridge, MA: MIT Press, 1997) at 67; and I.M. Young, *Inclusion and Democracy* (Oxford: Oxford University Press, 2000).

44 From 1991 to 2001, I served as a Member of the Legislative Assembly of British Columbia and held numerous cabinet portfolios. See Introduction at 10–11.

45 See W. Magnusson, 'Local Autonomy and Community Politics' in W. Magnusson, C. Doyle, R.B.J. Walker, & J. De Marco, eds., *After Bennett: A New Politics for British Columbia* (Vancouver: New Star Books, 1986).

46 For information on the treaty, implementing legislation, and Nisga'a government, see 'Nisga'a Lisims Government,' online: Nisga'a Lisims Government http://www.nisgaalisims.ca.

47 See P. Hirsh, *Associative Democracy* (Amherst: University of Massachusetts Press, 1993).

48 R. Williams, 'Bologna and Emilia Romagna – A Model for Economic Democracy' (paper presented to the Annual Meeting of the Canadian Economics Association, Calgary, May–June 2002), online: B.C. Co-operative Association http://www.bcca.coop/pdfs/BolognaandEmilia.pdf. See generally, R. Putnam, *Making Democracy Work: Civic Traditions in Modern Italy* (Princeton: Princeton University Press, 1993).

49 Transformations of this kind were proposed in British Columbia in the late 1990s in relation to the Insurance Corporation of British Columbia and British Columbia Hydro. Converting such entities into consumer-run cooperatives would have made them more directly accountable to the public they served and provided a democratic alternative to privatization or to turning them into not-for-profit corporations of the kind the federal government established to run its airports and harbours. These proposals did not proceed, however, when they proved too controversial to gain support within government.

50 In this respect, the process might be thought of as an extension of what James Fishkin refers to as 'deliberative polling': see Fishkin, *supra* note 43.

51 For a full account of this process, see J. MacDonald, *Randomocracy: A Citizen's Guide to Electoral Reform in British Columbia* (Victoria: FCG Publications, 2005).

52 As a consequence, a second referendum on electoral reform was held after this essay was written in conjunction with the 12 May 2009 general election in British Columbia. In this referendum, the proposal for electoral reform was defeated with less than 40 per cent support. However, a seven-point decline from 2004 in voter turnout (from 58 to 51 per cent) provided further evidence of voter dissatisfaction with the current electoral system.

53 After this essay was written, proposals to establish mixed-member proportional representation systems were defeated in referenda held in Prince Edward Island in 2005 and in Ontario in 2007.

8 Wealthcare: The Politics of the *Charter* Revisited[*]

Every man for himself said the elephant as he danced among the chickens.

Tommy Douglas

Of Health and Wealth

'Health is wealth' is one of my Irish mother-in-law's favourite sayings. In *Chaoulli v. Quebec (A.G.)*,[1] however, the Supreme Court of Canada turned this aphorism on its head. In a four-to-three decision, the Court held that, given the failure of the Quebec government to provide timely access to Medicare services, Quebeckers have a constitutional and/or quasi-constitutional[2] right to purchase private health insurance to access corresponding services from commercial health care providers.

What would be the implications of this decision if it were applied and implemented across the country? One is that Canadians who can afford private health insurance would have access to better medical care than those who cannot. Another is that those who exercise their right to buy private health insurance would have a weaker stake in ensuring that the Medicare system provides timely and effective medical services. Indeed, where the private and public systems competed for the same health care professionals, those with private insurance would have an interest in the most qualified of these being diverted into the private system, where their services could be accessed on a preferred basis.

What about the implications for the public health care system?

* Originally published in C.M. Flood, K. Roach, & L. Sossin, eds., *Access to Care, Access to Justice: The Legal Debate over Private Health Insurance in Canada* (Toronto: University of Toronto Press, 2005) at 116–38. Copyright © 2005 by Andrew Petter.

Would the introduction of private health insurance, in addition to improving the quality of health care for those who can afford it, compromise the quality of health care for those who cannot? Many believe that the answer to this question is 'yes.' They argue that a two-tier system of health care would siphon resources from and weaken support for Medicare, making it more difficult to manage the public system effectively. Others disagree. They argue that expanding private medical services would increase the overall capacity of the health care system and thereby reduce pressure on the public system. Still others argue that the risk to Medicare from private health insurance is uncertain but, insofar as it exists, the more prudent strategy for reducing wait times is not to expand private medical services for the few, but to improve public medical services for all.[3]

Debate over the relative merits of a one-tier or two-tier health care system has been at the heart of Canadian politics for almost forty years. This debate has engaged Canadians at all levels. It has prompted countless community groups, professional bodies, and public interest organizations to hold forums, to undertake studies, and to produce position papers. It has been the subject of numerous public commissions, and it has played a part in virtually every federal and provincial election campaign since the mid-1960s. Moreover, the debate has been about values and ideology as much as it has been about costs and benefits. In many ways it has been a debate about the fundamental nature of Canada. Do we want a country in which health care is viewed as a market commodity, with access determined by one's economic status? Or do we want a country in which health care is viewed as a public good, with access determined by one's medical needs? Or we do we think that it's somehow possible to have both?

Since the introduction of our national Medicare plan almost forty years ago, the position that has prevailed in this debate has been the one favouring retention of a single-payer model of public health insurance for core medical services. This has remained true despite the considerable stress experienced by the public health care system in recent years. Thus the 2002 Romanow Report[4] and the subsequent health care accord reached by Canada's first ministers[5] rejected private health insurance in favour of improving medical services in the public system. Indeed, to say that the single-payer model has prevailed understates the reality. Canada's commitment to a universal public health care system is widely regarded by citizens as a core social value and a defining national achievement. This too was reaffirmed recently when Tommy

Douglas, best known as the father of Medicare, was voted the greatest Canadian in a nationwide competition undertaken by the CBC.[6]

Now a majority of judges on the Supreme Court of Canada has told us in *Chaoulli* that they know better. In the majority's eyes, the single-payer model of health insurance and its goal of providing equal health care services for all, far from embodying this country's commitment to social justice, violates the rights of those who could gain access to medical services more quickly by purchasing private health insurance. Moreover, according to the Court, there is no evidence that the introduction of private health insurance would compromise the quality of Canadian health care. Never mind the trial judge's finding that the 'effect of establishing a parallel private health care system would be to threaten the integrity, proper functioning and viability of the public system.'[7] Never mind the recommendations of various public commissions that the single-payer model should be retained. Never mind the decisions of different governments over the years that have rejected two-tier health care. All of this can be ignored in *Charterland*, where judges get to decide what qualifies as evidence and what can be cast aside as mere 'assertions of belief'[8] or 'socio-political discourse that is disconnected from reality.'[9]

Thus, with the benefit of a one-day hearing, three of four majority judges were able to conclude that prohibiting private health insurance 'is not necessary or even related to the provision of quality public health care'[10] – a conclusion they based on a review of second-hand information concerning the health care experience of other Western democracies. The efficiency and apparent dependability of this methodology makes one wonder why the federal government allowed the Romanow Commission to hold months of hearings, gather hundreds of submissions, and spend $15 million before releasing its recommendations on the future of Canada's health care system. Apparently the job could have been done much more quickly, cheaply, and reliably simply by putting a reference to the Supreme Court.

Given the complex and contentious nature of the issues raised by *Chaoulli*, many expected that this would be a case in which the Court would be reluctant to substitute its opinion for that of the legislature. In past *Charter* cases involving complex issues and conflicting claims, Supreme Court judges have sometimes shown great deference to legislative choices, particularly where a statutory regime purports to protect the interests of vulnerable groups.[11] Apparently these considerations do not apply, however, when it comes to evaluating the intricacies and impacts of competing health care schemes. Notwithstanding testimony from experts and representations from anti-poverty and public health care advocacy organizations that two-tier health care would hurt the economically disadvantaged, who are more likely to suffer from poor health and who cannot afford private insurance,[12] three of the majority judges held that they had sufficient evidence to conclude that the legislation was 'arbitrary' and therefore contrary to 'the principles of fundamental justice.'[13] Ironically, these are the words of a Chief Justice who has previously maintained that the value judgments made by courts under the *Charter* are themselves 'essentially arbitrary' and who has urged judges to seek guidance in 'the dominant views being expressed in society at large on the question in issue.'[14]

What about the remedy adopted by the Court? If the Court's objective was to secure citizens' rights to access health care services, why did it not order the Quebec government to provide such access within the public system, as suggested in the factum of the Charter Committee on Poverty Issues and the Canadian Health Coalition?[15] This remedy would have preserved the single-payer model and its principle of equal access to health care based on one's medical need rather than one's personal wealth. It therefore would have enabled the Court to avoid the appearance that it was more concerned about protecting the rights of those with money than of those in need of medical care. Yet the Court shied away from this remedy, presumably because it would have required judges to assume responsibility for directing the public health care system. And managing government services, unlike dismantling them, is something that even activist judges are not prepared to do.

Some have suggested that the Court's judgment was intended as a 'wake-up call' to governments about the need to fix Medicare by reducing wait times for medically necessary procedures.[16] If this indeed was the motivation, the judges were playing a dangerous game based on questionable assumptions and with little regard for the consequences. First, there has in recent years been no lack of political pressure or commitment regarding the need to reduce wait times. This issue was a key component of the agreement reached in 2004 by federal and provincial governments to pump an additional $41 billion into the public health system over ten years.[17] Under that agreement, the Health Council of Canada was charged with developing benchmarks for reasonable wait times, and the provinces committed themselves to reporting on their success in meeting those benchmarks.[18] Thus this 'wake-up call' came at a time when no one seems to have been asleep. Second, by deciding that access to private health insurance is a *Charter* right, the Court has given constitutional legitimacy to those advocating a two-tier health care system for Canada, thereby unleashing political forces that may be difficult to contain.[19] There are many ways to arouse people from their slumbers. By tearing down a central pillar of the Medicare system, the Court opted for a wrecking ball over an alarm clock. Finally, the Court appears to have acted with disregard for the trade implications of its decision, ignoring the Romanow Report's admonitions that, to be protected as 'public services' under such agreements, health care services must be 'universally accessible on the basis of need rather than the ability to pay' and must be 'financed out of public revenues.'[20] By requiring governments to allow private insurers to fund core medical services in commercial health care facilities, the Court's ruling has threatened Canada's trade position.[21] In so doing, it may well have limited the capacity of governments to set future directions on health care policy, making it difficult if not impossible to restore a universal, single-payer system. In short, this is one wake-up call from which Canadians may never be allowed to get back to sleep.

If all of this sounds disturbing, it should. If it seems to suggest that the Court is engaging in political decision making, it does. If, on the other hand, it comes as a shock, it ought not to do so. The path trodden by the Court in *Chaoulli* was shaped by ideological norms and assumptions that have been part and parcel of the *Charter* enterprise from its inception; and the power invoked by the Court has been nurtured by Canadian politicians and scholars over the same period of time. This does not mean that the outcome in *Chaoulli* was inevitable – the strong dissenting judgment of the minority demonstrates that it was not – but it does mean that *Chaoulli* was a *Charter* calamity waiting to happen.

The Politics of the *Charter* Revisited

In the mid-1980s, as the Supreme Court of Canada was issuing its first decisions under the *Canadian Charter of Rights and Freedoms*, a vigorous debate took place amongst Canadian constitutional scholars about the political nature and consequences of the *Charter*. In that debate I and other progressive *Charter* sceptics argued that, beyond the confines of the criminal law, the *Charter* was more likely to serve the interests of the economically privileged than those of ordinary and disadvantaged Canadians.[22] The reason for this, we contended, was that *Charter* rights are grounded in an ideology of liberal legalism that holds that the main enemy of freedom is not disparities in wealth or concentrations of private power, but the state. This ideology finds expression in the fact that the rights set out in the *Charter* are predominantly negative in nature, with little in the way of positive economic or social entitlements. It is further animated by a belief that existing distributions of property are products of private initiative rather than state power, and that when courts protect these distributions through the application of the common law rules, they are acting as 'neutral arbiters' rather than as state actors.[23] Such property distributions are therefore regarded as the 'natural foundation' upon which *Charter* rights are bestowed and against which the constitutionality of state action is judged.

The ideology of liberal legalism, we maintained, removes from *Charter* scrutiny the major source of inequality in our society – the unequal distribution of property entitlements among private parties – and directs the restraining force of the *Charter* against the arms of the state best equipped to redress such inequality – the ostensibly democratic arms consisting of the legislature and the executive.[24] In so doing, it gives political meaning to the *Charter*'s open-ended provisions. For example, shaped by this ideology, equality rights do not guarantee citizens a right to be made substantively equal, but rather a right to be treated equally by government. Thus, section 15 of the *Charter* places no positive duties upon the state; it is satisfied by equal 'inaction' as much as it is by equal 'action.' Similarly, the right to security of the person in section 7, according to this ideology, does not require governments to implement measures to make people secure. In the *Charter* scheme of things, courts are to disregard threats to personal security emanating from the market and common law property rights. It is only when the 'normalcy' of the market is disrupted by legislative or executive action that section 7 rights are engaged.

Our conclusion was that the *Charter* shares much the same reverence for private markets and individual autonomy, and the same hostility towards legislative and executive action, as animated the common law. This did not mean that the entire legislative regime of social entitlements and economic regulation put in place in Canada following the Second World War would suddenly be dismantled under the *Charter*. Even if courts were so inclined, the political costs of doing so, thankfully, were too great for them to contemplate. What the *Charter* was more likely to do was to 'enable the judiciary to chisel away at certain aspects of that regime, and to erect barriers to future innovation.'[25] Nor did it mean that there would be no progressive *Charter* decisions. There would be some, though most would be 'those in which the courts uphold legislation – in other words, do nothing.'[26] In addition, there would be exceptional instances in which the *Charter* was used 'to expand the protection afforded by a particular regulatory scheme (subject to the right of legislatures to dismantle the scheme altogether).'[27] Thus, our view on the overall political impact of the *Charter* could be summed up as follows: 'At best, the *Charter* will divert progressive energies, inhibit market regulation, and legitimize prevailing inequalities in wealth and power. At worst, it will undermine existing programs and block future reform.'[28]

These arguments caused something of a stir at the time, though this must have been due to the pungency of our prose rather than to the novelty of our ideas. Certainly the positions we advanced were unique neither to us nor to Canada. A number of scholars in this country had previously raised similar concerns.[29] In England, John Griffith's well-known treatise, *The Politics of the Judiciary*, had critiqued the British legal system along the same lines.[30] And in the United States, John Hart Ely among others had written of the 'systematic bias' embedded in the system of rights favoured by the 'upper-middle, professional class from which most lawyers and judges, and for that matter most moral philosophers are drawn.'[31] These people, Ely argued, see their social and economic status most threatened by the regulatory and redistributive powers of the modern state. Thus, no one should be surprised that they regard as 'fundamental' those values that afford them protection from such state powers; '[b]ut watch most fundamental-rights theorists start edging toward the door when someone mentions jobs, food, or housing: those are important, sure, but they aren't *fundamental.*'[32]

Probably the most compelling exposé of liberal legalism's ideological hold on the *Charter*, however, came not in the form of academic writings, but in the Supreme Court of Canada's own 1986 decision in *Dolphin Delivery.*[33] In a judgment that offended progressive proponents of the *Charter* even more than it did sceptics, the Court unanimously held that a common law injunction prohibiting unionized workers from picketing a private corporation did not constitute state action and was therefore not reviewable as a breach of the *Charter* right to freedom of expression. It is hard to imagine a more blatant illustration of the privileged position that the *Charter* accords property rights and the institutions that protect them. Not surprisingly, the decision provoked a barrage of indignation from progressive academics of all *Charter* persuasions. *Charter* proponents excoriated the Court for renouncing the

Charter's progressive possibilities;[34] *Charter* critics lamented the politics of the decision but welcomed its candid acknowledgment of the *Charter*'s regressive propensities.[35]

The Politics of the *Charter* Refined

In the wake of the critical commentary concerning *Dolphin Delivery* and other early *Charter* decisions, judges who were troubled by the political dimensions of their *Charter* role sought to moderate the *Charter*'s regressive tendencies. This they did in two ways. First, they found reasons to defer to legislative choices where statutes provided protection to vulnerable groups,[36] where equality rights were invoked by those who were not socially disadvantaged,[37] or where there was a lack of conclusive social science evidence.[38] Second, they developed techniques that increased the *Charter*'s progressive potential. One such technique was simply to be receptive to negative and formal rights claims that were directed against legislative provisions that were inequitable and outdated, such as those that restricted a woman's right to abortion[39] or that openly discriminated against gays and lesbians.[40] Another technique was to develop equality rights doctrines requiring governments to ameliorate the adverse impacts of their policies upon disadvantaged groups[41] and allowing judges to extend rather than strike down underinclusive statutory benefits.[42] A third technique was to apply *Charter* rights to legislation that withdrew statutory protections, thereby imposing obligations on the state to reinstate some such protections in limited circumstances.[43] In addition, judges interpreting the common law increasingly took *Charter* values into account, despite their continued insistence that the *Charter* did not directly apply.[44]

These techniques enabled judges to counter the regressive pull of the *Charter* on a case-by-case basis. By operating as qualifications and exceptions, however, their effect was to ameliorate rather than alter the *Charter*'s regressive tendencies: constraining the legislative and executive arms of the state remained the central mission of the *Charter* enterprise. The major impact of these techniques, therefore, was to allow the courts to be more selective in their use of *Charter* rights and to opt for legislative refinements over invalidity, though almost always on the understanding that invalidity remained the default *Charter* position.[45]

Moreover, these techniques left it to individual judges to decide, according to their own beliefs and inclinations, when the *Charter*'s underlying ideology would be given full expression and when it would be held in check:

- In some cases judges decided that the *Charter* does not permit powerful interests to strike down legislation aimed at protecting vulnerable groups;[46] in other cases they reached the opposite conclusion.[47]
- In some cases judges deferred to legislative choices in the absence of conclusive social science evidence;[48] in other cases they did not.[49]
- In some cases judges invoked formal equality rights to strike down laws directed against gays and lesbians;[50] in other cases they found reasons to avoid doing so.[51]
- In some cases judges emphasized that equality rights are intended to protect the socially disadvantaged;[52] in other cases they emphasized that equality rights are available to members of advantaged groups.[53]
- In some cases judges were prepared to remedy a *Charter* breach by extending legislative benefits;[54] in other cases they were not.[55]
- In some cases judges held that withdrawing legislative protections violated the *Charter*;[56] in other cases they found that such withdrawals were justified.[57]
- In some cases judges invoked the *Charter* to modify the common law;[58] in other cases they declined to do so.[59]

Thus, in the process of moderating *Charter* decision making, the Court has developed its own constitutional brand of palm tree justice.

Judges have been encouraged in this process by the rise of dialogue theory and its effort to legitimize judicial review based not upon the ability of judges to find right answers, but rather upon the contention that *Charter* decision making engages judges in a democratic dialogue with legislatures. Dialogue theorists make two claims as to why this dialogue is democratic: first, they assume that the deliberations of judges in *Charter* cases will improve the quality of legislative decision making; second, they assert that under the *Charter* it is legislatures, not the courts, that usually get the final say.[60] I have explained elsewhere why I find these propositions unpersuasive,[61] and I will consider their contribution to *Chaoulli* later in this essay. Their significance here, however, is that neither provides a normative vision of rights to guide or constrain the courts in their enterprise.[62] On the contrary, by accepting that there are no right answers when it comes to *Charter* decision making, dialogue theorists provide no metewand with which to evaluate the appropriateness of judicial action; they essentially authorize judges to do whatever they want within the bounds that liberal legalism allows. Is it any wonder that the Court embraced this theory within months of it being committed to paper?

The Politics of the *Charter* Reaffirmed

Armed with a *Charter* whose rights remain rooted in the political assumptions of liberal legalism, and emboldened by a theory of judicial review that authorizes courts to do what they want, it was only a matter of time before a majority of the Supreme Court of Canada judges gave full vent to the *Charter*'s underlying ideology. This appears to be what has happened in the past few years. With the departure of some judges and the arrival of others,[63] the Court has shown itself more willing to succumb to the *Charter*'s regressive tendencies. This trend is evident in four contentious cases decided recently: *Gosselin v. Québec (Attorney General)*,[64] *Trociuk v. British Columbia (Attorney General)*,[65] *Auton (Guardian ad litem of) v. British Columbia (Attorney General)*,[66] and now *Chaoulli*.

In *Trociuk* and *Auton*, the Court drew on the *Charter*'s negative conception of rights to strengthen section 15's commitment to formal equality. In *Trociuk*, an 'estranged' biological father sought a declaration that legislation granting mothers control over the process of registering the births and names of their children violated his equality rights and was constitutionally invalid. The Court unanimously granted the declaration, rejecting the decision of the court below that the legislation was justified as a means of protecting the well-being of mothers and their children. In doing so, the judges embraced a conception of equality that presumed that genetic fathers have the same stake as genetic mothers in the process of registering births and naming children. This formal vision of equality was reinforced by the Court's willingness to see *Charter* equality rights used by a member of an historically advantaged group to challenge legislation that benefits those who have been historically disadvantaged. According to the Court, an absence of historical disadvantage is not a compelling factor against a finding of discrimination.

Trociuk involved a claim made on behalf of an historically advantaged group to gain greater influence in relation to government's birth registration and naming practices. *Auton*, on the other hand, involved a claim brought on behalf of a disadvantaged group to extend government health care benefits to better meet its medical needs. In the latter case, parents of autistic children maintained that, by refusing to fund certain autism therapies, the government had denied their children equal benefit of the law without discrimination, in violation of section 15 of the *Charter*. The Court dismissed this claim, holding that the denial of funding resulted from the procedures not being provided by designated 'medical practitioners' rather than from their being directed at persons with autism. According to the Court, the denial was therefore not discriminatory. In reaching this conclusion, the Court rejected arguments that the government had a duty under section 15 to ensure that its definition of funded services did not have adverse impacts upon those with autism and, if it did, to ameliorate these impacts. Invoking the hollow logic of formal equality, the judges held that the duty to ameliorate went no further than requiring governments to provide equal access to procedures that were already funded; it did not require government to fund new procedures.[67]

Trociuk and *Auton* mark a reaffirmation of the Court's commitment to liberal legalism in relation to section 15; *Gosselin* and *Chaoulli* do the same in relation to section 7. These latter cases, however, more clearly expose the ideological assumptions and political workings of the *Charter*, in much the same way that *Dolphin Delivery* did almost twenty years earlier. Louise Gosselin was a Quebec woman whose social assistance benefits had been cut by legislation reducing benefits for all persons under the age of thirty. These cuts, she maintained, had left her in a position of abject poverty, thereby denying her *Charter* right to security of the person. The Court rejected this claim, with a majority of judges holding that section 7 did not place positive obligations on the state to ensure that Gosselin enjoyed security of the person, only negative obligations not to deprive her of such security. And as the judges saw it, '[s]uch a deprivation does not exist in the case at bar.'[68] In reaching this conclusion, the Court, much like its predecessor in *Dolphin Delivery*, simply assumed that the state is not implicated in the distribution and maintenance of property entitlements in our society. Here, as there, one is expected to accept that such entitlements – and the whole regime of laws and institutions that helped create and preserve them – are prepolitical and not subject to *Charter* review. Thus the *Charter* guarantees personal security not to individuals who 'naturally' *lack* such entitlements, but only to individuals who 'naturally' *enjoy* such entitlements and who wish to resist government efforts to take them away or restrict their use.

Louise Gosselin represented individuals on one side of this line. George Zeliotis and Jacques Chaoulli represented those on the other.

Zeliotis was a retired businessman who had become frustrated with wait times in the Quebec health care system; Chaoulli was a physician who wished to provide private health care services to patients in the province. They both resented Quebec legislation that prevented individuals from purchasing private health insurance for core medical services provided through the public system. They maintained that this prohibition deprived Quebeckers of their rights to life and personal security in section 1 of the *Quebec Charter of Human Rights and Freedoms*, and to life and security of the person in section 7 of the Canadian *Charter*. A majority of the Supreme Court agreed, holding that the legislation violated one or both of these by denying those who had money timely access to medically necessary services.[69] In doing so, the majority rejected the holding of the trial judge and the claims of experts, governments, and public interest groups that allowing private health insurance would drain resources from and otherwise jeopardize the public Medicare system. The majority was equally unpersuaded by arguments that such a move would weaken public solidarity and commitment to Medicare and would promote social inequality by allowing more health care services to be allocated based on wealth rather than need.

The political message and meaning of *Gosselin* and *Chaoulli* become even clearer when these cases are considered together. Despite the *Charter*'s fine words, the social rights it confers do not speak to the security of all Canadians, nor to their actual equality. In *Charterland*, persons who lack property enjoy few meaningful social entitlements no matter how much suffering they endure. On the one hand, the *Charter* places no positive obligation on the state to provide them with the basic necessities of life; on the other hand, they have little to gain from the negative rights that the *Charter* confers on those with property to prevent the state from restricting that property's use for constitutionally protected ends. Thus while the *Charter* provides Louise Gosselin no right to call upon the state to provide her with food, clothing, or shelter, it provides her the right to purchase private health insurance in the marketplace – if only she had the money to do so. Like champagne and lobster tails, *Charter* rights are only valuable to those who can afford them.

Indeed, the situation facing disadvantaged Canadians is even worse than this. As cases such as *Trociuk* and *Chaoulli* demonstrate, the disadvantaged not only have little to gain in the way of social benefits from the *Charter*, but they also have much to lose. The reason, of course, is that rights are not commodities to be given away, but rather entitlements governing the relationships amongst individuals within a society. The extent to which the socially advantaged make gains in *Charter* rights, therefore, is often the same extent to which the socially disadvantaged incur losses in statutory rights, such as a mother's right to register the birth and name of her child or the right of poor Canadians to a universal system of public health care. Moreover, in the *Charter* scheme of things, constitutional rights are to be accorded presumptive priority over statutory rights. Once a *Charter* right is made out, the onus shifts to the state to satisfy a court based on convincing evidence that the statutory right is required in order to achieve an important social purpose. If the court is not satisfied, the *Charter* right prevails, regardless of how important or well established the statutory right is perceived to be. For those who take *Charter* rights seriously, there is no room for applying a precautionary principle, even in relation to a single-payer Medicare system that has been nurtured and cherished for almost forty years and upon which so many Canadians depend.

The Politics of Dialogue Theory

The decisions of the Court in *Chaoulli* and in the other three cases discussed above provide strong evidence that the political assessment of the *Charter* that I and other sceptics offered twenty years ago continues to hold true. The *Charter* today remains animated by a negative conception of rights and by a formal vision of equality that favours those with property and market power. Yet it is also true, as discussed previously, that judges can when they wish find ways to resist the *Charter*'s regressive tendencies, both by being strategic in deciding when to defer to legislative choices and by developing creative mechanisms to moderate the impact of the *Charter* within the limits allowed by liberal legalism. Thus while the incidence of poverty and the gap between rich and poor in this country have grown since the *Charter*'s inception,[70] it would seem far-fetched to suggest that the *Charter* has been a major contributor to these trends. The *Charter*'s greater influence has likely been to legitimize governments that have pursued regressive policies such as privatization, program cuts, and weakening progressive tax regimes, and to condition Canadians to accept such policies and their consequences as a legitimate feature of a 'free and democratic society.'

What is remarkable about *Chaoulli*, therefore, is not what it discloses about the politics of the *Charter*, but what it discloses about the politics of the Court, or at least of four of its members. By relying on the Canadian and Quebec *Charters* to pull down a key pillar of Medicare

– a program that lies at the heart of Canada's commitment to social justice – these judges displayed a degree of judicial activism that caught many legal scholars, including this one, by surprise. What accounts for this development? There are many possible factors, but one that should not be overlooked is the contribution of dialogue theory. I have already referred to the basic elements of this theory and its justification of judicial decision making based on the claim that, in the *Charter* interplay between courts and legislatures, it is the latter that usually get the final say. I have also noted that dialogue theorists concede that *Charter* decision making discloses no right answers and that they provide no normative vision to guide or constrain the *Charter* enterprise.

Dialogue theory has had a number of impacts on *Charter* decision making since it emerged in the academic literature and was embraced by the Court in the late 1990s. Most obviously, the theory has provided judges with a new, academically accredited justification for their decisions. And the beauty of the theory from a judicial point of view is that it can be used to justify virtually any decision that the courts choose to make. This, in turn, has allowed judges who have sought to moderate the *Charter*'s regressive tendencies to rely upon the theory to explain their use of creative remedies, such as extending underinclusive legislation rather than striking it down.[71] In this way, dialogue theory has helped courts appear more nuanced and progressive in their *Charter* decision making, thereby further enhancing the image and legitimacy of the *Charter* in the eyes of lawyers, scholars, and the community at large.

Another significant impact of dialogue theory on *Charter* decision making results from the reassurance it provides to judges that their judgments are transitory and that legislatures can remedy or reverse any problems that arise from their *Charter* decisions. I believe that this reassurance is misguided in that it underestimates the influence of courts and overestimates the capacity of governments.[72] In particular, it hugely discounts both the political force of *Charter* decisions and the constraints placed on governments by market forces and globalization. Misguided or not, however, it has encouraged judges to see their *Charter* role as that of advocates rather than arbiters, and their judgments as being missives directed at government rather than verdicts directed at society.[73]

By bolstering the *Charter*'s ostensible legitimacy, increasing public support for *Charter* decision making, and encouraging judges to perceive themselves as advocates rather than arbiters, dialogue theory has emboldened judges – including those who are prepared to give full expression to the *Charter*'s underlying ideology and regressive tendencies – to be more activist in their *Charter* decisions. This may not be what scholars who advanced the theory intended, but like those who ride to power on the back of a tiger, such scholars ought not to be surprised when they end up inside.[74] This metaphor is perhaps most aptly applied to dialogue theorists who support judicial activism. Kent Roach, for example, has characterized minimalist definitions of rights as unfortunate and has argued that dialogue theory, by freeing judges from the anxiety that they have the final say, gives them licence to 'err on the side of more robust approaches to judicial review.'[75] I suspect that the decision in *Chaoulli* does not represent the kind of 'robust approach' that Professor Roach had in mind. But since he provides no grounds for preferring one kind of judicial activism over another, he has no basis for protesting the fact that the majority in *Chaoulli* relied upon his views to support its decision.[76]

Other scholars have argued that dialogue theory militates in favour of judicial restraint. The leading proponent of this view is Patrick Monahan, who has maintained that the theory is best served by judges making 'minimalist rulings' that leave 'the greatest scope possible for potential responses by the legislative and executive branches.'[77] It might be argued that this version of dialogue theory, which was not referenced by the Court in *Chaoulli*, does not place its academic adherents on the back of the *Charter* tiger alongside their activist counterparts. This argument would have greater force were it not for the fact that Dean Monahan has recently voiced support – both as a scholar and as an advocate – for employing the *Charter* to challenge legislative restrictions on access to private health care.[78] By encouraging this degree of judicial activism, he has signalled that his earlier advocacy of 'minimalist rulings' can be either disregarded or reconciled with this result. Either way, it appears that he has avoided the back of the *Chaoulli* tiger only insofar as he has preferred to occupy its mouth.

Having helped cultivate the conditions for the Court's judgment in *Chaoulli*, it will be interesting to see what dialogue theorists, especially those who advocate judicial activism, have to say in response. Will they, for example, argue that the Court was not activist enough and that all would be well today if only the judges, instead of providing access to private health insurance, had ordered government to make improvements to the public health care system? This seems to be the position Professor Roach has advanced in the wake of *Chaoulli*;[79] however, it is a position that suffers from two major weaknesses. First, without a normative vision of rights to back them up, dialogue theorists offer no constitutional basis for preferring their remedy to the one embraced by the Court.[80] Second, it is a position that fails to account for the *Charter*'s underlying ideology. Activist dialogue theorists may place no constraints on judicial decision making, but liberal legalism and the institutional limits of courts most assuredly do. Thus while judges have been able to moderate the *Charter*'s regressive tendencies when it has suited their purpose, they have done so within an ideological paradigm and judicial structure that restricts their creative capacity. It is no coincidence therefore that most judges have balked at imposing major expenditures upon governments[81] or directing the delivery of government programs.[82] Such remedies smack too much of positive rights and political decision making for even dialogue-loving judges.[83]

Conclusion

In rising to new heights of judicial activism, the Supreme Court of Canada in *Chaoulli* has exposed the depths of the *Charter*'s regressive vision of rights. More disturbingly, it has embraced this vision to undermine a program that lies at the core of Canada's commitment to social justice, and it has done so at a time when that program is already under severe stress from the pressures exerted upon it by market forces and globalization. It is entirely possible, indeed likely, that the majority was acting out of the very best of intentions, perhaps believing that its decision would prod governments to address the deficiencies in the public health care system. But even judges ought to be mindful of where a road that is paved with good intentions can lead – particularly when it is a road that is strewn with hazards, and with which they have limited familiarity and navigational expertise. Thus while the majority may well have believed that its decision would help improve health care for Canadians, it is far more likely to have the opposite effect. By handing the imprimatur of constitutional rights to advocates of private medicine and two-tier health care, the Court has dealt a serious blow to the legitimacy of the single-payer model of health insurance as well as to the values of collective responsibility and social equality that this model seeks to uphold.

What can be done to counter this? As tempting as it might be to suggest that the notwithstanding clauses of the Quebec and Canadian *Charters*[84] should be invoked to overcome the decision in *Chaoulli* and to prevent future use of these documents to attack single-payer health insurance, I believe that the culture of constitutional rights that has built up in this country over the past many years, and the resulting pressures it has placed on the political process, make this unlikely. Moreover, the use of these clauses would leave the Court's rulings on rights unchallenged and could be construed by some as legislative acknowledgment of a *Charter* violation. In light of these considerations, a more productive strategy – albeit one that would also require a significant degree of political resolve – would be for the Quebec National Assembly to amend the *Quebec Charter* to stipulate that single-payer health insurance is consistent with its rights guarantees,[85] and for the federal government to put a reference question to the Supreme Court seeking a conclusive decision on the *Canadian Charter* issue.[86] The hope with respect to the reference would be that, with three new judges sitting on the Court,[87] at least two of these would concur with the three minority judges in *Chaoulli* to create a majority against there being a *Canadian Charter* violation.

I started this paper by referring to the views of judges on our health care system, and I will end it by doing the same. What follows are the words of a judge whose opinions were shaped not by a one-day judicial hearing consisting exclusively of lawyers' arguments, but rather by an eighteen-month commission in which he and other commissioners spoke with hundreds of people and received 1,500 submissions. The British Columbia Royal Commission on Health Care and Costs completed its work in November of 1991;[88] and here is what its chair, Justice Peter Seaton, had to say to the graduating class of the University of Victoria when he received an honorary degree in June of the following year:

> We Canadians take a lot for granted. I do not propose that we have a flag raising ceremony every morning. I do propose that we, as individuals, stop now and then and recognize what a decent society we live in. Professor Evans [a colleague on the Royal Commission] said of another society that, 'They do not mind throwing people overboard as long as they cannot hear the splash.' Most Canadians listen for the splash and they do care …
>
> The key is, we do not have one system for the rich and another for the poor. When people in authority are making decisions about health care, they are dealing with the health of themselves and their families. So long as that is the case, we will have a good system.
>
> If we move to a scheme in which those who can afford it have bet-

ter care, it will follow that those who have not got the money will get poorer care, and it will get poorer, and poorer. Those in charge will not be alarmed. It will be the health of 'other people' and 'other people's children' that is threatened ...[89]

Justice Seaton, sadly, is no longer with us. His views on health care, however, remain as relevant today as they ever were. As someone noted for his compassion and humility, he was a judge who understood that rights in a free and democratic society are best served when everyone has a stake in their protection, and that allowing those with money to buy their way out of collective responsibilities undermines the rights of all. Like most other Canadians, he listened for the splash. And I imagine that he would be saddened to learn that its sound has apparently been drowned out by *Charter* chatter in at least some chambers of the Supreme Court of Canada.

NOTES

1 *Chaoulli v. Quebec (A.G.)*, [2005] 1 S.C.R. 791 [*Chaoulli*].
2 Deschamps J. based her decision solely on the *Quebec Charter of Human Rights and Freedoms*. Her reasoning, however, is highly sympathetic to that of the three other majority judges, who found that the legislation also violated the *Canadian Charter of Rights and Freedoms*.
3 For discussion of these positions see Commission on the Future of Health Care in Canada, *Building on Values: The Future of Health Care in Canada – Final Report* (Saskatoon: Commission on the Future of Health Care in Canada, 2002) [Romanow Report].
4 *Ibid.*
5 Office of the Prime Minister, 'A 10-Year Plan to Strengthen Health Care' (16 September 2004), online: http://www.hc.-sc.ca/hcs-sss/delivery-prestation/fptcollab/2004-fmm-rpm/nr-cp_9_16_2-eng.php.
6 CBC News, 'Tommy Douglas crowned 'Greatest Canadian'' (30 November 2004), online: http://www.cbc.ca/arts/story/2004/11/29/TommyDouglasGreatestCanadian041129.html.
7 As cited in *Chaoulli, supra* note 1 at para. 242.
8 *Ibid.* at para. 138.
9 *Ibid.* at para. 85.
10 *Ibid.* at para. 140.

11 See *e.g. R. v. Edwards Books and Art Ltd.*, [1986] 2 S.C.R. 713; and *Irwin Toy v. Quebec (A.G.)*, [1989] 1 S.C.R. 927 [*Irwin Toy*].
12 See *e.g. Chaoulli v. Quebec (Attorney General)*, (Factum of the Charter Committee on Poverty Issues and the Canadian Health Coalition, Intervener, at para. 48), online: http://www.healthcoalition.ca/chaoulli-factum.pdf [Coalition & CCPI Factum].
13 *Chaoulli, supra* note 1 at para. 128.
14 B. McLachlin, 'The Charter: A New Role for the Judiciary?' (1991) 29 Alta. L. Rev. 540 at 545–7.
15 Coalition & CCPI Factum, *supra* note 12 at para. 48.
16 See *e.g.* Editorial: 'Medicare Ruling a Wake-Up Call,' *Toronto Star* (10 June 2005), A26; and comments by Health Minister Ujjal Dosanjh, as cited in Cristin Schmitz, 'Ruling may reshape Medicare: But gov't insists system won't be undermined,' *The StarPhoenix* (10 June 2005), B7.
17 Government of Canada, 'New Federal Investments on Health Commitments on 10-Year Actiomn Plan on Health' (16 September 2004), http://www.hc-sc.gc.ca/hca-sss/delivery-prestation/fptcollab/2004-fmm-rpm/bg-fi_inv-eng.php.
18 10-Year Plan, *supra* note 5.
19 Anyone who doubts the political significance of this decision need only consult Dr Chaoulli's speech at a Heritage Lecture in the United States: J. Chaoulli, 'A Victory for Freedom: The Canadian Supreme Court's Ruling on Private Health Care' (22 July 2005), online: http://www.heritage.org/Research/HealthCare/hl892.cfm. The judgment also influenced the Canadian Medical Association's endorsement of private-sector health services: see T. Lemmens & T. Archibald, 'The CMA's *Chaoulli* Motion and the Myth of Promoting Fair Access to Health Care,' in C.M. Flood, K. Roach, & L. Sossin, eds., *Access to Care, Access to Justice: The Legal Debate over Private Health Insurance in Canada* (Toronto: University of Toronto Press, 2005) at 323.
20 Romanow Report, *supra* note 3 at 242.
21 See T. Epps & D. Schneiderman, 'Opening Medicare to Our Neighbours or Closing the Door on a Public System? International Trade Law Implications of *Chaoulli v. Quebec*,' in C.M. Flood, K. Roach, & L. Sossin, eds., *Access to Care, Access to Justice: The Legal Debate over Private Health Insurance in Canada* (Toronto: University of Toronto Press, 2005) at 369.
22 This view was expressed in different forms by scholars such as Allan Hutchinson, Judy Fudge, Joel Bakan, Harry Glasbeek, and Michael Mandel, though the variant set out here derives from my own writings.

23 *Dolphin Delivery Ltd. v. Retail, Wholesale and Department Store Union, Local 580*, [1986] 2 S.C.R. 573 at 600 [*Dolphin Delivery*].

24 For a discussion of the democratic shortcomings of these arms of the state, see ch. 7, 'Look Who's Talking Now: Dialogue Theory and the Return to Democracy.'

25 Ch. 4, 'Canada's *Charter* Flight: Soaring Backwards into the Future' at 103.

26 *Ibid*. at 104.

27 *Ibid*.

28 *Ibid*. at 110.

29 See *e.g*. D. Schmeiser, 'Disadvantages of an Entrenched Canadian Bill of Rights' (1968) 33 Sask. L. Rev. 249; D. Smiley, 'The Case against the Canadian Charter of Human Rights' (1969) 2 Can. J. Pol. Sc. 277; R.A. Macdonald, 'Postscript and Prelude: The Jurisprudence of the Charter: Eight Theses' (1982) 4 Sup. Ct. L. Rev. 321; and P. Russell, 'The Political Purposes of the Canadian Charter of Rights and Freedoms' (1983) 61 Can. Bar Rev. 30.

30 J.A.G. Griffith, *The Politics of the Judiciary* (Manchester: Manchester University Press, 1977).

31 J.H. Ely, *Democracy and Distrust: A Theory of Judicial Review* (Cambridge, MA: Harvard University Press, 1980) at 59.

32 *Ibid*. (original emphasis).

33 *Dolphin Delivery, supra* note 23.

34 See *e.g*. D. Beatty, 'Constitutional Conceits: The Coercive Authority of Courts' (1987) 37 U.T.L.J. 83.

35 See *e.g*. ch. 3, 'Private Rights/Public Wrongs: The Liberal Lie of the *Charter*.'

36 See *e.g*. *Irwin Toy, supra* note 11.

37 See *e.g*. *R. v. Turpin*, [1989] 1 S.C.R. 1296 [*Turpin*].

38 See *e.g*. *R. v. Sharpe*, [2001] 1 S.C.R. 45 [*Sharpe*]. The Court's approach in such cases is discussed at length in S. Choudhry, 'Worse Than *Lochner*?' in C.M. Flood, K. Roach, & L. Sossin, eds., *Access to Care, Access to Justice: The Legal Debate over Private Health Insurance in Canada* (Toronto: University of Toronto Press, 2005) at 75.

39 *R. v. Morgentaler*, [1988] 1 S.C.R. 30.

40 *M. v. H.*, [1999] 2 S.C.R. 3 [*M. v. H.*].

41 See *e.g*. *Eldridge v. British Columbia (Attorney General)*, [1997] 3 S.C.R. 624.

42 This strategy was adopted in *Vriend v. Alberta*, [1998] 1 S.C.R. 493 [*Vriend*], where the Court extended prohibitions on discrimination in Alberta human rights legislation to include discrimination on the basis of sexual orientation, rather than declare such prohibitions constitutionally invalid.

43 In *Dunmore v. Ontario (Attorney General)*, [2001] 3 S.C.R. 1016 [*Dunmore*], for example, the Court found that legislation excluding agricultural workers from Ontario's labour relations regime violated their freedom of association, though the Court made it clear that the *Charter* did not require them to be provided the same protection afforded to other workers.

44 See *e.g. Pepsi-Cola Canada Beverages (West) Ltd. v. R.W.D.S.U., Local 558*, [2002] 1 S.C.R. 156 [*Pepsi-Cola*].

45 One possible exception is *Dunmore, supra* note 43, in which the Court held that government had a positive obligation to reinstate some measure of legislative protection for agricultural workers. Even here, however, the degree of protection required by the Court appears to have been more symbolic than real.

46 See *e.g. Irwin Toy, supra* note 11.

47 See *e.g. RJR-MacDonald Inc. v. Canada (Attorney General)*, [1995] 3 S.C.R. 199.

48 See *e.g. Sharpe, supra* note 38.

49 See *e.g. Thomson Newspapers Co. v. Canada*, [1998] 1 S.C.R. 877.

50 See *e.g. M. v. H., supra* note 40.

51 See *e.g. Egan v. Canada*, [1995] 2 S.C.R. 513.

52 See *e.g. Turpin, supra* note 37.

53 See *e.g. Law v. Canada*, [1999] 1 S.C.R. 497.

54 See *e.g. Nova Scotia (Workers' Compensation Board) v. Martin; Nova Scotia (Workers' Compensation Board) v. Laseur*, [2003] 2 S.C.R. 504.

55 See *e.g. Schachter v. Canada*, [1992] 2 S.C.R. 679.

56 See *e.g. Dunmore, supra* note 43.

57 See *e.g. Newfoundland (Treasury Board) v. Newfoundland and Labrador Assn. of Public Employees (N.A.P.E.)*, [2004] 3 S.C.R. 381 [*Newfoundland Pay Equity*].

58 See *e.g. Pepsi-Cola, supra* note 44.

59 See *e.g. Hill v. Church of Scientology of Toronto*, [1995] 2 S.C.R. 1130.

60 See *e.g.* P.W. Hogg & A.A. Bushell, 'The *Charter* Dialogue between Courts and Legislatures (or Perhaps the *Charter of Rights* Isn't Such a Bad Thing After All)' (1997) 35 Osgoode Hall L.J. 75; and K. Roach, *The Supreme Court on Trial: Judicial Activism or Democratic Dialogue* (Toronto: Irwin Law, 2001).

61 Ch. 6, 'Rip Van Winkle in *Charterland.*'

62 Professor Roach concedes as much when he states that 'dialogue is not a theory of judicial review that will tell judges how to decide hard cases,' and then seeks to justify the judicial role in *Charter* dialogues by reference to a 'legal process tradition' that is no less devoid of normative content: K. Roach, 'Dialogic Judicial Review and Its Critics' (2004) 23 Sup. Ct. L. Rev. 49.

63 The past five years have seen the departure of Justices Arbour, Iacobucci, Gonthier, L'Heureux-Dubé, and Cory, and the arrival of Justices LeBel,

Deschamps, Fish, Abella, and Charron, though the latter two were not appointed until after *Chaoulli* was heard and thus did not take part in *Chaoulli* or the other three decisions discussed in this section. (After this essay was written, Justices Major and Bastarache also left the Court and were replaced by Justices Rothstein and Cromwell.)

64 [2002] 4 S.C.R. 429 [*Gosselin*].

65 [2003] 1 S.C.R. 835 [*Trociuk*].

66 [2004] 3 S.C.R. 657 [*Auton*].

67 See B.L. Berger, 'Using the Charter to Cure Health Care: Panacea or Placebo?' (2003) 8 Rev. Const. Stud. 20.

68 *Gosselin, supra* note 64 at para. 81.

69 Deschamps J. on the basis of the Quebec *Charter*, and three other judges on the basis of the Quebec and Canadian *Charters*.

70 K. Scott & R. Lessard, 'The Social Determinants of Health: Income Inequality as a Determinant of Health' (summary of presentations, November 2002), online: http://www.phac-aspc.gc.ca/ph-sp/oi-ar/02_income-eng.php.

71 See *e.g. Vriend, supra* note 42.

72 Ch. 6, 'Rip Van Winkle in *Charterland*.'

73 One prominent dialogue theorist, for example, refers to the courts' involvement in *Charter* dialogues as 'contributions to political debates, and not judicial supremacy': Roach, 'Dialogic Judicial Review,' *supra* note 62 at 52.

74 This allusion is borrowed from President Kennedy: J.F. Kennedy, 'Inaugural Address' (20 January 1961).

75 Roach, 'Dialogic Judicial Review,' *supra* note 62 at 72. It is worth noting, however, that in the wake of *Chaoulli*, Professor Roach now allows that constitutional minimalism may not be such a bad thing after all in relation to section 7 cases: K. Roach, 'The Courts and Medicare: Too Much or Too Little Judicial Activism,' in C.M. Flood, K. Roach, & L. Sossin, eds., *Access to Care, Access to Justice* (Toronto: University of Toronto Press, 2005) 184 at 189–90.

76 *Chaoulli, supra* note 1 at para. 89, citing Roach, *ibid.* It is more than a little ironic that the passage the Court quotes comes from a section of this article in which Professor Roach is trying to counter arguments that his justification of dialogue theory lacks normative foundation.

77 P. Monahan, 'The Supreme Court of Canada in the 21st Century' (2001) 80 Can. Bar Rev. 374 at 392.

78 See S.H. Hartt & P. Monahan, 'The Charter and Health Care: Guaranteeing Timely Access to Health Care for Canadians,' C.D. Howe Institute, Commentary, no. 164 (May 2002). Dean Monahan also served as counsel for Senator Kirby *et al.* in the *Chaoulli* case.

79 Roach, 'The Courts and Medicare,' *supra* note 75.

80 There was no clearer evidence of this than the fact that the majority in *Chaoulli* relied on Professor Roach's characterization of the judicial role within his version of dialogue theory to support its decision: *Chaoulli, supra* note 1 at para. 89.

81 See *e.g. Newfoundland Pay Equity, supra* note 57.

82 See *e.g. Auton, supra* note 66.

83 Professor Roach comes close to conceding this point in his response to *Chaoulli* when he acknowledges that '[c]ourts may be reluctant to issue more complex remedies that attempt to achieve systemic reforms of the public system even though such remedies may be necessary to ensure that the promise of *Chaoulli* is realized for all Canadians': Roach, 'The Courts and Medicare,' *supra* note 75 at 185.

84 *Quebec Charter of Human Rights and Freedoms,* R.S.Q. c. C-12, s. 52; *Charter of Rights and Freedoms,* s. 33.

85 I am indebted to Martha Jackman for this suggestion.

86 Given that Justice Deschamps based her decision solely on the *Quebec Charter*, the obvious rationale for a reference would be to end the legal uncertainty created by the 3–3 split on the *Canadian Charter* issue.

87 Justices Abella and Charron and the replacement for Justice Major, who will retire later this year. (After this essay was written, Justice Rothstein was appointed to replace Justice Major and Justice Cromwell was appointed to replace Justice Bastarache.)

88 British Columbia Royal Commission on Health Care and Costs, *Closer to Home: The Report of the British Columbia Royal Commission on Health Care and Costs* (Victoria: Crown Publications, 1991).

89 From an unpublished address to the graduating class of 1992 by the late Justice Peter Seaton, excerpted in a letter to the editor by my colleague, Hamar Foster, in *The Advocate* 63, no. 5 (2005): 772–3.

9 Taking Dialogue Theory Much Too Seriously (or Perhaps *Charter* Dialogue Isn't Such a Good Thing After All)[*]

Introduction

In their influential 1997 article 'The *Charter* Dialogue between Courts and Legislatures (or Perhaps the *Charter of Rights* Isn't Such a Bad Thing After All),'[1] Peter Hogg and Allison Bushell maintained that certain structural features of the *Canadian Charter of Rights and Freedoms* give legislatures the capacity to respond to court decisions that invalidate laws by enacting modified laws accomplishing the same legislative objectives. According to the authors, this capacity 'greatly diminished' any concern about the legitimacy of judicial review because it showed that *Charter* decisions are not a major obstacle to democratic decision making.[2] They argued that this diminished concern was justified despite the high degree of discretion exercised by courts in interpreting the *Charter*, which they acknowledged 'inevitably remakes the constitution into the likeness favoured by the judges.'[3]

My initial response to this thesis was mixed.[4] On the one hand, I applauded the authors' acknowledgment of the subjective nature of *Charter* decision making and, in light of this, their willingness to reject traditional defences of judicial review based upon the rule of law. I also welcomed their use of democracy as the yardstick of constitutional legitimacy, their acceptance of legislative engagement on rights issues, and their support for legislative supremacy in relation to matters of social and economic policy. Finally, I saw some benefit in the thesis's potential to encourage judges to lessen their attachment to liberal legal-

* Originally published in (2007) 45 Osgoode Hall L.J. 147–67. Copyright © 2007 by Andrew Petter.

ism and to edge away from the regressive assumptions that animated *Charter* jurisprudence in the 1980s.

Other aspects of the thesis, however, I found problematic. First, I observed that the thesis was devoid of normative content and that it exerted no moral claim to support or guide the involvement of judges in *Charter* decision making. It applied to any and all *Charter* interpretations, offering reassurance on the basis that, no matter what judges decided, legislatures could find ways to reassert their policy objectives. For this reason, I argued that the thesis at best mitigated, rather than legitimated, the courts' role under the *Charter*. Second, I maintained that the thesis seriously underestimated the extent to which judicial decision making under the *Charter* influences public policy in Canada. This it did by: discounting the privileged position that courts occupy in *Charter* dialogues; treating all legislative responses to court decisions alike, without regard to the extent to which those responses maintained the legislatures' policy objectives; and ignoring the extent to which judicial interpretations of *Charter* rights permeate public discourse, drive policy decisions, and influence every aspect of political life. Finally, I saw disturbing implications for democracy in the fact that Canadian constitutional scholars had no difficulty advancing a thesis that both acknowledged the political nature of judicial review and defended its legitimacy.

I was not alone in pointing out problems and deficiencies in the arguments concerning *Charter* dialogue presented by Hogg and Bushell.[5] Not surprisingly, however, these shortcomings did not discourage the courts and some *Charter* enthusiasts from embracing a thesis that purported to legitimize the role of judges while placing no constraints on their decision-making authority.[6] As a consequence, what might properly have been regarded as a modest case for moderating concerns about the undemocratic effects of *Charter* decisions has been invoked by judges and scholars over the past decade as though it represented a fully fledged theory of judicial review. Moreover, while the thesis advanced by Hogg and Bushell in 1997 implicitly spoke to the desirability of judges showing deference to the policy-making role of legislatures, the thesis has since been harnessed by some courts and commentators to justify more, not less, judicial activism.[7]

Hogg, Bushell Thornton, and a new co-author recently returned to the dialogue debate with '*Charter* Dialogue Revisited – or "Much Ado about Metaphors."'[8] They might have used this opportunity to reiterate the limitations of their original thesis, to correct its deficiencies, and to repudiate its misapplication by courts and scholars. Unfortunately, they have for the most part gone in the opposite direction, abandoning some of the limitations of their original thesis, adding to its deficiencies, and encouraging its judicial and academic misuse. In short, like so many others, they have fallen prey to the temptation to take dialogue theory much too seriously.

In this response, I do not propose to replicate the criticisms of dialogue theory that I have advanced previously. Instead I intend to focus on two propositions that are central to the revised thesis presented by the authors:

1 That structural features of the *Charter* – particularly the reasonable limits clause found in section 1 – result in a weaker form of judicial review providing legislatures broader scope to pursue their policy objectives than would otherwise be the case; and,
2 That the capacity of legislatures to respond to court decisions under the *Charter*, while not justifying judicial review, significantly diminishes concerns about the legitimacy of judicial review.

I contend that neither of these propositions is sustainable.

A Weaker Form of Judicial Review (or Not)

The thesis presented by Hogg and Bushell in 1997 was predicated on the claim that Canada has a weaker form of judicial review than is thought to exist in the United States, where 'the anti-majoritarian objection to judicial review could not be ignored.'[9] The reason for this, according to the authors, is that the *Charter* contains features that enable legislatures to respond to court decisions invalidating legislation and thereby continue to pursue their policy objectives, albeit in different ways. The authors identified four such features, the most significant of which is the reasonable limits clause in section 1. They supported this claim by identifying sixty-six *Charter* cases in which a law had been held to be invalid by the Supreme Court of Canada or lower courts and by showing that 80 per cent of these cases had triggered some legislative response.[10] They held this data out as evidence of dialogue and as support for their claim that the *Charter* had established a weaker form of judicial review.

In their most recent article, Hogg and his co-authors, Allison A. Bushell Thornton and Wade K. Wright ('the authors'), reassert this claim in succinct and definitive terms:

In 1997, the literature on judicial review was predominantly American, and the Canadian contributions naturally drew inspiration from the American literature. Most Canadian writers assumed a 'strong form' of judicial review, under which courts usually have the last word. Our study made clear that in Canada we had a weaker form of judicial review that rarely had the effect of actually defeating the purpose of the legislative body.[11]

They also update their data to show that, of the twenty-three Supreme Court cases decided since their 1997 article in which a law was held to be invalid under the *Charter*, 61 per cent elicited some legislative response.[12]

How persuasive is the authors' claim that this level of legislative response is evidence that section 1 and other *Charter* features have produced a weaker form of judicial review in Canada? The answer, sadly, is that it is not at all persuasive. There are various reasons for this, chief amongst which are: (1) their focus on quantitative rather than qualitative analysis of *Charter* decisions and legislative responses; (2) their inattention to the extent and nature of constitutional dialogues in the United States; and (3) their failure to consider the significance of legislatures' lack of use of the override clause in section 33.

(1) The Importance of Qualitative Analysis

Let us turn first to the authors' focus on quantitative rather than qualitative analysis of *Charter* decisions and legislative responses. According to the authors, any legislative response to a *Charter* decision invalidating a law is evidence of dialogue. Thus their count of legislative responses over the two periods they surveyed includes eight cases in which the legislature simply repealed the laws found to be unconstitutional by the courts, and several others in which the legislature 'merely implemented the changes the reviewing court had suggested.'[13] These cases were included, they said, because it would cast the notion of dialogue 'too narrowly to discount those remedial measures that have merely followed the directions of the court, either by repealing or amending an unconstitutional law.'[14] Whether or not one finds this explanation convincing, what it reveals is that the presence of *Charter* dialogue, as defined by the authors, is no indication of the strength of judicial review. Such strength can be measured only by attending to the nature as well as the number of legislative responses.

To demonstrate this point, consider a situation in which every *Char-*

ter decision declaring a law to be invalid resulted only in a subsequent repeal of that law or other amendment required by the court. Under Hogg and Bushell's definition of dialogue, this situation would constitute a 100 per cent rate of dialogue. Yet by no stretch of the imagination could it be said that this situation provided evidence of a weak form of judicial review. On the contrary, the fact that legislatures in this example gave effect to the judgments of the court in each and every case would suggest an incredibly strong and effective form of judicial review.

There is, in other words, nothing remarkable or revealing about the fact that legislatures respond to judicial decisions that strike down laws. Indeed, given that legislative responses are often required in order to give effect to such decisions, and to accommodate their impacts upon other aspects of legislative schemes, it would be more remarkable if legislatures did *not* respond. In assessing the strength of judicial review, therefore, it is necessary to consider the degree to which *Charter* rulings that strike down laws enable legislatures to achieve their original policy objectives. The only way this can be assessed is through a comprehensive qualitative analysis of the cases – one that evaluates the substance of the court rulings, their impact upon the legislatures' policy objectives, and the extent to which legislative responses were successful in overcoming, as opposed to accommodating, these impacts. Qualitative analysis is also required in order to identify the secondary impacts of judicial decisions upon legislative policy, as well as the extent to which *Charter* decisions may affect other government policies and future policy making.

The value of qualitative analysis is well illustrated by examining the Supreme Court of Canada's decision in *Schachter v. Canada*.[15] The Court in that case confirmed a ruling of the Federal Court that it was a contravention of the guarantee of equality in section 15(1) of the *Charter* to deny biological parents access to benefits that were available to adoptive parents under the *Unemployment Insurance Act*.[16] This left Parliament with a choice: either increase benefits for biological parents, or decrease them for adoptive parents. Parliament's response, tabled in 1989 as part of Bill C-21 following the Federal Court's decision and enacted in 1990, was a bit of both, making such benefits available to all parents for ten weeks, rather than for the fifteen weeks that adoptive parents had previously enjoyed.[17] Hogg and Bushell chalk this up as another example of *Charter* dialogue, noting that '[s]ection 15(1) leaves room for different legislative choices of this kind, such that democratically elected bodies are still ultimately responsible for setting their own budgetary priorities, albeit in a way that does not discriminate against disadvantaged groups.'[18] This rosy assessment discounts the extent to which Parliament's response to *Schachter* required it to deviate from its original policy objectives, both by reducing the duration of benefits made available to adoptive parents and by giving biological parents access to benefits that it had not previously provided them.[19] This response represented a major alteration in the statutory scheme; it also required a substantial expenditure of funds that had not previously been authorized by Parliament.[20]

Yet these are only the direct consequences of the decision. In the zero-sum world of public finance, the \$500 million in new costs imposed upon the Unemployment Insurance (UI) program as a result of this response and Parliament's response to *Tétrault-Gadoury v. Canada*[21] – in which the Court ordered that UI benefits be extended to those who are sixty-five years of age and older – impelled the government to seek further savings within the UI system.[22] Such savings were achieved through additional legislative amendments that increased the number of work weeks required to qualify for UI benefits, reduced the number of weeks for which UI benefits were provided, and toughened the penalties for workers who left their jobs without cause, who refused a suitable job, or who were dismissed for misconduct.[23] These amendments resulted in at least 30,000 people losing UI benefits, with female, immigrant, elderly, and disabled workers being the hardest hit.[24] These are not minor policy consequences. On the contrary, they are changes that influenced and continue to influence the lives of thousands of Canadians.

What this qualitative analysis reveals – and what quantitative analysis cannot – are the significant first- and second-order impacts that *Schachter* and *Tétrault-Gadoury* had upon public policy in Canada. Moreover, it is safe to assume that their impacts were even more far-reaching than this, as governments across Canada reviewed and revised other statutory schemes in light of these rulings, and incorporated these rulings into their analyses of new legislative initiatives.[25] Yet the authors minimize the importance of such qualitative analysis. While they refer to the substance of some judicial decisions and statutory sequels to illustrate their argument, they insist that all legislative responses, regardless of whether they accommodate or overcome court rulings, are evidence of dialogue.[26] To the same effect, they maintain that judicial review can be characterized as 'weak' even though it exerts 'considerable judicial influence on the legislative process';[27] and they dismiss suggestions that resulting policy distortions raise serious questions concerning the legitimacy of that influence.

The dialogue thesis advanced by the authors relies upon quantitative rather than qualitative analysis of *Charter* cases to measure their impact on legislative policy, even while qualitative analysis of *Charter* cases abounds in Canadian constitutional scholarship. One of Canada's leading constitutional scholars, for example, has drawn upon his extensive qualitative analysis of *Charter* cases (albeit focused more on judicial decisions than on legislative responses) to reach the following conclusion concerning the impact of section 1:

> During the public debate that preceded the adoption of the *Charter*, there was controversy about the desirability of a limitation clause, the conventional view being that the clause 'weakened' the *Charter*. But s. 1 has probably had the effect of strengthening the guaranteed rights. [Section 1] has been interpreted as imposing stringent requirements of justification. Those requirements may be more difficult for the government to discharge than the requirements that would have been imposed by the courts in the absence of a limitation clause.[28]

This assessment challenges a central tenet of the dialogue thesis presented by the authors, namely, that section 1 of the *Charter* has resulted in a weaker form of judicial review. Yet nowhere do they mention this assessment, let alone answer it. This omission is extraordinary given that the constitutional scholar whose qualitative analysis led to this contrary view is none other than Peter Hogg, in a passage penned in 1992 and repeated in the 2006 edition of his constitutional law treatise.[29]

So which Peter Hogg are we to believe? Is it the Peter Hogg who argued in '*Charter* Dialogue' and '*Charter* Dialogue Revisited' that section 1 weakened judicial review under the *Charter*? Or is it the Peter Hogg who argued in his book, *Constitutional Law of Canada*, that section 1 probably strengthened judicial review under the *Charter*? It is difficult to say. What one can say, however, is that the qualitative analysis of the cases engaged in by the latter Peter Hogg provides a stronger basis on which to make such an assessment than the predominantly quantitative analysis of the cases employed by the former Peter Hogg.[30]

(2) Lessons on Dialogue from the United States

Even if one were to accept the flawed proposition that *Charter* dialogues, as defined by Hogg and Bushell, provide evidence of a weaker form of judicial review, this would not justify the conclusion that Canadian judicial review is so weak that it can escape the legitimacy debate that they acknowledge 'could not be ignored' in the United States.[31] To support this conclusion, one would need to examine the extent to which legislatures in the United States have been able to respond to constitutional rulings in which laws were struck down by courts. It is true that the United States Constitution does not contain an express limitation clause like section 1 of the *Charter*; but as Hogg acknowledges in the above passage from his treatise, the absence of such a clause does not prevent the courts from routinely reading limitations into the constitutional rights themselves. Indeed, as Hogg also points out in his treatise, the proportionality test adopted by the Supreme Court of Canada in *R. v. Oakes*[32] to give meaning to section 1 of the *Charter* 'bears striking similarities' to the test articulated six years earlier in relation to commercial expression by the United States Supreme Court.[33] Nor is the use of such 'means–ends' tests rare in American jurisprudence. On the contrary, judicial scrutiny of means–ends relationships 'may well be the most frequently invoked technique in the judicial review of the validity of federal and state legislation.'[34]

In order to sustain the argument that Canadian judicial review is significantly weaker than its American counterpart, therefore, serious attention must be given to the existence of constitutional dialogues in the United States. Incredibly, beyond a footnote in their first article referring to 'conceptions of "dialogue"' in the American literature,[35] the authors neglect to do this.[36] This is made even more remarkable by the fact that dialogue was identified as a 'central motif' in American constitutional scholarship well before the concept was introduced into the Canadian constitutional lexicon.[37] The following characterization of judicial review in the United States, taken from Barry Friedman's 1993 essay 'Dialogue and Judicial Review,' could just as easily have come from Hogg and Bushell's article on the Canadian *Charter* published four years later:

> I call the process of judicial review that actually occurs in the workaday world *dialogue*. The term emphasizes that judicial review is significantly more interdependent and interactive than generally described. The Constitution is not interpreted by aloof judges imposing their will on the people. Rather, constitutional interpretation is an elaborate discussion between judges and the body politic.[38]

Similar views have been voiced by members of the American judiciary, as in this excerpt from a speech delivered in 1993 by Justice Ruth Bader Ginsburg: '[J]udges play an interdependent part in our democracy. They do not alone shape legal doctrine but ... they participate in a dialogue with other organs of government, and with the people as well.'[39]

What conclusions can be drawn from the American scholarship concerning constitutional dialogue? Above all, such scholarship provides strong support for the view – acknowledged by Hogg in his treatise but overlooked in these articles on dialogue – that the existence or absence of an express limitation clause does not determine the extent to which judicial decisions are influential or conclusive. The United States Supreme Court has developed what Harry H. Wellington has referred to as 'a whole family of procedural or structural doctrines' that allow the Court to say to other governmental entities: 'You may be able to achieve the substantive result you desire, but you must proceed toward your objective in a different fashion from the one you have used.'[40]

The extent and impact of such structural doctrines have been exhaustively examined in Dan Coenen's recent study, 'A Constitution of Collaboration: Protecting Fundamental Values with Second-Look Rules of Interbranch Dialogue.'[41] Coenen documents nine structural doctrines (many with multiple subcategories) through which the United States Supreme Court 'initiates a dialogue with and among non-judicial actors, often deferring to decisions of political branches on how to resolve constitutional issues, so long as those decisions bear the earmarks of deliberation and care.'[42] He also identifies three 'quasi-structural rules' and four 'quasi-structural tools' that facilitate interbranch dialogue. Coenen's study shows such doctrines to be so pervasive that, based on its findings, Mark Tushnet has questioned whether the United States 'could get along quite well with subconstitutional doctrine and no substantive judicial review.'[43]

In sum, there is strong evidence in the United States, as in Canada, that constitutional decision making by the courts frequently produces 'dialogues' with other branches of government. Indeed, the structural and quasi-structural devices that Coenen identifies as facilitating dialogue in the United States are more numerous than the *Charter* devices identified by the authors. This does not mean that constitutional dialogues occur more frequently in the United States (though there is no reason to assume that they do not, particularly if the definition of dialogue includes legislative responses acquiescing to court decisions). What it *does* mean is that if the authors wish to make the case that Canada enjoys a weaker form of judicial review, they need to undertake a comprehensive qualitative assessment of judicial decisions and legislative responses in both countries.

Another point that emerges clearly in the American literature is the importance of distinguishing amongst opportunities for dialogue on the basis that some pose more serious obstacles than others for the attainment of governmental objectives.[44] Unlike the authors, American scholars accept that assessing the significance of dialogues requires one to attend to the nature, as well as the frequency, of legislative responses, the influence of the courts in shaping those responses, and the degree to which such responses involve policy compromises and deviations from legislative goals. As a result, American scholars are not prone to speaking of constitutional dialogues as answering anti-majoritarian criticisms of judicial review. Rather, they understand that, while the existence of such dialogues may influence debates over the legitimacy of judicial review, it in no way resolves them.[45]

(3) The Significance of the Insignificance of Section 33

One feature of the Canadian *Charter* that has no explicit or implicit counterpart in the United States Constitution is section 33, which allows legislatures to override *Charter* decisions by including a notwithstanding clause in statutes. The authors refer to section 33 as one of the structural features of the *Charter* that enables dialogue, and they invoke it to support their claim that legislatures have the last word even where a legislative objective is held to be unconstitutional. However, the section does not feature prominently in their analysis. The reason they give is that the section in practice 'has become relatively unimportant, because of the development of a political climate of resistance to its use.'[46]

I agree that the political climate in Canada has rendered the use of section 33 insignificant. However, this is not true of its non-use. The relative strength or weakness of judicial review, after all, is a function of political as well as textual opportunities and constraints. Like Sherlock Holmes's famous clue of the dog that did not bark,[47] the failure of legislatures to invoke section 33 speaks volumes. Given that section 33 was part of the original *Charter* bargain, the degree of political resistance that has built up to its use provides a powerful indicator of the dominance of legalism over democracy in the realm of *Charter* decision making.[48] Thus while legislatures have *de jure* powers to override courts under section 33, the political inability of legislatures to exercise such powers gives courts *de facto* final say over the constitutional acceptability of legislative objectives. Moreover the existence of section 33 allows courts to claim that their decisions are reversible and therefore have democratic as well as legal legitimacy.[49] This situation nicely illustrates the extent to which the *Charter* privileges judicially defined norms and places pressure on legislatures to accede to such norms even when they are legally empowered to resist them. In this way, it further calls into question the degree of influence attributed to legislatures by the authors.

Far from supporting the claim that Canada has a weaker form of judicial review, therefore, section 33 provides further grounds for doubting this proposition. Yet all of this seems lost on the authors, who are happy to point to section 33 as a device supporting dialogue when it helps bolster their thesis, while acknowledging that it is of little practical importance when it does not.

A Legitimate Form of Judicial Review (or Not)

The arguments marshalled by the authors to support their claim that the *Charter* establishes a weaker form of judicial review have not changed significantly from those presented in 1997. The same cannot be said, however, of their arguments in favour of the *Charter*'s legitimacy. Hogg and Bushell began their first article by expressing a high degree of scepticism about traditional justifications for judicial review:

> The view that the *Charter* is a 'bad thing' is commonly based on an objection to the legitimacy of judicial review in a democratic society. Under the *Charter*, judges, who are neither elected to their offices nor accountable for their actions, are vested with the power to strike down laws that have been made by the duly elected representatives of the people.
>
> The conventional answer to this objection is that all of the institutions of our society must abide by the rule of law, and judicial review simply requires obedience by legislative bodies to the law of the constitution. However, there is something a bit hollow and unsatisfactory in that answer. The fact is that the law of the constitution is for the most part couched in broad, vague language that rarely speaks definitively to the cases that come before the courts. Accordingly, judges have a great deal of discretion in 'interpreting' the law of the constitution, and the process of interpretation inevitably remakes the constitution into the likeness favoured by the judges. This problem has been captured in a famous American aphorism: 'We are under a Constitution, but the Constitution is what the judges say it is.'[50]

It was against this premise of judges exercising discretion in a manner that reflects their own likenesses that Hogg and Bushell first presented their case for dialogue. They supported their claim that the *Charter* was 'not such a bad thing after all' not by contending that there was a satisfactory justification for the powers given to courts to decide *Charter* cases (they suggested the opposite), but rather by contending that such powers could be overcome through the capacity of legislatures to respond to judicial decisions. Indeed, they were so confident of this legislative capacity that they were emboldened to say that 'the critique of the *Charter* based on democratic legitimacy cannot be sustained.'[51]

Even this overblown statement, from which they quickly retreated,[52] cannot disguise the fact that Hogg and Bushell's original thesis had more to do with mitigating than legitimating the role of the courts under the *Charter*. It was the asserted inability of judicial decisions to undermine legislative democracy that, in their eyes, made the *Charter* 'not so bad.'[53] In other words, judicial review is more acceptable when it is less effective; and by implication, judicial deference is to be favoured so that courts can, as Patrick Monahan puts it, 'create the space needed to permit such dialogue to occur.'[54] It came as no surprise, therefore, when Hogg subsequently argued that courts should accord even greater deference to legislatures that re-enact laws previously struck down by the courts.[55] Based on this understanding of Hogg and Bushell's analysis, and its failure to provide a moral claim to support or guide judges' involvement in *Charter* decision making, I maintained that their thesis did not amount to a justification for judicial review. On the contrary, by celebrating the fact that court decisions under the *Charter* are ultimately less influential than is sometimes supposed, it called into question why courts should be allowed to make such decisions in the first place.[56]

In '*Charter* Dialogue Revisited,' the authors concede the point that 'dialogue theory does not provide a justification for judicial review.'[57] At the same time, they abandon the premise of the 1997 article that the subjective nature of *Charter* interpretation renders conventional theories of judicial review 'hollow and unsatisfactory.'[58] Instead they embrace such theories with the zeal of converts, arguing that judicial review is justified on moral, political, and legal grounds. The moral justification, they maintain, is 'the idea that individuals have rights that must be "taken seriously," which means that they cannot be taken away simply by an appeal to the general welfare.'[59] In support of this tautological assertion they cite Ronald Dworkin's 1977 book, *Taking Rights Seriously*.[60] The political and legal justifications they provide are not any more original: the former referring to the 'democratic process' that gave rise to the *Charter* and the 'popular support' it enjoys; and the latter relying on the fact that 'the *Charter* is now part of the Constitution of Canada.'[61] All of this, of course, was well known to Hogg and Bushell in 1997, and none of it comes close to answering the claim made in their original article that, regardless of the political history and legal status of the *Charter*, the discretion it bestows upon courts 'inevitably remakes the constitution into the likeness favoured by judges.'[62] Moreover, the reference to Dworkin is particularly ironic for two reasons. First, his is one of the 'avalanche' of 'ingenious theories to justify judicial review' that Hogg and Bushell identified with the United States, and that they implied was neither convincing nor required to counter the anti-majoritarian objections to judicial review in Canada.[63] Second, a key aspect of Dworkin's contribution to this avalanche is his assertion that there are 'right answers' to constitutional questions – a claim that flat out contradicts Hogg and Bushell's prior arguments.[64]

This shift is significant not only because it represents a renunciation of Hogg and Bushell's previous views, but also because it undermines the coherence of their thesis. That thesis, it will be recalled, was aimed at countering the anti-majoritarian objection to judicial review. The capacity of legislatures to respond to judicial decisions was deemed to be a 'good thing' because it meant that the power of courts to interfere with democratic decision making was diminished. This made sense if one proceeded from Hogg and Bushell's assumption that there was no satisfactory justification for such interference. It does not make sense, however, if one takes the revised view of these authors and their new co-author, Wright, that such interference is justified on other grounds, and particularly if one takes the view that it is based on a judicial capacity to discern 'right answers.' In this case, the ability of legislatures to respond to judicial decisions with anything other than compliance represents a potential threat to the 'legitimate' values that judicial review is designed to protect. The question of whether that capacity is a 'good thing' or a 'bad thing,' therefore, can only be assessed with reference to those values and to the extent to which they are reinforced or undermined by legislative dialogues. Yet the authors offer no such assessment – nor could they, given that beyond asserting that the purpose of the *Charter* is to take rights seriously (and the suggestion that such values 'often include the concerns of an aggrieved minority'[65]), they provide no clue as to what values (or minorities) it is designed to protect – let alone what it might mean to take them seriously.

Thus by trying to remedy one problem (their lack of a justification for judicial review), the authors have unwittingly created another even bigger problem (the abandonment of their justification for legislative dialogues). Further evidence of this can be found in their new claim that dialogue theory does not militate for or against judicial restraint[66] and in their insistence that Hogg's prior call for courts to show increased deference to legislation re-enacted following adverse *Charter* rulings 'cannot be right.'[67] Here we see the product of a dialogue theory that has been diverted from its original mission of mitigating judicial powers that *cannot* be justified and that has been assigned new duties mitigating judicial powers that *can* be justified. Yet if such rights can be justified, why do judicial decisions enforcing them need to be mitigated? Is it to enable legislatures to correct judicial error? If so, some substantive theory of rights is required to ascertain when such error has occurred. Is it to guard against unintended disruption to legislation from justifiable judicial decisions? If so, the legislative role is reduced to refining the exercise of judicial power. In the reconstituted world of *Charter* dialogue that the authors have created, legislatures that do more than acquiesce to judicial decisions run the risk of thwarting *Charter* rights and subjecting themselves to further judicial censure. Moreover, given the lack of an articulated set of values to guide *Charter* decision making, legislatures have no basis for measuring the appropriateness of their actions, other than waiting for courts to tell them what they have done wrong.

Conclusion

When all is said and done, the dialogue thesis advanced by the authors appears to boil down to the unremarkable insight that legislatures have the capacity to modify legislation following adverse *Charter* rulings by the courts. Given that such modifications include repealing provisions found to be unconstitutional by the courts and repairing other provisions in light of such repeals, it would be much more surprising if legislatures did not have this capacity. Nor is it extraordinary that legislatures are often given an opportunity to refashion legislation struck down by the courts on the basis of a means–ends analysis. These and other opportunities to respond to decisions about rights are a common feature of constitutional jurisprudence in other jurisdictions, including the United States.

In addition to their banality, the above propositions do not tell us much of anything about the legitimacy of judicial review. The authors now concede that dialogue theory does not provide a justification for judicial review. Moreover, the extent to which it answers anti-majoritarian objections to judicial review can be assessed only by means of qualitative analyses of the degree to which *Charter* decisions constrain democratic policy. In this regard, Hogg's own qualitative analysis suggests that a key feature of the *Charter* that he and his co-authors maintain weakens judicial review has, in fact, had the opposite effect. If he is right about this, dialogue theory is further undermined. Even if he is wrong, however, he and his co-authors have thrown themselves on the horns of another painful dilemma by abandoning their previous scepticism about the legitimacy of judicial review and by embracing a theory which holds that rights 'cannot be taken away by an appeal to the general welfare.' How this theory can be reconciled with one that celebrates the capacity of legislatures to reassert majoritarian preferences through *Charter* dialogues – including the capacity to override *Charter* rights by means of section 33 – is, to put it mildly, a mystery.

By shifting ground in this way, the authors have transformed a thesis that was coherent but unconvincing into one that is simply incoherent. Yet no one should think for this reason that dialogue theory is about to loosen its hold on the constitutional imagination of Canadian courts. As suggested by their subtitle, 'Or "Much Ado about Metaphors,"' dialogue theory's appeal derives more from its power as a metaphor than from its force as an argument. By portraying judicial review as a contribution to deliberative engagement, the dialogue metaphor recasts judges as advocates within a democratic process rather than as arbiters within an authoritarian regime. Similarly, by representing judicial decisions under the *Charter* as transitory and reversible by legislatures, the dialogue metaphor purports to relieve judges of responsibility for the consequences of their *Charter* rulings without constraining their *Charter* powers.

Given the ongoing pressure felt by courts to defend a form of judicial review that was imposed upon them, and in the absence of a more compelling justification for *Charter* decision making, it is hardly surprising that judges would embrace a metaphor that offers them all of this and that comes with a seal of academic approval. For these reasons, dialogue theory will likely continue to thrive as a metaphor, notwithstanding its deficiencies as an argument. Metaphors, it seems, have something in common with idols. Where the need is great and there is a constituency that wants to believe, their capacity to engender reverence is not impaired by their likelihood of being false.

NOTES

1 P.W. Hogg & A.A. Bushell, 'The *Charter* Dialogue between Courts and Legislatures (or Perhaps the *Charter of Rights* Isn't Such a Bad Thing After All)'
   (1997) 35 Osgoode Hall L.J. 75 ['*Charter* Dialogue'].
2 *Ibid*. at 80.
3 *Ibid*. at 77.
4 See ch. 6, 'Rip Van Winkle in *Charterland*.'
5 See *e.g.* F.L. Morton, 'Dialogue or Monologue?' (1999) 20 Policy Options 23;
   C.P. Manfredi & J.B. Kelly, 'Six Degrees of Dialogue: A Response to Hogg
   and Bushell' (1999) 37 Osgoode Hall L.J. 513; *idem*, 'Dialogue, Deference
   and Restraint: Judicial Independence and Trial Procedures' (2001) 64 Sask.
   L. Rev. 323; J. Webber, 'Institutional Dialogue between Courts and Legislatures in the Definition of Fundamental Rights: Lessons from Canada (and
   elsewhere)' in W. Sadurski, ed., *Constitutional Justice, East and West: Democratic Legitimacy and Constitutional Courts in Post-Communist Europe in a
   Comparative Perspective* (The Hague: Kluwer Law International, 2002) 61; K.
   Ewing, 'Human Rights' in P. Cane & M. Tushnet, eds., *The Oxford Handbook
   of Legal Studies* (Oxford: Oxford University Press, 2003) 309; M. Tushnet,
   'Judicial Activism or Restraint in a Section 33 World' (2003) 53 U.T.L.J 89;
   R. Knopff, 'How Democratic Is the *Charter*? And Does It Matter?' (2003)
   19 Sup. Ct. L. Rev. (2d) 199; and A.C. Hutchinson, 'Judges and Politics: An
   Essay from Canada' (2004) 24 L.S. 275.
6 The Supreme Court of Canada embraced the dialogue thesis in *Vriend v.
   Alberta*, [1998] 1 S.C.R. 493 [*Vriend*]. For examples of academic support for
   the thesis, see P.J. Monahan, 'The Supreme Court of Canada in the 21st
   Century' (2001) 80 Can. Bar Rev. 374; K. Roach, *The Supreme Court on Trial:
   Judicial Activism or Democratic Dialogue* (Toronto: Irwin Law, 2001).
7 See *e.g. Vriend, ibid.*; Roach, *The Supreme Court on Trial, ibid*. For discussion
   of how dialogue theory can encourage courts to become more activist, see
   ch. 8, 'Wealthcare: The Politics of the *Charter* Revisited,' at 180–2.
8 P.W. Hogg, A.A. Bushell Thornton, & W. Wright, '*Charter* Dialogue Revisited – or "Much Ado about Metaphors"' (2007) 45 Osgoode Hall L.J. 1
   [*Charter* Dialogue Revisited].
9 Hogg & Bushell, '*Charter* Dialogue,' *supra* note 1 at 77.
10 *Ibid*. at 97.
11 Hogg, Bushell Thornton, & Wright, '*Charter* Dialogue Revisited,' *supra* note
   8 at 4.
12 *Ibid*. at 51.
13 Hogg & Bushell, '*Charter* Dialogue,' *supra* note 1 at 98.

14 *Ibid.*
15 *Schachter v. Canada*, [1992] 2 S.C.R. 679 [*Schachter*].
16 *Unemployment Insurance Act, 1971*, S.C. 1970–71–72, c. 48, s. 30, as am. by
    S.C. 1980–81–82–83, c. 150, s. 4, 32(1), as am. by S.C. 1980–81–82–83, c. 150,
    s. 5.
17 *An Act to amend the Unemployment Insurance Act and the Employment and
    Immigration Department and Commission Act*, S.C. 1990, c. 40, s. 24 [*Unem-
    ployment Insurance Amendment*]. [UI has since been rebranded 'Employ-
    ment Insurance.']
18 Hogg & Bushell, '*Charter* Dialogue,' *supra* note 1 at 91.
19 Members of Parliament voiced considerable frustration during committee
    hearings on Bill C-21, with the choice they were forced to make following
    Schachter between decreasing benefits for adoptive parents and increasing
    benefits for biological parents. Responding to pleas from a government
    MP that a way be found to restore adoptive parents' benefits to fifteen
    weeks, the Minister of Employment and Immigration admitted that, while
    she was 'very sensitive to the situation of adoptive parents' and had given
    'considerable thought to this problem,' she had not been able to find a
    solution: House of Commons, *Minutes of Proceedings and Evidence of the
    Legislative Committee on Bill C-21*, 34th Parl., no. 19 (3 October 1989) at 19:31
    [English translation].
20 It is worth noting that a principal reason given by the Supreme Court of
    Canada for deciding to remedy the *Charter* violation by striking down
    the benefit provided to adoptive parents, rather than extending it to bio-
    logical parents, was that the costs of such an extension would constitute
    an intrusion into the legislative domain 'substantial enough to change
    potentially the nature of the scheme as a whole.' *Schachter*, *supra* note 15
    at 723. To the same effect, Hogg, in his constitutional text, says that the
    'remedy of extension directly alters the statutory scheme and requires new
    expenditures by the federal government that have never been authorized
    by Parliament,' noting that 'a court faced with an under-inclusive statute
    has an unpalatable choice between the draconian remedy of nullifica-
    tion and the radical remedy of extension.' P.W. Hogg, *Constitutional Law
    of Canada*, student ed. (Toronto: Thomson Carswell, 2006) at 900. Appar-
    ently it is his view that the 'unpalatable choice' that a court faces in such
    situations becomes a delectable exercise in democracy when imposed on
    legislatures.
21 *Tétrault-Gadoury v. Canada*, [1991] 2 S.C.R. 22 [*Tétrault-Gadoury*].
22 J. Bakan, *Just Words: Constitutional Rights and Social Wrongs* (Toronto: Uni-
    versity of Toronto Press, 1997) at 59.

23 *Unemployment Insurance Amendment, supra* note 17.

24 Bakan, *supra* note 22.

25 The federal Department of Justice, for example, 'routinely reviews new
   legislation for potential Charter violations' by trying 'to gauge the courts'
   likely response to legislation, based on existing case law.' M.A. Hennigar, 'Expanding the "Dialogue" Debate: Canadian Federal Government
   Responses to Lower Court Charter Decisions' (2004) 37 Can. J. of Pol. Sci.
   3 at 16–17. Similar reviews take place within all provincial governments.
   A sense of how this process influences policy making can be gleaned from
   the following remarks of Jean-Pierre Blackburn, MP, during the debate on
   Bill C-21: 'When we, as members of Parliament, want to introduce amendments, we feel there is always something hanging over our heads: namely
   the famous rule that our amendment may run counter to the Charter. I find
   this rather disturbing. It is like a form of blackmail. As soon as a member
   tries to move an amendment, he or she is told that it may not be in keeping
   with the Charter. This fear prevents us from working in the interest of all
   Canadians.' House of Commons, *supra* note 19.

26 It is interesting to observe in this regard that if the authors did nothing
   more than classify legislative responses confined to repealing laws struck
   down by courts, together with legislative non-responses, as examples of
   'acquiescence' rather than of 'dialogue,' their analysis would show that
   legislatures acquiesced to court rulings in 34 per cent (30 of 88) of all the
   Charter cases they surveyed, and in 43 per cent (10 of 23) of the recent
   Charter cases they surveyed in their second article. It appears difficult to
   reconcile this substantial and growing rate of legislative acquiescence with
   the view that judicial review is a weak influence on legislative decision
   making in Canada. This is particularly so given that such cases do not
   include those like *Quebec Assn. of Protestant School Boards v. Quebec (A.G.)*,
   [1984] 2 S.C.R. 66 and *Baron v. Canada*, [1993] 1 S.C.R. 416, in which legislatures merely implemented legislative changes recommended by the courts,
   nor those like *Schachter*, *supra* note 15, and *Tétrault-Gadoury*, *supra* note 21,
   in which legislatures were impelled by *Charter* rulings to undertake other
   major changes in legislative policy.

27 Hogg, Bushell Thornton, & Wright, '*Charter* Dialogue Revisited,' *supra* note
   8 at 39.

28 P.W. Hogg, *Constitutional Law of Canada*, student ed. (Toronto: Thomson
   Carswell, 1992) at 853.

29 Hogg, *Constitutional Law of Canada*, 2006, *supra* note 20 at 827.

30 Though the qualitative analysis of *Charter* cases in Hogg's text would
   provide an even stronger basis for such an assessment if it devoted as

much attention to legislative responses as it does to the judicial decisions themselves.

31 Hogg & Bushell, '*Charter* Dialogue,' *supra* note 1 at 77.

32 *R. v. Oakes*, [1986] 1 S.C.R. 103.

33 Hogg, *Constitutional Law of Canada*, 2006, *supra* note 20 at 827, n. 4a.

34 G. Gunther & K.M. Sullivan, *Constitutional Law*, 13th ed. (Westbury: Foundation Press, 1997) at 108n2.

35 Hogg & Bushell, '*Charter* Dialogue,' *supra* note 1 at 79n12.

36 Though in a separate article written on his own in 2004, Hogg acknowledges that legislative sequels undoubtedly occur in the United States and that judicial review in that country may not be as strong as is sometimes supposed: P.W. Hogg, 'Discovering Dialogue' (2004) 23 Sup. Ct. L. Rev. (2d) 3 at 4.

37 S. Ingber, 'Judging without Judgment: Constitutional Irrelevancies and the Demise of Dialogue' (1994) 46 Rutgers L. Rev. 1473 at 1479n10. Examples of other recent American scholarship discussing the existence of constitutional dialogues in the United States include the following: L. Fisher, *Constitutional Dialogues: Interpretation as Political Process* (Princeton: Princeton University Press, 1988); B. Friedman, 'Dialogue and Judicial Review' (1993) 91 Mich. L. Rev. 577; and D.T. Coenen, 'A Constitution of Collaboration: Protecting Fundamental Values with Second-Look Rules of Interbranch Dialogue' (2001) 42 Wm. & Mary L. Rev. 1575.

38 Friedman, *ibid.* at 653.

39 R.B. Ginsburg, 'Speaking in a Judicial Voice' (1992) 67 N.Y.U.L. Rev. 1185 at 1198.

40 H.H. Wellington, *Interpreting the Constitution: The Supreme Court and the Process of Adjudication* (New Haven: Yale University Press, 1991) at 35.

41 Coenen, *supra* note 37.

42 *Ibid.* at 1583.

43 M. Tushnet, 'Subconstitutional Constitutional Law: Supplement, Sham, or Substitute?' (2001) 42 Wm. & Mary L. Rev. 1871 at 1880.

44 Coenen, *supra* note 37 at 36. See also the debate between Professors Tushnet and Coenen as to whether judges take advantage of such obstacles to drive substantive outcomes by means of structural decisions: Tushnet, *ibid.*; D.T. Coenen, 'Structural Review, Pseudo-Second-Look Decision Making, and the Risk of Diluting Constitutional Liberty' (2001) 42 Wm. & Mary L. Rev. 1881.

45 See generally Fisher, *supra* note 37.

46 Hogg & Bushell, '*Charter* Dialogue,' *supra* note 1 at 83.

47 A.C. Doyle, 'Silver Blaze' in *The Memoirs of Sherlock Holmes* (Oxford: Oxford University Press, 2000) 3.
48 This is due not only to the greater authority that courts command over matters that are represented as 'questions of law,' but also to the fact that under the *Charter*, courts get to speak the language of 'rights' while legislatures are relegated to speaking in language of 'limits'; and, in order to invoke section 33, legislatures are required to argue that rights 'do not matter.' See J. Waldron, 'Some Models of Dialogue between Judges and Legislators' (2004) 23 Sup. Ct. L. Rev. (2d) 7 at 34–39. See also Webber, *supra* note 5 at 97, noting that constitutional rights assume 'a superordinate importance, resistant to balancing,' and that any effort by legislators to influence their application is seen 'as an illegitimate attempt to impair fundamental liberties.'
49 See *e.g. Vriend, supra* note 6; B. McLachlin, 'Courts, Legislatures, and Executives in the Post-Charter Era' in P. Howe & P.H. Russell, eds., *Judicial Power and Canadian Democracy* (Montreal: McGill-Queen's University Press, 2001) 63 at 68–9.
50 Hogg & Bushell, '*Charter* Dialogue,' *supra* note 1 at 76–7 [footnotes omitted].
51 *Ibid.* at 105.
52 P.W. Hogg & A.A. Thornton, 'Reply to "Six Degrees of Dialogue"' (1999) 37 Osgoode Hall L.J. 529 at 534.
53 For discussion of the implications of this view for legislative democracy, see ch. 7, 'Look Who's Talking Now: Dialogue Theory and the Return to Democracy.'
54 Monahan, *supra* note 6 at 396.
55 Hogg, 'Discovering Dialogue,' *supra* note 36 at 5.
56 Ch. 6, 'Rip Van Winkle in *Charterland*,' at 141.
57 Hogg, Bushell Thornton, & Wright, '*Charter* Dialogue Revisited,' *supra* note 8 at 29.
58 Hogg & Bushell, '*Charter* Dialogue,' *supra* note 1 at 77.
59 Hogg, Bushell Thornton, & Wright, '*Charter* Dialogue Revisited,' *supra* note 8 at 28.
60 R. Dworkin, *Taking Rights Seriously* (London: Duckworth, 1977).
61 Hogg, Bushell Thornton, & Wright, '*Charter* Dialogue Revisited,' *supra* note 8 at 28.
62 Hogg & Bushell, '*Charter* Dialogue,' *supra* note 1 at 77.
63 *Ibid.* at 77–8.
64 It also contradicts the views of another Canadian proponent of dialogue

theory, Kent Roach, who titles an entire chapter of his book on the subject 'The Myths of Right Answers,' with much of that chapter devoted to questioning Dworkin's claim that right answers can be derived from moral principles. See Roach, *supra* note 6 at 225–38.

65 Hogg, Bushell Thornton, & Wright, '*Charter* Dialogue Revisited,' *supra* note 8 at 45.

66 *Ibid.* at 47.

67 *Ibid.* at 48.

10 Legalize This: The *Chartering* of Canadian Politics*

I fought the law and the law won.

Sonny Curtis

In the period immediately following the enactment of the *Canadian Charter of Rights and Freedoms*,[1] a number of academic commentators predicted that a major impact of the *Charter* would be to 'legalize' politics in Canada.[2] In my twenty-five years of experience with the *Charter* – as a government lawyer, as a constitutional law professor, and as a provincial cabinet minister – I have become ever more aware of how prescient these commentators were.[3] Since the *Charter* came into force in 1982, issues of rights in Canada have increasingly become identified and understood as being legal rather than political in nature. This development, which reflects a global trend in favour of 'legalizing' public affairs, has been encouraged by politicians as much as by lawyers and has produced two spheres of public discourse: a sphere of justice and rights that has become the primary domain of lawyers and courts; and a sphere of policy and interests that remains the principal preserve of politicians and legislatures. Moreover, there can be no question as to which sphere dominates in the event of conflict. For all the talk of 'dialogue' between courts and legislatures, those who speak in the language of justice and rights have a huge rhetorical and political advantage over those who speak in the language of policy and interests.

The 'legalization' of politics has increased the stature and author-

---

* Originally published in J. Kelly and C. Manfredi, eds., *Contested Constitutionalism: Reflections on the Canadian Charter of Rights and Freedoms* (Vancouver: UBC Press, 2009) at 33–49. Copyright © 2009 by UBC Press. Reprinted by permission of UBC Press.

ity of lawyers and legal discourse within Canadian society and has diminished the importance and influence of politicians and democratic engagement. These shifts can be seen most clearly in the context of *Charter* litigation, where contentious issues of public policy, such as abortion, unemployment insurance, regulation of commercial advertising, Medicare, Sunday closing of retail stores, same-sex marriage, obscenity laws, judicial salaries, collective bargaining, the powers of customs officials, and even cruise missile testing have become the subjects of legal argument and judicial decision making.[4] However, 'legal' politics within the courts are only the tip of a much larger iceberg – one that shows no signs of diminishing due to global warming. The judicial arena is just one of many forums in which law and/or lawyers direct political debate and shape public policy in the name of upholding *Charter* rights. Indeed it is no exaggeration to say that such influence has become pervasive within Canadian government and civil society. In this essay I draw upon my experiences and those of others to explore some of the ways in which this influence has manifested itself.

The Legalization of Government Policy Making

As will be evident to those who have been engaged in public policy processes both before and after 1982, the *Charter* has significantly altered the way in which governments in Canada go about making decisions. The federal Department of Justice 'now routinely reviews new legislation for potential Charter violations, and recommends to the responsible minister or parliamentary committee whether such limitations may be "reasonable" and sustained under a section 1 analysis.'[5] Existing legislation is also reviewed to ensure its consistency with new *Charter* decisions. Comparable legislative review procedures exist in all provincial governments. Such processes, as Matthew Hennigar has observed,

[do] not occur within a legal vacuum, but typically [involve] bureaucratic actors attempting to gauge the courts' likely response to legislation, based on existing case law. To this extent, there is usually, if not always, an external judicial influence on internal legislative-executive discussions on constitutional rights.[6]

In addition to reviewing new and existing legislation to ensure its consistency with the *Charter*, government lawyers regularly incorporate their understanding of *Charter* requirements in the day-to-day guid-

ance they give government employees, in the legal opinions they issue
to ministries, in the advice they provide to the Attorney General, and in
the decisions they make during the processes of legislative drafting. In
these various ways, government lawyers, and the court decisions upon
which they rely, exert huge influence on public policies without those
policies ever being tested in court.[7]

The extent of this influence is amplified by two related factors. The
first is that government lawyers tend to be risk averse in their approach
to the *Charter*. This means that, on the margins, they are more inclined
to advise that a law or practice violates the *Charter* than that it does
not. The reason for this is obvious: a government lawyer is much more
likely to be criticized for being wrong in predicting that a law or practice complies with the *Charter* than for being wrong in predicting that
it does not. This likelihood is in part because the latter advice, if heed-
ed, will never get tested in court. Moreover, even if advice of a *Charter*
violation is ignored, government officials are not prone to being dis-
pleased because a law or practice that they were told was unconstitutional survives *Charter* challenge. On the contrary, they are likely to be
delighted, as I was as Minister of Forests when a government lawyer
successfully defended the ministry's handling of a forest tenure from
a constitutional challenge that he had originally advised could not be
won. When the decision came down, I penned him a congratulatory
note (though I refrained from doing so a second time when the decision was upheld on appeal). The second factor that amplifies the influence of policy advice provided in the form of *Charter* opinions is the
reverence accorded such advice by public servants who are not lawyers. Given their lack of familiarity with the law and the legal system,
non-lawyers within government are frequently intimidated by legal
opinions, particularly those that speak of possible violations of constitutional rights. Thus government officials generally go out of their way
to accommodate such opinions in their decision-making processes.[8] As
a result, *Charter* issues seldom reach the ministerial level, and when
they do, cabinet ministers themselves are disinclined to assume the
political risk of proceeding with a policy that they are told is likely to
violate the *Charter*.

In one of the rare instances where a cabinet of which I was a member decided to proceed with a policy in the face of an adverse *Charter*
opinion, the decision was taken only because the policy in question –
the imposition of strict spending limits on third parties in provincial
election campaigns – was seen by ministers as being central to both

the government's mission and its ability to compete fairly in the next election. Even then, the decision to proceed might have gone the other way had I and other lawyers in cabinet not challenged the certitude of the legal opinion and persuaded the Attorney General to seek further legal advice on the matter from outside counsel (a course not generally welcomed by lawyers within ministries of the attorney general – or anywhere else for that matter).[9]

An exception to the tendency of cabinet ministers to heed legal advice relating to the *Charter* sometimes arises with respect to legal opinions advising that new policies are required. While cabinet ministers are loath to run the political risk of proceeding with government policies that the courts are likely to strike down under the *Charter*, the political calculus tends to be quite different with respect to policies that the *Charter* is said to require, particularly if those policies are controversial or do not accord with government priorities. In these situations, ministers may find it convenient to avoid incurring the political costs associated with implementing such policies by deferring their decisions and leaving the issues to be resolved by the courts. The British Columbia cabinet of which I was a member, for example, decided not to act on legal advice recommending that it introduce legislation giving francophone parents greater control over their children's French-language educational programs, preferring to wait until there was a court decision requiring it to do so.

Perhaps the most obvious example of politicians hiding behind the courts to avoid dealing with a contentious political issue raised by the *Charter* is the federal Liberals' handling of the same-sex marriage controversy.[10] In the years between 2000 and 2003 the government avoided dealing with this issue simply by saying that it was before the courts. Finally, after the British Columbia and Ontario Courts of Appeal determined that the *Charter* required civil rights of marriage to be extended to same-sex couples, and further appeal became politically unpalatable, Prime Minister Jean Chrétien announced that his government would propose legislation to recognize the union of same-sex couples across Canada. However, rather than bring this legislation directly to Parliament for a vote, where it would have divided the Liberal caucus and created a difficult political situation in advance of a federal election, the government referred the draft bill to the Supreme Court of Canada to seek the Court's opinion concerning its constitutionality.[11] The Court reference provided a pretext for the government to delay parliamentary debate on the legislation for a further nineteen months, thereby diffusing the issue for a period that extended past the election. Moreover, when the Supreme Court finally issued its judgment supporting the constitutionality of same-sex marriage legislation, the government was able to rely upon that ruling to justify introducing such legislation in Parliament. In sum, by seeking a constitutional reference, the government succeeded both in delaying and diffusing a contentious political issue, and in garnering constitutional legitimacy for its decision.

The Role of Attorneys General in Legalizing Politics

Not surprisingly, the *Charter* has greatly enhanced the powers of attorneys general, who, as chief law officers of the Crown, can use it to directly influence public policy. This is frequently done without consulting cabinet, and almost always without consulting the legislature. The most obvious example of this influence relates to decisions concerning the conduct of *Charter* litigation, such as which arguments to make in court and which cases to appeal. Though these decisions can have a profound impact upon government powers and legislation, final say over them resides with attorneys general rather than with cabinets or legislatures. Within the federal government, for example, decisions concerning appeals to the Supreme Court of Canada are the responsibility of the Attorney General of Canada and turn on an assessment of whether 'the public interest *requires* an appeal.'[12] The Attorney General (or sometimes the Deputy Attorney General) bases this decision upon advice received from the National Litigation Committee, which is composed of a number of senior lawyers from the Department of Justice.[13] It is true that decisions concerning the conduct of *Charter* litigation at both the federal and provincial levels often involve attorneys general or their legal officers taking advice from other government officials. Government lawyers, for example, will commonly seek instructions from client ministries concerning whether, and on what basis, to defend a ministry policy that is attacked in court, as happened in relation to the forest tenure that became the subject of a constitutional challenge when I was Minister of Forests.

Similarly, attorneys general will sometimes seek advice from their cabinet colleagues and/or the premier or prime minister on civil litigation decisions affecting major public policy, such as whether to appeal a ruling striking down significant legislation. The federal Attorney General's decision not to appeal appellate court rulings striking down the common law prohibition on same-sex marriage, for example, was discussed at the cabinet level and was ultimately announced by the Prime Minister.[14] As Attorney General of British Columbia, I spoke with both the Premier and Cabinet before deciding not to appeal a trial court decision striking down the third-party election spending restrictions that were enacted following the cabinet deliberations referred to earlier in this essay.[15] While my decision to forgo the appeal was influenced by legal considerations (particularly the existence of a case from another province that raised the same issue and was likely to reach the Supreme Court of Canada first), the political dimensions of the case were such that I did not feel comfortable making a final determination without first consulting the political executive.

While attorneys general and their law officers sometimes make decisions concerning *Charter* litigation in consultation with others in the executive branch, there are two things that need to be noted in evaluating the significance of these decisions on the legalization of politics. The first is that such decisions are ultimately an attorney general's to make (though an attorney general would be foolish not to take seriously the advice given by cabinet on a highly contentious political issue such as same-sex marriage or election spending).[16] The second is that, regardless of the influence exerted on such decisions by other members of the executive branch, the decisions themselves remain artefacts of a legal process that involves the use of the *Charter* to shape public policy without legislative deliberation or oversight.

This process is well illustrated by the reaction of the Attorney General of Canada to the 1988 decision of the Federal Court in *Schachter v. Canada*.[17] The trial judge in that case held that a provision of the *Unemployment Insurance Act* providing fifteen weeks of parental leave benefits to adoptive parents contravened the guarantee of equality rights in section 15(1) of the *Charter* by not extending equivalent benefits to biological parents.[18] The Attorney General decided not to appeal this aspect of the decision, thereby leaving Parliament under a constitutional obligation to provide equal benefits to both groups of parents.[19] This obligation was addressed the following year, when the Minister of Employment and Immigration tabled Bill C-21, which proposed to provide parental leave benefits to all parents for ten weeks.[20] This proposal represented a major alteration in the statutory scheme, both by reducing benefits for adoptive parents and by granting new benefits to biological parents. Moreover, given the much larger numbers of biological parents, it required a substantial expenditure of public funds not previously authorized by Parliament.

The frustration felt by Members of Parliament (MPs) concerning the constitutional constraints placed upon them by the trial court decision in *Schachter* is evident from the remarks of Jean-Pierre Blackburn, MP, during committee debate on Bill C-21:

> When we, as members of Parliament, want to introduce amendments, we feel there is always something hanging over our heads: namely the famous rule that our amendment may run counter to the Charter. I find this rather disturbing. It is like a form of blackmail. As soon as a member tries to move an amendment, he or she is told that it may not be in keeping with the Charter. This fear prevents us from working in the interest of all Canadians.[21]

This same frustration seems to have been shared by then Employment and Immigration Minister Barbara McDougall, who, during that same committee debate, stated in relation to requests to restore the benefits being taken away from adoptive parents:

> I am very sensitive to the situation of adoptive parents. We gave considerable thought to this problem when the Bill was being drafted. The problem still exist [*sic*]. In fact, there are two problems. There is the problem of the Charter of Rights and Freedoms, and that regarding the situation of natural parents and adoptive parents. In addition, the system is open and much more costly. We are trying to find a solution.
>
> Before my appearance here today, I had not found a solution. I am sorry, but that is simply the case.[22]

What the Minister did not say was that the option of seeking to preserve Parliament's ability to provide differential benefits for adoptive parents by appealing the trial judge's ruling had been taken away by the Attorney General of Canada, who, whether he consulted Cabinet (as seems likely) or not, made the decision to accept this limitation on legislative powers without ever consulting Parliament.

Some attorneys general have gone even further in using their authority over *Charter* litigation to defeat legislative powers. Ian Scott, acting as Attorney General of Ontario, saw no problem with conceding in court that certain legislative provisions violated the *Charter*.[23] In *Re Blainey and Ontario Hockey Association et al.*, he joined with the plaintiff in submitting that the *Ontario Human Rights Code* was unconstitutional in exempting sports organizations from its prohibition on sexual discrimination.[24] Similarly, in *Paul and Wright v. The Minister of Consumer and Commercial Relations*, he conceded that the *Vital Statistics Act* was unconstitutional in requiring a child to be given the father's surname.[25] In the latter case at least, he took this stance after introducing an amendment in the legislature that would have changed the law, but that had not yet been enacted. In the former case, however, he argued against the constitutionality of the provision without having tabled amending legislation; even more incredibly, he maintained this position in the Ontario Court of Appeal even after the impugned provision had been upheld by the trial judge.[26]

The *Charter* sometimes gives attorneys general the opportunity to challenge the constitutionality of laws outside provincial jurisdiction. As Attorney General of British Columbia, I asked the Director of Vital Statistics to withhold his decision to deny a marriage licence to a lesbian couple while I sought a court declaration that the federal common law prohibition on same-sex marriage was unconstitutional. While I took this decision in the knowledge that the court action did not threaten provincial powers, and having sought and obtained the support of the Premier, there can be no question that it had profound political ramifications and was controversial amongst provincial legislators (including some in my own party).

The Legalization of Political Advocacy and Discourse

Just as the *Charter* has changed the way in which governments make policy, it has also altered the way in which organized groups practise political advocacy.[27] Prior to the enactment of the *Charter*, the use of the courts to influence public policy by such groups was 'exceptional.' Since the enactment of the *Charter*, however, there has been a 'transformation' through which interest group litigation has become 'an established form of collective action' for all categories of organized interests.[28] Canadian feminists, for example, have committed huge amounts of time and energy to pursuing their political objectives through legal mobilization, guided in large measure by lawyers working with the Women's Legal Education and Action Fund (LEAF).[29] Groups, such as unions, corporations, civil libertarians, social conservatives, gay and lesbian rights organizations, market libertarians, religious bodies, anti-poverty advocates, and professional associations, have likewise invested heavily in *Charter* litigation. Moreover, given that the *Charter* is an instrument that can cut many ways, these groups have frequently found it necessary to participate in *Charter* cases in order to defend as well as advance their interests.

The inevitable consequence of the shift to litigation as a mechanism for political advocacy has been to increase the influence of law and lawyers within such organized groups.[30] This trend further feeds the tendency of such groups to look to courts rather than legislatures and governments to address their concerns. The overall impact, as Michael Mandel demonstrated in his examination of the court challenge brought against cruise missile testing by Operation Dismantle, is to downplay or even demobilize other forms of political action.[31] This is partly because litigation consumes huge amounts of time and money that cannot then be devoted to public education, lobbying and other grassroots initiatives. It is also because the legal forms and forums in which *Charter* issues are argued makes them less comprehensible and accessible to the public and thus drains them of their political meaning.

This process is exacerbated by the nature of the discourse that such litigation produces in the media and the popular press. Lawyers and law professors, whose opinions and oratory prior to the *Charter* were confined mostly to courtrooms and classrooms, are now regularly asked to share publicly their constitutional views on any and all political issues. These views are invariably packaged as their legal understanding of how the issues in question ought best to be addressed by the courts under the *Charter*. When commenting on court judgments, such commentary is usually comprised of *ex post facto* legal explanations of how and why a court reached a particular decision, with muted if any criticism of the outcome. This posture is hardly surprising given that judges are regarded as the ultimate authorities on constitutional interpretation. Even lawyers and groups that lose a *Charter* case will generally try to find something positive to say about the court's judgment, if only to justify their efforts to their clients, their supporters, or themselves. Thus when Operation Dismantle's *Charter* claim against cruise missile testing was unanimously dismissed by the Supreme Court of Canada, the group characterized the decision as 'a victory for the strength of the Charter and the civil rights and liberties of Canadians' because it recognized a judicial power to review cabinet decisions.[32] Similarly, when a majority of the Supreme Court rejected Louise Gosselin's claim that cuts to her social assistance payments violated her *Charter* rights, the Charter Committee on Poverty Issues, which had intervened in support of her claim, issued a press release in which one of its members welcomed the views of the dissenting judges and expressed relief 'that the majority accepted the possibility the Charter will be found in a future case to protect the right to adequate food, clothing and housing.'[33]

The legalization of political discourse generated by the *Charter* is not confined to political advocacy groups and constitutional pundits. Politicians regularly invoke the *Charter* to explain, criticize, and debate public policy. Cabinet ministers welcome opportunities to rely on the *Charter* to support legislative measures or government actions, particularly where they are politically controversial. Thus when introducing the legislation giving francophone parents in British Columbia greater control over their children's French-language educational programs, the first words from the Minister of Education's mouth were these:

> This bill will enable francophones living in British Columbia to have management and control of their children's francophone educational program, as provided for in Canada's Charter of Rights and Freedoms. Courts have interpreted section 23 of the Charter as requiring that francophone parents have management and control of francophone education, and this legislation is designed to provide that management and control through the Francophone Education Authority.[34]

In the same vein, I should confess that my public explanation as Attorney General for seeking a court order declaring the common law prohibition on same-sex marriage to be unconstitutional relied in large part upon a legal opinion that had been prepared by my Ministry and that I released to the media.

Opposition Members of the Legislative Assembly (MLAs) also commonly invoke the *Charter* to strengthen or legitimize their criticisms of government measures, as they did in British Columbia when challenging the introduction of laws that prohibited the publication of hate propaganda[35] and that placed protective zones around abortion clinics (thereby prohibiting harassment of people using or providing abortion services).[36] By invoking the *Charter*, these MLAs were able to give their criticisms a patina of constitutional legitimacy that made them less likely to offend the ethnic communities and the women that these measures were designed to protect.

The flip side of such *Charter*-based criticism is *Charter*-based justification, through which ministers and others defend their actions by invoking legal opinions to demonstrate their compliance with the *Charter*. This technique, which Kent Roach refers to as '*Charter*-proofing,' was used extensively by the federal government to defend the anti-terrorism legislation it introduced in 2001.[37] By claiming that the legislation had been reviewed and found by government lawyers to be consistent with the *Charter*, the government sought to conflate the question of whether the legislation was politically justifiable with the issue of whether it was constitutionally acceptable.

Politicians have also taken to using *Charter* discourse to try to manufacture political issues. Perhaps the most blatant example of this was Prime Minister Paul Martin's surprise promise during a leaders' debate in the 2006 federal election campaign to repeal the notwithstanding clause in section 33 of the *Charter*.[38] Martin clearly hoped that the ploy would create a wedge issue between himself and Conservative leader Stephen Harper, thereby diverting public attention from political difficulties he and his party were experiencing. As it turned out, the manoeuvre was too blatant and was widely interpreted as a disingenuous act of political desperation. This assessment was reinforced by the fact that Martin had previously vowed to invoke the notwithstanding clause, if necessary, to prevent courts from imposing same-sex marriage on religious organizations.[39]

Legalization in Action – A Top Three List

I have thus far discussed some of the ways in which the legalization of politics in Canada has manifested itself under the *Charter*, including the explosion of *Charter* litigation in the courts, the increased influence of lawyers within government, the enhanced powers of attorneys general, and the legalization of political advocacy and discourse. I will now focus on three examples that demonstrate the degree to which Canadian politics has become legalized in recent years. In the same spirit that *Charter* enthusiasts put forward their 'top ten' lists of Supreme Court decisions to mark the twenty-fifth anniversary of the *Charter*, I offer the following as my 'top three' list of political legalisms, presented in ascending order of audacity.

Number 3: Canada Takes the Charter to the United Nations

Canada, being a signatory to the International Covenant on Economic, Social, and Cultural Rights (ICESCR),[40] is required to report periodically to the Committee on Economic, Social, and Cultural Rights on what it is doing to fulfil its obligations under the ICESCR. In the 1990s, as Canadian governments were embarking on major cutbacks to social programs, Canada turned to the *Charter* to provide evidence that it was meeting its ICESCR commitments. In its 1993 report to the committee, for example, the Canadian delegation referenced the *Charter*'s capacity to encompass economic and social rights and the Supreme Court of Canada's use of the ICESCR in its interpretation of the *Charter*. As noted by the committee in its consideration of the Canadian report:

> The committee was informed that the Charter of Rights and Freedoms guarantees, in section 7, the right to security of the person and, in section 15, the equal benefit and protection of the law. It notes with satisfaction that Canadian courts have applied these provisions to cover certain economic and social rights, and that the Supreme Court of Canada has, on occasion, turned to the International Covenant on Economic, Social and Cultural Rights for guidance as to the meaning of provisions of the *Charter*.[41]

Five years later, when the 1998 report was due, the Canada Assistance Plan (CAP) had been replaced with a block transfer that gave provinces greater flexibility with respect to social programs.[42] This change posed a major problem for the Canadian delegation, as CAP had been highlighted in previous reports as a key instrument through which Canada was fulfilling its ICESCR obligations:

> The Government informed the Committee in its 1993 report that *CAP* set national standards for social welfare, required that work by welfare recipients be freely chosen, guaranteed the right to an adequate standard of living, and facilitated court challenges to federally-funded provincial social assistance programmes which did not meet the standards proscribed in the *Act*.[43]

Faced with the embarrassment of having to justify CAP's elimination, the Canadian delegation again trotted out the *Charter* as evidence of Canada's continuing commitment to meeting its obligations under the ICESCR. According to its report, 'the Canadian Charter of Rights and Freedoms plays a similar role at the domestic level regarding the protection of economic, social and cultural rights to that of the International Covenant on Civil and Political Rights at the international level.'[44] The delegation went on to say that section 7 of the *Charter* 'may be interpreted to include the rights protected under the Covenant' and that the Supreme Court of Canada 'has also held section 7 as guaranteeing that people are not to be deprived of basic necessities.' It noted further that the 'Government of Canada is bound by these interpretations.'[45]

These efforts to use the *Charter* to demonstrate Canada's continuing commitment to its obligations under the ICESCR are disturbing for a

number of reasons. First, they rely on selective and strained interpretations of *Charter* jurisprudence. Second, these same interpretations have
been strongly opposed by Canadian governments in domestic courts.
Third, they are not isolated examples: Canada has used the same tactic
in relation to the Convention on the Rights of the Child, insisting in
1995 that Convention rights were subject to *Charter* protection, while
arguing the opposite in court a few years later.[46] At a more fundamental
level, these practices are disturbing because they show how the *Charter*
can be used to legalize even international politics, allowing Canadian
delegations to invoke legal interpretations of abstract constitutional
rights as a substitute for providing real evidence of substantive social
progress and as a smokescreen for the country's political failings.

Number 2: Senators Take Their Report to the Supreme Court of Canada

In 2002 the Standing Senate Committee on Social Affairs, Science, and
Technology, chaired by Senator Michael Kirby, released its report on
Canada's health care system.[47] The report recommended that governments establish a 'health care guarantee' that would oblige them
to provide patients with timely access to medically necessary health
care within public or private health delivery systems. According to the
report, failure to provide patients such a guarantee, while preventing
them from purchasing medically necessary services, would violate
their rights to life and security under section 7 of the *Charter*. The Kirby
Report was seen as a contender to the report of the Royal Commission
on the Future of Health Care, also released in 2002 by Commissioner
Roy Romanow.[48] The Romanow Report placed greater emphasis on the
need to maintain a single-payer model of health care insurance, calling
for sweeping changes and a 'health covenant' to ensure the sustainability of a universally accessible, publicly funded health care system.

In 2003, Kirby and nine other senators on his committee sought leave
in their official capacity to make arguments as interveners before the
Supreme Court of Canada in *Chaoulli v. Quebec (Attorney General)*,[49]
which involved a *Charter* challenge to Quebec legislation prohibiting
the sale of private health insurance in the province for core medical
services. Their application was contested by the respondent Attorney
General of Canada on a number of grounds, including that it would
create:

> a whole new forum for political discussion incongruent with the proper
> functioning and role of Parliament by allowing a particular group of par-

liamentarians holding a particular point of view a second forum to make their case, without the balance of divergent legislators' views; it would also open the door to Senators or members of the House of Commons opposed to the views of their colleagues to also seek to intervene in order to put forward ... their own point of view.[50]

The Court finessed these objections by granting intervener status to the senators in their individual capacities, whereupon they proceeded to file arguments based on their report in support of the appellants and in opposition to the position of the Government of Canada. In particular, they submitted that, absent a 'health care guarantee,' the prohibition on private health insurance violated patients' rights under section 7 of the *Charter*.[51] These arguments ultimately found favour with three of the four majority judges, thereby contributing to the Court's decision to declare the Quebec legislation invalid.

Here we see an example of the legalization of politics in its purest and most potent form: members of an unelected Senate committee, not content to influence public policy through normal parliamentary channels, transformed their political recommendations into legal arguments in order to persuade an unelected court to make a constitutional ruling that undermined the policies of both an elected federal government and an elected provincial legislature. Moreover, given its inconsistency with the principles of the *Canada Health Act*,[52] this ruling undermined the policies of an elected House of Commons and of the very Parliament to which those senators belonged.

Number 1: Law Professors Take the Charter to Parliament

It used to be that law professors were academic mortals like all others. But that was before the *Charter*. Now law professors are exalted interpreters of constitutional rights, second only to judges – and a close second at that. Consider the case of the 134 law professors who, in 2005, signed an open letter to then Opposition Leader Stephen Harper. The letter told Harper that if, as anticipated, he opposed proposed government legislation extending the right to marry to same-sex couples and offered amendments to limit the definition of marriage to opposite-sex couples, it would be 'legally necessary' for him to use the *Charter*'s notwithstanding clause. 'You must be completely honest with Canadians about the unconstitutionality of your proposal,' the letter went on to say. 'The truth is, there is only one way to accomplish your goal: invoke the notwithstanding clause.'[53]

What was extraordinary about this advice was that it came in the wake of a Supreme Court of Canada decision in which the Court, while holding that same-sex marriage was constitutionally permissible, refused to say whether it was constitutionally *required*. One of the reasons given by the judges for refusing to address this issue was that it 'ha[d] the potential to undermine the uniformity that would be achieved by the adoption of the proposed legislation.'[54] Yet as the judgment itself noted, such uniformity would have been undermined only if the Court had concluded that same-sex marriage was *not* constitutionally required.[55] It is apparent, therefore, that the judges believed that the 'potential' existed for the Court to reach this result – and the constitutional status of the prohibition on same-sex marriage remained an open question in their minds. Thus, while the law professors purported to be certain that Harper's position was unconstitutional, the judges of the Supreme Court clearly signalled that they were not.

What makes the law professors' advice even more troubling is that, at the time the letter was written, Parliament remained the one major federal institution that had not been given a chance to consider the issue of same-sex marriage following appellate court judgments holding that it was constitutionally required. The Attorney General had considered the issue and decided not to pursue appeals. The cabinet and the Prime Minister had considered the issue and had decided to prepare draft legislation and refer it to the Supreme Court of Canada. The Supreme Court had considered the issue and had decided that same-sex marriage legislation was constitutionally permissible (but, as discussed, not that it was constitutionally required). Given that the outcome of these various processes was to propose legislation to Parliament, one might have assumed that Parliament should have been given a meaningful opportunity to debate the legislation. One might particularly have thought that MPs, as the elected representatives of the people, should have been entitled to make their own best judgment on the merits of the legislation – including its constitutional merits. Yet 134 law professors disagreed, suggesting that those opposed to same-sex marriage were not legally entitled to advance their position in Parliament without first conceding, by invoking the notwithstanding clause, that it contravened the *Charter*.

Now I have long been a supporter of the right of same-sex couples to marry. Indeed I was the first attorney general in the Commonwealth to support such a right both by speaking out politically and by seeking a declaration in court under the *Charter*. I am also a law professor. But the notion of law professors using their position as constitutional authorities to tell elected MPs that they are legally required to concede a breach of *Charter* rights in respect of a matter that was explicitly left open by the Supreme Court of Canada strikes me as more than a tad presumptuous. When I made this point at a recent conference, a law professor who had signed the letter suggested to me that I was over-reacting. The letter, she said, was simply a political strategy to support same-sex marriage rights. Excuse me? I believe that was my point! One hundred thirty-four law professors engage in a political strategy by using their status as legal experts to challenge the constitutional capacity of elected MPs to advance a policy with which those professors disagree. Sounds like a pretty compelling example of legalized politics to me.

Conclusion

The legalization of politics foreseen by some commentators at the time of the *Charter*'s enactment has become well established in Canada over the past three decades. This process has increased the influence of lawyers and legal discourse within Canadian society while diminishing that of politicians and democratic engagement. Moreover, such legalization has not been confined to the judicial arena: it has had a profound influence on the way political issues are considered and treated within governments, legislatures, and society at large. One aspect of legalized politics that I find especially troubling is the use of the *Charter* by public officials as a means of escaping political responsibility. Having been in government, I understand how tempting it can be to invoke the *Charter* to bolster a political argument or to delay making a decision; I have even succumbed to this temptation myself on occasion. What disturbs me is that such tendencies seem to have become endemic and that politicians and other public officials are turning to the *Charter* with increased regularity to justify or avoid taking positions on contentious issues, to shift political responsibility to the courts, and to try to discredit the political views of others.

I have made no secret of my concern that these developments, combined with other forces, are contributing to an impoverishment of Canadian democracy.[56] It would be a mistake, however, to assume that all legalization of politics is unnecessary and undesirable. To the extent that societies make defined commitments to values such as due process and the rule of law, it is important that we have lawyers, both inside and outside of government, charged with the responsibility of ensuring that elected and unelected officials adhere to these commitments. My concern for legalized politics, therefore, is not absolute, but is directed at the use of law to address politically contested matters that should, in my view, be the subject of democratic engagement and decision making. This is a concern that I hope would be shared by others who espouse the values of democracy, including those who seek to justify judicial review on the basis that it forms part of a 'democratic dialogue' with legislatures.[57] It is, after all, not much of a dialogue and hardly democratic if the same legal norms and interpretations are driving decisions at both ends.

NOTES

1 *Canadian Charter of Rights and Freedoms,* Part I of the *Constitution Act, 1982,* being Schedule B to the *Canada Act 1982* (U.K.), 1982, c.11 [*Charter*].
2 See *e.g.* P.H. Russell, 'The Political Purposes of the Canadian Charter of Rights and Freedoms,' (1983) 61 Canadian Bar Rev. 51; H. Glasbeek & M. Mandel, 'The Legalization of Politics in Advanced Capitalism: The Canadian Charter of Rights and Freedoms,' (1984) 2 Socialist Studies 84; M. Mandel, *The Charter of Rights and the Legalization of Politics in Canada* (Toronto: Wall and Simpson, 1989).
3 I served as an articling student and lawyer with the Constitutional Branch of Saskatchewan Justice from 1982 to 1984; as law professor at Osgoode Hall Law School and the University of Victoria Law School from 1984 to the present; and as a Member of the Legislative Assembly of British Columbia from 1991 to 2001, where I held numerous cabinet portfolios, including Aboriginal Relations, Forests, Health, Finance, Intergovernmental Relations, Advanced Education, and Attorney General.
4 It is true, of course, that judicial policy making on issues such as abortion and obscenity occurred prior to the *Charter* in the context of common law decision making and statutory interpretation. The judicial policy making that takes place under the *Charter*, however, is qualitatively different in that it is based on a constitutional mandate to give political meaning to open-ended rights and in that the policy-making authority of judges takes precedence over that of elected legislators.
5 M.A. Hennigar, 'Expanding the "Dialogue" Debate: Federal Government Responses to Lower Court Charter Decisions,' (2004) 37 Can. J. of Pol. Sci. 3 at 16.
6 *Ibid.* at 16–17.

7 J.B. Kelly, *Governing with the Charter* (Vancouver: UBC Press, 2005) at 245–9.
8 J.L. Hiebert, *Charter Conflicts: What Is Parliament's Role?* (Montreal: McGill-Queen's University Press, 2002) at 11–12.
9 The resulting legislation was subsequently challenged and struck down by the Supreme Court of British Columbia as being contrary to the guarantee of freedom of expression in section 2(b) of the *Charter: Pacific Press v. British Columbia (Attorney General)*, [2000] 5 W.W.R. 219 (B.C.S.C.) [*Pacific Press*]. As explained later in this essay, this decision was not appealed, but the same issue was later addressed by the Supreme Court of Canada in *Harper v. Canada (Attorney General)*, [2004] 1 S.C.R. 827, in which a majority of judges disapproved of the *Pacific Press* decision and held that similar third-party spending restrictions in federal legislation were justified under section 1 of the *Charter*.
10 For a fuller discussion of this issue see M.A. Hennigar, 'Reference re Same-Sex Marriage: Making Sense of the Government's Litigation Strategy,' in J.B. Kelly & C.P. Manfredi, eds., *Contested Constitutionalism: Reflections on the Canadian Charter of Rights and Freedoms* (Vancouver: UBC Press, 2009) at 209.
11 *Reference re Same-Sex Marriage*, [2004] 3 S.C.R. 698.
12 Department of Justice Canada, *Federal Prosecution Service Deskbook* (Ottawa: Department of Justice Canada, 2000), Sec. 22.3 [emphasis in original].
13 M.A. Hennigar, 'Why Does the Federal Government Appeal to the Supreme Court of Canada in Charter of Rights Cases? A Strategic Explanation,' (2007) 41 L. & Soc. Rev. 225 at 231.
14 *Ibid.*; T. MacCharles, 'It was an issue of rights,' *Toronto Star* (2 October 2004), online: http://www.emergence.qc.ca/default.aspx?scheme=2484. This may have been done because the decision not to appeal was announced together with the decision to propose legislation recognizing the union of same-sex couples and to refer this legislation to the Supreme Court of Canada. See Government of Canada, 'Statement by the Prime Minister on Same Sex Unions' (17 June 2003), online: Canada News Centre http://news.gc.ca.
15 *Pacific Press, supra* note 9.
16 M.A. Hennigar, 'Conceptualizing Attorney General Conduct in Charter Litigation: From Independence to Central Agency,' *Canadian Public Administration* 51, no. 2 (2008): 193 at 201.
17 *Schachter v. Canada*, [1988] 3 F.C. 515.
18 *Unemployment Insurance Act, 1971*, S.C. 1970–71–72, c. 48, ss. 32 [as am. by R.S.C. 1980–81–82–83, c. 150, s. 4] and 32(1) [as am. by R.S.C. 1980–81–82–83, c. 150, s. 5].
19 The Attorney General did appeal the remedy granted by the Federal Court

in that it extended the benefits to biological parents rather than strike the section down. This appeal had the effect of prolonging the trial judge's order that the operation of his judgment be suspended pending appeal: see *Schachter v. Canada*, [1992] 2 S.C.R. 679.

20 *An Act to Amend the Unemployment Insurance Act and the Employment and Immigration Department and Commission Act*, S.C. 1990, c. 40, s. 24.
21 Canada, House of Commons, *Minutes of Proceedings and Evidence of the Legislative Committee on Bill C-21*, 34th Parl., no. 12:2 (3 October 1989) [English translation] [*Minutes*].
22 *Ibid.*
23 See I. Scott, 'Law, Policy, and the Role of the Attorney General: Constancy and Change in the 1980s' (1989) 39 U.T.L.J. 109 at 124–6.
24 *Blainey v. Ontario Hockey Association* (1985), 52 O.R. (2d) 225 (H.C.); *Ontario Human Rights Code*, R.S.O. 1980, c. 340, s. 2.
25 *Paul and Wright v. The Minister of Consumer and Commercial Relations*, unreported decision of the High Court of Justice of Ontario, 9 December 1985; *Vital Statistics Act*, R.S.O. 1980 c. 525 [as am. by R.S.O. 1981 c. 66, and R.S.O. 1983, c. 34].
26 *Blainey v. Ontario Hockey Association* (1986), 54 O.R. (2d) 513 (C.A.).
27 For a comprehensive analysis of interest-group use of political advocacy, see T. Riddell, 'Explaining the Impact of Legal Mobilization and Judicial Decisions: Official Minority Language Education Rights outside Quebec,' in J.B. Kelly and C.P. Manfredi, eds., *Contested Constitutionalism* (Vancouver: UBC Press, 2008) at 250–77.
28 G. Hein, 'Interest Group Litigation and Canadian Democracy,' in P. Howe & P. Russell, eds., *Judicial Power and Canadian Democracy* (Montreal: McGill-Queen's University Press, 2001) at 222.
29 See C.P. Manfredi, *Feminist Activism in the Supreme Court of Canada: Legal Mobilization and the Women's Legal Education and Action Fund* (Vancouver: UBC Press, 2004); G. Brodsky and S. Day, *Canadian Charter Equality Rights for Women: One Step Forward or Two Steps Back?* (Ottawa: Canadian Advisory Council on the Status of Women, 1989).
30 See M. Smith, *Lesbian and Gay Rights in Canada: Social Movements and Equality Seeking, 1971–95* (Toronto: University of Toronto Press, 1999).
31 M. Mandel, *The Charter of Rights and the Legalization of Politics in Canada*, rev. ed. (Toronto: Thompson Educational Publishing, 1994) at 74–81.
32 *Ibid.* at 78, quoting *Toronto Star* (9 May 1985), A1.
33 B. Morton in Charter Committee on Poverty Issues, Press Release, 'Gosselin Decision from Supreme Court' (19 December 2002), online: http://dawn.thot.net/gosselin1.html.

34 British Columbia, Legislative Assembly, *Hansard*, 6 (18 June 1997) at 4588 (Hon. P. Ramsey).
35 *Human Rights Amendment Act*, R.S.B.C. 1993, c. 27.
36 *Access to Abortion Services Act*, R.S.B.C. 1996, c. 1.
37 K. Roach, 'The Dangers of a Charter-Proof and Crime-Based Response to Terrorism,' in R. Daniels, P. Macklem, & K. Roach, eds., *The Security of Freedom: Essays on Canada's Anti-Terrorism Bill* (Toronto: University of Toronto Press, 2001) at 131.
38 'Martin wraps campaign in constitutional pledge,' *CBC News* (10 January 2006), online: http://www.cbc.ca/news/story/2006/01/09/elxn-debates-look.html.
39 J. Tibbets, 'Martin won't force gay marriages on churches,' *CanWest News Service* (19 December 2003), online: http://www.canada.com/national/features/samesexmarriage/story.html?id=ee4d2e69-d040-4e5f-8830-0cb2bb7d8bbd.
40 Much of the information in this section is drawn with permission from S. Labman, 'Charter Maybes = Starving Babies?' (2002) [unpublished]; *International Covenant on Economic, Social, and Cultural Rights* (1976), 993 U.N.T.S. 3, [1976] C.T.S. 46.
41 United Nations Economic and Social Council, Committee on Economic, Social, and Cultural Rights, *Consideration of Reports Submitted by States Parties under Articles 16 and 17 of the Covenant: Concluding Observations of the Committee on Economic Social, and Cultural Rights (Canada)*, Geneva (10 June 1993), E/C 12/1993/5 at para. 93.
42 R.S.C. 1985, c. C-1 [CAP].
43 United Nations Economic and Social Council, Committee on Economic, Social, and Cultural Rights, *Consideration of Reports Submitted by State Parties under Articles 16 and 17 of the Covenant: Concluding Observations of the Committee on Economic, Social, and Cultural Rights (Canada)*, Geneva (4 December 1998), E/C 12/1/Add.31 at para. 19.
44 *Implementation of the International Covenant on Economic, Social, and Cultural Rights*, Third Periodic Report: Canada (20 January 1998), E/1994/104/Add.17 at para. 8.
45 *Review of Canada's Third Report on the Implementation of the International Covenant on Economic, Social, and Cultural Rights: Responses to the Supplementary Questions Emitted by the United Nations Committee on Economic, Social, and Cultural Rights* (E/C/12/Q/CAN/1) *on Canada's Third Report on the International Covenant on Economic, Social and Cultural Rights*, E/1994/104/Add.17 at Question 53.

46 C. Scott, 'Canada's International Human Rights Obligations and Disadvantaged Members of Society: Finally into the Spotlight?' *Constitutional Forum* 10, no. 4 (1999): 97 at 107.

47 Canada, The Standing Senate Committee on Social Affairs, Science, and Technology, *The Health of Canadians – The Federal Role*, vol. 6, online: http://www.parl.gc.ca/37/2/parlbus/commbus/senate/com-e/SOCI-E/rep-e/repoct02vol6-e.htm.

48 Canada, Royal Commission on the Future of Health Care in Canada, *Building on Values: The Future of Health Care in Canada*, Final Report, online: http://www.cbc.ca/healthcare/final_report.pdf.

49 *Chaoulli v. Quebec (Attorney General)*, [2005] 1 S.C.R. 791.

50 *Ibid.*, Response of the Attorney General of Canada to the Motion for Leave to Intervene of Senator Kirby *et al.* at 3.

51 *Ibid.*, (Factum of the Interveners Senator Michael Kirby *et al.*), online: http://www.law.utoronto.ca/healthlaw/docs/chaoulli/Factum_Senate.pdf.

52 *Canada Health Act*, R.S.C. 1985, c. C-6.

53 Open letter from Canadian law professors to Stephen Harper (25 January 2005), online: http://www.law.utoronto.ca/samesexletter.html.

54 *Reference re Same-Sex Marriage*, [2004] 3 S.C.R. 698 at para. 69.

55 *Ibid.* at para. 70.

56 For discussion of other factors contributing to an impoverished Canadian democracy, and what might be done to address them, see ch. 7, 'Look Who's Talking Now: Dialogue Theory and the Return to Democracy.'

57 See *e.g.* P.W. Hogg & A.A. Bushell, 'The *Charter* Dialogue between Courts and Legislatures (or Perhaps the *Charter of Rights* Isn't Such a Bad Thing After All),' (1997) 35 Osgoode Hall L.J. 75; and K. Roach, *The Supreme Court on Trial: Judicial Activism or Democratic Dialogue* (Toronto: Irwin Law, 2001).

Conclusion

Courage my friends, 'tis not too late to build a better world.

Tommy Douglas

When I began my journey into *Charterland* in 1982, the *Canadian Charter of Rights and Freedoms* was regarded by many social activists and political progressives as the culmination of Pierre Elliott Trudeau's commitment to creating a 'just society' in Canada. From his appointment as prime minister in 1968 to the end of the 1970s, that commitment had most clearly been expressed in the Trudeau government's development of national programs aimed at increasing income security, improving health care, and enhancing Canada's ability to determine its own economic destiny. Following introduction of these programs, income inequality and poverty rates dropped significantly in Canada from the mid-1970s to the mid-1980s, countering trends in the United States.[1] Many expected that the *Charter*, with its commitments to 'liberty,' 'security,' and 'equality,' would build on this progress and guarantee Trudeau's promise of a society in which 'all Canadians will have the means and the motivation to participate' and 'groups which have not fully shared in the country's affluence will be given a better opportunity.'[2]

Now, almost three decades later, it is evident that this expectation was ill-founded. Far from helping secure a more democratic and egalitarian society, the *Charter* has provided support for a very different political project. The rise of neo-conservatism in the 1980s, which paved the way for economic globalization in the 1990s, eroded the fiscal and regulatory capacities of government, shifted powers back to the market, and ate away at Canadians' sense of national purpose and collective responsibility. In the new reality of the 1990s, the main functions of government became reducing its involvement in the economy, withdrawing support for social programs, and convincing Canadians that the best hope for improving their well-being was through increased participation in the global marketplace. The consequence was a levelling off of Canadian rates of income inequality and poverty from the mid-1980s to the mid-1990s, followed by significant increases in these rates, above those of most other OECD countries, from the mid-1990s to the mid-2000s. Thus by the mid-2000s, Canada's poverty rate, which had fallen below the OECD average in the mid-1990s, again exceeded that average, and Canada's level of income inequality surpassed the OECD average for the first time in thirty years.[3]

While it would be a mistake to claim that these changes came about as a result of the *Charter*, it is equally wrong to disregard the part the *Charter* has played in facilitating and legitimizing them. By constructing a constitutional regime of rights using the architecture of liberal legalism, the introduction of the *Charter* reinforced the notion that the main threat to Canadians' rights is not poverty or income disparity, but rather the state. At the same time, the *Charter* shaped Canadians' understandings concerning the fundamental entitlements of citizens and, by implication, the fundamental responsibilities of governments in a 'free and democratic society.' According to the ideological assumptions of liberal legalism, the *Charter* right to 'liberty,' for example, does not guarantee Canadians the resources and capacities to realize their full potential as citizens, nor the freedom to resist restrictions placed upon them by those who command market power. *Charter* 'liberty' provides relief only from government interference in their lives, leaving them to sink or swim in the marketplace according to their own means and devices. Similarly, the *Charter* right to 'security of the person' places no obligations on governments to ensure that people have adequate food, clothing, or shelter. In the *Charter* scheme of things, governments are free to disregard threats to personal security that emanate from the marketplace. Only threats to personal security stemming from government interference with that market merit constitutional scrutiny. Informed by these same ideological assumptions, the *Charter* right to 'equality' does not require governments to promote equality of condition by correcting or compensating for systemic social disparities. Governments' obligations are limited to providing citizens with equality of treatment. The result is that equality of inaction is as constitutionally worthy as equality of action – and is a lot easier to achieve.

The consequence of entrenching a charter with these attributes was to create a superordinate regime of rights that was hospitable to government cutbacks, privatization, and deregulation, and that provided

234 The Politics of the *Charter*

constitutional legitimacy to governments pursuing these policies. Politicians favouring these approaches could confidently claim that their policies respected and protected the fundamental rights of Canadians. At the same time, the *Charter* imposed constitutional costs on politicians advocating redistributive or interventionist policies. In addition to facing traditional resistance from established interests, such politicians now had to contend with the political risks of their proposals being derided as unconstitutional, as well as the legal risks of their being stymied by government lawyers or castigated in the courts.

While these pressures may seem minor in relation to the larger political and economic forces that have been at work over the past three decades, they have exerted significant normative influence on the political margins, where policy making actually occurs. Moreover, these pressures have been amplified by the *Charter*'s broader societal impact on rights discourse and political behaviour. Since the introduction of the *Charter*, organizations promoting the rights of workers, women, and other disempowered and disadvantaged groups have devoted enormous energy and resources to *Charter* advocacy and litigation. Such strategies have been utilized by these groups not only as a matter of choice to try to advance their political interests, but also as a matter of necessity to protect those interests from being undermined by *Charter* claims asserted by corporations and other dominant groups. This process of legalizing rights advocacy has diverted large amounts of time and money from other forms of political mobilization and engagement. More significantly, it has normalized and neutralized rights discourse by associating it with a legal system whose ideological assumptions exclude the structural causes of poverty and inequality from *Charter* scrutiny, thereby legitimizing governments that disavow responsibility for addressing such structural concerns.

～

The *Charter*'s role in facilitating and legitimizing the rise of neo-conservatism, imposing constitutional costs on those advocating interventionist and redistributive policies, and diverting and dissipating the energies and resources of civil society groups represents its major political influence over the past three decades, outstripping that of individual court decisions. This is not to suggest that court decisions have been inconsequential. Such decisions have served an important function in explicating and justifying the character and content of *Charter* rights. Their immediate instrumental impact, however, has been sporadic. This is in part due to costs and other barriers and limitations associated with constitutional litigation, including the fact that such litigation reviews policy only in relation to particularized facts and issues. However, it is also because courts, while embracing the underlying ideology of liberal legalism, have been loath to give full effect to that ideology. The result has been a varied and inconsistent record of judicial policy making.

In some *Charter* cases the hand of liberal legalism has been used by the Supreme Court of Canada to sweep aside legislative policies aimed at curbing market power. Examples include: *Southam*[4] (striking down investigative search powers under the former *Combines Investigation Act*); *RJR-Macdonald*[5] (striking down legislative prohibitions on tobacco advertising); and *Chaoulli*[6] (striking down legislative prohibitions on private health insurance). The last case, in particular, is remarkable for its willingness to meddle with a health care system upon which all Canadians depend in order to vindicate an individual's right to gain access to market medicine. If future cases were to follow the reasoning of the majority in *Chaoulli* who relied on the *Canadian Charter*,[7] they could impair the integrity of Canada's single-payer Medicare regime and, with it, forty years of political endeavour to create a public health care system in which all Canadians have a common stake.

In other cases that hand has been restrained by the Court resorting to the 'reasonable limits' clause and other limiting language of the *Charter*. Examples include: *Irwin Toy*[8] (upholding legislation prohibiting children's television advertising); *Canadian Newspapers*[9] (upholding a requirement that courts, when requested, ban publication of the identity of complaints in sexual assault cases); *Harper*[10] (upholding third-party spending restrictions in federal election campaigns); and *Kapp*[11] (upholding a fishing licence granted to Aboriginal bands under section 15(2) of the *Charter*).

The Court in some cases has relied on liberal legal orthodoxies to reject efforts by labour and disadvantaged groups to harness *Charter* rights to achieve progressive ends. Examples include: *Dolphin Delivery*[12] (holding that common law restrictions on secondary picketing are not subject to *Charter* scrutiny); *Delisle*[13] (holding that the exclusion of Royal Canadian Mounted Police members from labour relations legislation did not violate their freedom of association); *Granovsky*[14] (upholding legislation denying Canada Pension Plan benefits to persons who failed to meet normal qualifying requirements due to a temporary disability); *Gosselin*[15] (sustaining Quebec legislation providing much reduced welfare benefits for young persons); and *Auton*[16] (upholding the exclusion of an autism therapy from funding under the British Columbia health plan).

In other cases the Court has tried to leaven the *Charter*'s regressive tendencies by seizing opportunities to produce progressive results where those opportunities correspond with, or at least do not seriously offend, liberal legal precepts. Examples include: *Morgentaler*[17] (striking down legislative restrictions on abortion); *Schachter*[18] (invalidating differential parental benefits for biological and adoptive parents under the Unemployment Insurance [UI] program); *Eldridge*[19] (requiring public health facilities to provide sign-language interpretation for persons with hearing disabilities); *Vriend*[20] (extending human rights code prohibitions to include discrimination on the basis of sexual orientation); and *Health Services and Support-Facilities Subsector Bargaining Assn.*[21] (striking down legislation invalidating collective agreements and limiting the scope of collective bargaining).

Though these latter decisions have produced some important benefits, their progressive impacts have been constrained both by the ideological limitations imposed by the *Charter* – particularly its inability to address structural issues within the political economy and its indisposition to placing positive obligations on government[22] – and by doctrinal limitations imposed by the Court. As a result of these limitations:

- The *Morgentaler* decision, while removing legal impediments to abortion services,[23] did nothing to ensure that medical facilities would be made available to deliver such services. Thus the availability of abortion services has actually declined in Canada since 1988.[24]
- The requirement in *Schachter* that parental leave benefits be equalized prompted the federal government to reduce support for adoptive parents and to seek savings elsewhere in the UI system in order to recover the costs associated with this and another *Charter* decision extending UI benefits to persons over sixty-five.[25] These cuts resulted in 30,000 people losing UI benefits, with female, immigrant, elderly, and disabled workers being the hardest hit.[26]
- The decisions in *Eldridge* and *Vriend* have not, as some suggested, opened the door to 'a new paradigm of substantive equality' that would enable judges to place positive obligations on governments to meet the needs of vulnerable groups.[27] The Court has instead

sealed this door more tightly in subsequent cases such as *Gosselin*, *Auton*, and *Kapp*.[28]

The recent decision in *Health Services*, heralded by many for its belated acceptance that 'freedom of association' includes the right of workers to bargain collectively, suffers from both forms of limitations. By affirming that '[t]he *Charter* applies only to state action,'[29] the Court made it clear that the decision does not represent a paradigmatic shift in *Charter* thinking. Rather, the majority recast unions as bearers of collective bargaining rights within the existing *Charter* paradigm. Consequently, the decision has no direct impact upon private-sector employment relations; it can only be invoked against governments in their capacities as legislators or employers. For this reason alone, the decision will be of marginal benefit to workers. As Joel Bakan has noted, the forces primarily responsible for eroding labour's power are economic; thus protecting workers' rights 'only from direct state interference' does 'nothing to curb rapid erosion of workers' collective power.'[30]

In addition, the decision in *Health Services* was carefully tailored by the Court to address the egregious conduct of the British Columbia government, which had, without consultation, stripped the unions in question of their contractual rights and prevented them from negotiating key employment issues. For this reason too, the judgment will likely have limited purchase in future *Charter* litigation. As the majority made clear, the right the case recognizes is purely procedural and does not guarantee any 'substantive or economic outcome';[31] it does not protect any particular 'model of labour relations' or 'bargaining method';[32] and it is violated only where 'the essential integrity of the process of collective bargaining' has been compromised.[33] For such a violation to occur, the Court must determine *both* that the state substantially interfered with workers' ability to pursue their goals collectively *and* that the process denied them an opportunity for meaningful consultation and good faith negotiation. Thus, provided governments meet the procedural requirements of consulting in good faith, they remain free to impose whatever agenda they wish. In the words of the majority: 'Even where a matter is of central importance to the associational right, if the change has been made through a process of good faith consultation it is unlikely to have adversely affected the employees' right to collective bargaining.'[34]

Charter rights have their greatest potential to produce progressive impacts in those areas where government policies represent the major source of oppression faced by disadvantaged groups. Examples include: criminal law (where the Court has enhanced protections afforded to persons subject to criminal investigation and proceedings); gay and lesbian entitlements (where the Court has invoked formal equality to strike down legislation that discriminates on the basis of sexual orientation); and immigration (where the Court has strengthened protections available to refugee claimants, as well as persons facing detention, extradition, and deportation). Yet even in these areas, courts have sometimes been reluctant to disrupt government policies, and the *Charter* record has been mixed.

I will leave it for others to comment on the voluminous and varied *Charter* record in the area of criminal law.[35] With respect to gay and lesbian rights, however, the Court has both upheld and struck down legislation denying spousal benefits to same-sex couples.[36] And while holding in *Reference re Same-Sex Marriage* that Parliament could replace the common law definition of marriage with one that included same-sex couples, the Court refused to decide whether prohibiting same-sex marriage violated the *Charter's* equality guarantees.[37] It is also worth noting that, while recent cases have favoured the recognition of gay and lesbian rights, this trend followed developments pioneered in provincial and territorial legislatures.[38]

In the area of immigration, the Court has made some disquieting decisions, particularly in relation to deportation and detention. While insisting that persons facing deportation to countries where they may face torture be permitted to see and respond to the cases made against them, and be provided with written reasons, the Court has held that the minister may nonetheless deport such persons where appropriate procedures have been followed and appropriate factors have been taken into account.[39] Similarly, while finding it insufficient for a judge alone to review evidence supporting the detention of immigrants subject to security certificates, the Court has held that a special counsel system that also denies detainees access to evidence brought against them would suffice.[40] Such a system was subsequently denounced by the United Kingdom Parliament Joint Committee on Human Rights as being '"Kafkaesque" or like the Star Chamber.'[41]

In summary, while the ideology of liberal legalism that animates *Charter* rights is hostile to the regulatory and redistributive powers of government, the instrumental impact of constitutional litigation has been irregular and erratic. This is partly due to the inherent limitations of the litigation process; however, it is also due to the capacity of the Court to calibrate and control the instrumental products of that ideology on a case-by-case basis. These techniques have enabled the Court to moderate the regressive force of *Charter* rights and to exploit their progressive potential within the limits that legal liberalism allows. Of course, it always remains open to the Court to unleash that force when it chooses (as it did in *Chaoulli*), confident in the knowledge that it can contain it in subsequent cases, even by overruling itself if necessary (as it did in *Health Services*). The overall impact has been to increase the Court's capacity to make and vary decisions based on political conditions and the judicial temper of the times.

~

The techniques employed by the Court to engage in more selective and varied judicial policy making under the *Charter* have added fuel to the debate concerning the legitimacy of judicial review. The question at the core of this debate is what justification the *Charter* provides for preferring the decisions of unelected judges to those of elected legislators. The Supreme Court of Canada's early efforts to address this question by representing its *Charter* jurisprudence as the objective outcome of 'purposive reasoning' strained credulity even when they were first made in cases such as *Motor Vehicle Reference*[42] and *Morgentaler*. (This is especially so given that the Court in the first case disregarded the intentions of the *Charter*'s framers and in the second issued a split decision on the contentious issue of abortion.) Moreover, this justification was further discredited as it became increasingly apparent that *Charter* decisions are driven by political norms and policy considerations as much as they are by legal principles and judicial precedents.

Some constitutional scholars responded to this reality by trying to recast *Charter* decisions by the courts as legitimate contributions to a 'dialogue' with legislatures in which the latter get the final say.[43] While quickly embraced by the Court,[44] 'dialogue theory' has been widely criticized both for exaggerating the capacity of legislatures to overcome court decisions and for failing to provide a normative justification for judges' involvement in the policy-making process. In the wake of this criticism, leading proponents of this theory have now conceded that '[d]ialogue theory is not a theory of judicial review'[45] and 'does not provide a justification for judicial review.'[46] Instead they have argued that judicial review is justified based on the ability of judges to engage in 'good faith interpretation of the constitutional text'[47] and 'the idea that individuals have rights that ... cannot be taken away simply by an appeal to the general welfare.'[48] Not only do these arguments replicate, albeit murkily, previous claims that judges have some corner on the truth (the very claims that dialogue theory was intended to replace), but they also render incoherent the central contention of dialogue theory – the claim that *Charter* rights are justified by the ability of legislatures to overcome court decisions.

The result has been to leave dialogue theory in something of a shambles. Moreover, attempts by dialogue theorists to revert to justifications for judicial review that rely on judges' abilities to protect individuals from the general welfare, and to make good faith interpretations of the *Charter* text, have been disclaimed by recent decisions of the Court. In *Chaoulli*, for example, the claimants' medical interest in seeking access to private health insurance was not significantly different from that of other Canadians.[49] Thus those judges who invoked the *Charter* to strike down the prohibition on private health insurance did so based on their view that such prohibitions unduly restrict the access of 'ordinary Canadians' to health care services.[50] In other words, their judgment was founded on an assessment not of what policy best protected individuals from the general welfare, but rather of what policy best served the general welfare. As noted by the dissenting judges in *Chaoulli*:

> This way of putting the argument suggests that the Court has a mandate to save middle-income and low-income Quebeckers from themselves, because both the Romanow Report and the Kirby Report found that the vast majority of 'ordinary' Canadians want a publicly financed single-tier (more or less) health plan to which access is governed by need rather than wealth and where the availability of coverage is not contingent on personal insurability.[51]

Thus, while some scholars may continue to believe that the justification for judicial review rests on the ability of judges to protect individuals from the general welfare, the Supreme Court of Canada made it clear in *Chaoulli* that it does not share this view.

The stark differences of opinion amongst the judges in *Chaoulli* and other cases concerning the meaning and application of *Charter* rights also undercut the claim that *Charter* adjudication is justified by the capacity of judges to make 'good faith interpretations of the constitutional text.' The mere fact that judges make their *Charter* interpretations in 'good faith' does nothing to justify their decisions in the absence of some accompanying evidence that such interpretations produce 'right' or at least 'good' answers.[52] Not only do dialogue theorists fail to provide such evidence, but the Court's dramatic reversal of opinion in *Health Services*, on top of the mass of divided decisions like *Chaoulli*, demonstrates that even the judges themselves do not accept this position. In *Health Services* the majority ruled that two decades of *Charter* decisions denying workers a right to bargain collectively 'do not withstand principled scrutiny and should be rejected.'[53] If the Court can discard as unprincipled a key component of *Charter* jurisprudence for the past twenty years, it is difficult to see what basis remains for the rest of us to rely on other 'good faith' *Charter* interpretations. It seems almost as if the Supreme Court of Canada has come to accept what dialogue theorists apparently cannot – namely, that the quest for legitimacy of judicial review is, as Lawrence Tribe has described it, futile.[54]

~

If the *Charter of Rights and Freedoms* is not an effective or legitimate instrument for promoting social justice in Canada, where are we to turn? The *Charter* journey I have taken over the past three decades has strengthened my conviction that political mobilization and democratic engagement remain the best strategies at our disposal. Some may consider this view drearily conventional; others may regard it as wildly naive. Yet from my perspective as a democrat who desires social equality and opposes political privilege,[55] I see no better alternatives.

The social injustices and disparities that exist in Canada are products of the underlying political economy. Challenging these injustices and disparities requires us to employ tools and strategies that are able to affect the structures and operations of that political economy. Given its preoccupation with controlling state power and its disregard for the influence of capital and markets, the *Charter* is peculiarly ill-equipped to perform this function. This is additionally so given that the *Charter* is administered by the judiciary, an inherently conservative institution. For these reasons, the *Charter* has served as an impediment to, more than an agent for, progressive politics.

Democratic institutions do not suffer from these same disabilities. History has shown such institutions capable of curbing market power and redistributing wealth, though economic globalization and associated international trade regimes have undoubtedly made it more difficult for them to do so in recent years. And while these institutions have been deficient in their democratic practices, popular forces have nonetheless been able to utilize them to achieve progressive ends. Admittedly the results have been mixed, and democratic governments have frequently been captured by dominant interests or pressured by the power of capital to make significant compromises. Yet notwithstanding these constraints, such governments have in the past made major strides in building a more just society. In Canada their accomplishments include Medicare, a strong public education system, an unemployment insurance plan, provincial social assistance plans, a national pension plan, and human rights codes (which, unlike the *Charter*, are designed to constrain market power).[56]

This is not to suggest that those advocating progressive change should rely on the same mechanisms and strategies in the future as they have in the past. On the contrary, we must enhance the capacity and legitimacy of democratic institutions to pursue progressive policies. To this end, the deficiencies of parliamentary institutions should be addressed through electoral and other reforms, in order to make them more representative of and accountable to the people they serve. At the same time, we need to broaden our focus from the singular objective of expanding the welfare state to a more diverse set of strategies aimed at countering the forces of legalized politics and economic globalization. Such strategies require us to harness the capacity of civil society to educate and mobilize citizens, to build social capital, to develop cooperative economies, and to foster international alliances to influence transnational policies.

This, to be sure, is an ambitious political agenda. Yet it is no more ambitious for its day than the agenda pursued more than sixty years ago by Tommy Douglas and his colleagues when they faced down vested interests and forged the progressive policies that transformed Canadian society in the postwar era. Moreover, while today's challenges are very different from those of the mid-twentieth century, nothing in my *Charter* travels has dissuaded me in my belief that one thing at least remains the same – the enduring wisdom of Tommy Douglas's conviction that democratic mobilization by ordinary people provides the best hope of attaining social justice for all.

NOTES

1 *Growing Unequal? Income Distribution and Poverty in OECD Countries* (Paris: OECD Publishing, 2008) [*Growing Unequal*].

2 Pierre Elliott Trudeau, Official Statement by the Prime Minister, 'The Just
   Society,' 10 June 1968. Reproduced in Pierre Trudeau, *The Essential Trudeau*,
   ed. R. Graham (Toronto: McClelland and Stewart, 1998) at 18–19.

3 *Growing Unequal, supra* note 1.

4 *Hunter v. Southam Inc.*, [1984] 2 S.C.R. 145.

5 *RJR-MacDonald Inc. v. Canada (Attorney General)*, [1995] 3 S.C.R. 199.

6 *Chaoulli v. Quebec (A.G.)*, [2005] 1 S.C.R. 791 [*Chaoulli*].

7 Chief Justice McLachlin and Justices Major and Bastarache based their
   decisions on the *Canadian Charter of the Rights and Freedoms* and on the *Quebec Charter of Human Rights and Freedoms*, while Justice Deschamps based
   her decision solely on the *Quebec Charter* and thus did not find it necessary
   to decide whether there was a *Canadian Charter* violation.

8 *Irwin Toy v. Quebec (Attorney General)*, [1989] 1 S.C.R. 927.

9 *Canadian Newspapers Co. v. Canada*, [1988] 2 S.C.R. 122.

10 *Harper v. Canada (Attorney General)*, [2004] 1 S.C.R. 827.

11 *R. v. Kapp*, 2008 SCC 41 [*Kapp*].

12 *Dolphin Delivery Ltd. v. Retail, Wholesale and Department Store Union, Local
    580*, [1986] 2 S.C.R. 573.

13 *Delisle v. Canada (Deputy Attorney General)*, [1999] 2 S.C.R. 989.

14 *Granovsky v. Canada (Minister of Employment and Immigration)*, [2000] 1
    S.C.R. 703.

15 *Gosselin v. Quebec (Attorney General)*, [2002] 4 S.C.R. 429 [*Gosselin*].

16 *Auton (Guardian ad litem of) v. British Columbia (Attorney General)*, [2004] 3
    S.C.R. 657 [*Auton*].

17 *R. v. Morgentaler*, [1988] 1 S.C.R. 30 [*Morgentaler*].

18 *Schachter v. Canada*, [1992] 2 S.C.R. 679 [*Schachter*].

19 *Eldridge v. British Columbia (Attorney General)*, [1997] 3 S.C.R. 624 [*Eldridge*].

20 *Vriend v. Alberta*, [1998] 1 S.C.R. 493 [*Vriend*].

21 *Health Services and Support-Facilities Subsector Bargaining Assn. v. British
    Columbia*, [2007] 2 S.C.R. 391 [*Health Services*].

22 The Supreme Court has held that the *Charter* imposes positive obligations
    in two cases where government withdrew previously established protec-
    tions for agricultural workers and women: *Dunmore v. Ontario (Attorney
    General)*, [2001] 3 S.C.R. 1016 [*Dunmore*] and *Newfoundland (Treasury Board)
    v. Newfoundland and Labrador Assn. of Public Employees (N.A.P.E.)*, [2004] 3
    S.C.R. 381 [*N.A.P.E.*]. However, these obligations were minimal in the case
    of *Dunmore* and were negated by the reasonable limits clause in the case of
    N.A.P.E. Moreover, *Dunmore* has been distinguished and *N.A.P.E.* has been
    ignored in subsequent *Charter* cases in which these aspects of the decisions
    have been invoked by *Charter* claimants: see *Gosselin, supra* note 15 (dis-

244 The Politics of the *Charter*

tinguishing *Dunmore*) and *Health Services, ibid.* (ignoring *N.A.P.E.*). For an excellent critique of the Court's failure to address *N.A.P.E.* in its treatment of the equality rights claim in *Health Services*, see J. Fudge, 'Conceptualizing Collective Bargaining under the Charter: The Enduring Problem of Substantive Equality' (2008) 42 Sup. Ct. L. Rev. (2d), 213 at 227–43.

23 It is worth noting that the decision left open the possibility of Parliament enacting less restrictive legislation to criminalize abortion. The federal government proposed such legislation as Bill C-43, *An Act in respect of Abortion*, 2d Sess., 34th Parl., 1989–90. However while this bill passed in the House of Commons, it was defeated by a tied vote in the Senate.

24 See T. Wilson, *Protecting Abortion Rights in Canada* (Ottawa: Canadian Abortion Rights Action League, 2003), online: http://www.canadiansforchoice. ca/caralreport.pdf, which conducted a survey of hospitals providing abortion services to support its empirically based conclusion that 'women in all parts of Canada are finding it increasingly difficult to obtain an abortion at a hospital in or near their community' (at 2). This survey provided the baseline for a later study that determined that the number of Canadian hospitals providing accessible abortion services dropped from 17.8 per cent in 2003 to 15.9 per cent in 2006: J. Shaw, *Reality Check: A Close Look at Accessing Abortion Services in Canadian Hospitals* (Ottawa: Canadians for Choice, 2006), online: http://www.canadiansforchoice.ca/report_english.pdf.

25 *Tétreault-Gadoury v. Canada* [1991] 2 S.C.R. 22.

26 J. Bakan, *Just Words: Constitutional Rights and Social Wrongs* (Toronto: University of Toronto Press, 1997) at 59.

27 B. Porter, 'Beyond Andrews: Substantive Equality and Positive Obligations after Eldridge and Vriend' *Constitutional Forum* 9, no. 3 (1998): 71 at 78.

28 In *Kapp, supra* note 11, this was the effect of the majority's holding that s. 15(1) and s. 15(2) of the *Charter* 'work together' to promote a 'vision of substantive equality' by 'preventing discriminatory distinctions' under s. 15(1) while allowing governments that 'wish to combat discrimination' to develop 'programs aimed at helping disadvantaged groups improve their situation' under s. 15(2): at para. 16. The clear implication is that s. 15, while preventing governments from making discriminatory distinctions, permits but does not oblige them to improve the social conditions of vulnerable groups.

29 *Health Services, supra* note 21 at para. 88.

30 J. Bakan, *supra* note 26 at 85.

31 *Health Services, supra* note 21 at para. 91.

32 *Ibid.*

33 *Ibid.* at para. 129.

34 *Ibid.* For extended critiques of the *Health Services* decision and its implications, see J. Fudge, *supra* note 22, and E. Tucker, 'The Constitutional Right to Bargain Collectively: The Ironies of Labour History in the Supreme Court of Canada,' *Labour/Le Travail* 61 (2008): 151.
35 For discussion of the limited impact of the *Charter* in the area of criminal law, see K. Roach, 'A Charter Reality Check: How Relevant Is the Charter to the Justness of Our Criminal Justice System' (2008) 40 Sup. Ct. L. Rev. (2d) 717.
36 Compare *e.g. Egan v. Canada*, [1995] 2 S.C.R. 513 with *M. v. H.*, [1999] 2 S.C.R. 3.
37 *Reference re Same-Sex Marriage*, [2004] 3 S.C.R. 698.
38 British Columbia, for example, enacted legislation between 1992 and 2000:

- including sexual orientation as a prohibited ground of discrimination in human rights legislation (1992);
- extending workplace medical benefits to same-sex partners of government employees (1992);
- enabling same-sex partners to adopt as couples (1996);
- providing same-sex couples the same custody, maintenance, and support rights and responsibilities as heterosexual couples (1997);
- allowing same-sex couples to register cohabitation and division of property agreements (1997);
- providing pension benefits for the same-sex partners of public sector employees (1998);
- enabling lesbians, gays, and bisexuals to make medical decisions on behalf of same-sex partners who become incapacitated (2000); and
- amending the definition of spouse in numerous statutes to ensure that same-sex couples are treated equally in areas such as inheritance, estates, property law, and conflict of interest provisions (2000).

See 'A Chronology of Advances in LGBT Rights in Canada, and in BC,' British Columbia Teachers' Federation, online: http://bctf.ca/SocialJustice.aspx?id=6100.
39 *Suresh v. Canada (Minister of Citizenship and Immigration)*, [2002] 1 S.C.R. 3.
40 *Charkaoui v. Canada (Citizenship and Immigration)*, [2007] 1 S.C.R. 350.
41 UK House of Lords, House of Commons Joint Committee on Human Rights, 'Nineteenth Report of Session 2006–07,' 16 July 2007, online: http://www.publications.parliament.uk/pa/jt200607/jtselect/jtrights/157/15702.htm.
42 *Reference Re s. 94(2) of Motor Vehicle Act (British Columbia)*, [1985] 2 S.C.R. 486.

43 The leading proponents of this view were P.W. Hogg & A.A. Bushell, 'The *Charter* Dialogue between Courts and Legislatures (or Perhaps the *Charter of Rights* Isn't Such a Bad Thing After All)' (1997) 35 Osgoode Hall L.J. 75, and K. Roach, *The Supreme Court on Trial: Judicial Activism or Democratic Dialogue* (Toronto: Irwin Law, 2001).

44 *Vriend, supra* note 20 at paras. 136–9.

45 K. Roach, 'Dialogic Judicial Review and Its Critics' (2004) 23 Sup. Ct. L. Rev. (2d) 49 at 51.

46 P.W. Hogg, A.A. Bushell Thornton, & W. Wright, '*Charter* Dialogue Revisited – or "Much Ado about Metaphors"' (2007) 45 Osgoode Hall L.J. 1 at 29.

47 Roach, *supra* note 45 at 69.

48 Hogg, Bushell Thornton, & Wright, *supra* note 46 at 28.

49 The trial judge ruled based on the evidence that it was 'hard to conclude that the delays that occurred resulted from lack of access to public health services, and in fact even Mr. Zeliotis's complaints about delays are questionable': *Chaoulli, supra* note 6 at para. 211 [English translation]. The Supreme Court majority avoided this point by holding that the appellants need not show that they were 'personally affected by an infringement' and awarding standing based on the public interest test enunciated in *Minister of Justice of Canada v. Borowski*, [1981] 2 S.C.R. 575: *ibid.* at para. 35. Moreover, it is unlikely that Mr Zeliotis, given his medical history, would have qualified for private health insurance had it been available.

50 *Chaoulli, ibid.* at para. 124.

51 *Ibid.* at para. 175.

52 Roach addresses this point by arguing that, though courts do not produce 'right answers,' the process judges use to reach decisions is more constrained and is qualitatively different from the one used by legislators: *supra* note 45, at 67–75. On this general point he gets no disagreement from me (though we clearly disagree about the nature and consequences of those constraints and differences). Absent evidence that this judicial process produces 'right' or least 'good' answers, however, I fail to see how this argument furthers his case for *Charter* legitimacy.

53 *Health Services, supra* note 21 at 22.

54 L.H. Tribe, *Constitutional Choices* (Cambridge, MA: Harvard University Press, 1985) at 3.

55 See the Introduction to this work, where I characterize my political philosophy in these terms and explain its influences on my views of the *Charter*.

56 Human Rights Codes are designed to prevent employers, landlords, and others who wield market power from using that power to discriminate against employees, renters, and other members of the public.

Index

220; *Ford v. Quebec (Attorney
General)*, 127; *Quebec Association of
Protestant School Boards v. Quebec,*
26, 36–7, 44n30, 49n89
Laskin, Chief Justice Bora: cases, 53,
57, 68–9, 76n67; views, 53, 57
law professors, 224–6
legal aid. *See* public funding
legal counsel right, 24, 25, 45n37
legal rights, 24, 141; liberty and
security, 50–1, 60, 129, 172, 177–9;
moral innocence and, 54, 66–71;
principles of fundamental justice,
50–1, 52–4, 64–6, 73n16, 75n44;
substantive interpretation of
section 7, 58–64. *See also British
Columbia Motor Vehicle Reference*;
due process; immigrant and refugee rights
legalized discourse, 11, 219, 220–3,
226
legislation: favouring disadvantaged
Canadians, 40, 82, 102–3. *See also*
judicial review of legislation;
legislative responses to judicial
review; legislatures; *names of
specific acts*
legislative responses to judicial
review, 97n49, 137, 142; dialogue
theory and, 12, 145n19, 153, 191,
192–204, 207n26; striking down
v. remediation, 36, 90–1, 109,
113n26, 139, 152, 153, 174, 180–2,
206n20. *See also* judicial review of
legislation
legislatures, 147n46, 149, 243n22;
democratic shortcomings, 150,
155–7; exclusion from public
policy oversight, 215–18, 224;
legalization of political discourse,

13, 220–1; legislative supremacy,
12, 150, 152–5, 190; parliamentary
reform, 155–9. *See also* legislative
responses to judicial review
lesbian rights. *See* gay and lesbian
rights
liability: absolute v. strict liability,
66–7, 75n59
liberal ideology. *See* liberal legalism
liberal legalism, 8, 9, 14, 92–3, 140–1,
193–4, 233, 238–9; constitutional
principles and, 77–9, 81–2, 84–7,
93, 100–3, 150–2, 171–2, 179, 233–5,
238; dialogue theory and, 140–1,
142, 176–7, 182; *Dolphin Delivery*,
79, 84–8, 88–9, 91, 173–4; rejection
of, 138–9, 140, 152–5, 182
liberty. *See* freedom; legal rights
litigation costs, 22–6, 42n17, 104–5
local governments, 159
Lord's Day Act (Canada). *See* Sunday
closing laws
low-income Canadians. *See* disadvantaged Canadians

MacDonald, Roderick, 32–3
MacDougall (R. v.), 69–71
marginalized Canadians. *See* disadvantaged Canadians
market power, 32, 83–4, 108, 172;
Charter review and, 8, 9, 12, 172–3,
179, 233, 235; regulation, 9, 20,
32–3, 109, 172–3, 232–3, 241–2,
246n56. *See also* business interests;
Combines Investigation Act (Canada); corporate rights; property
rights
Martin, Paul, 221
Martland, Justice Ronald, 21
McDougall, Barbara, 217